EMPATHY FOR THE DEVIL

How to Help People Overcome Drugs and Alcohol Problems

Phil Harris

RHP

Russell House Publishing

Published in 2007 by:
Russell House Publishing Ltd.
4 St. George's House
Uplyme Road
Lyme Regis
Dorset DT7 3LS

Tel: 01297-443948
Fax: 01297-442722
e-mail: help@russellhouse.co.uk
www.russellhouse.co.uk

© Phil Harris

British Library Cataloguing-in-publication Data:
A catalogue record for this book is available from the British Library.

ISBN: 978-1-903855-54-6

Typeset by TW Typesetting, Plymouth, Devon
Printed and bound by Biddles Ltd, King's Lynn, Norfolk

About Russell House Publishing

Russell House Publishing aims to publish innovative and valuable materials to help managers, practitioners, trainers, educators and students.

Our full catalogue covers: social policy, working with young people, helping children and families, care of older people, social care, combating social exclusion, revitalising communities and working with offenders.

Full details can be found at www.russellhouse.co.uk and we are pleased to send out information to you by post. Our contact details are on this page.

We are always keen to receive feedback on publications and new ideas for future projects.

Contents

To Jessica Gwyther

Acknowledgements

During the long course of writing this book I have remained indebted to many colleagues and friends alike. Special thanks must go to Jessica Gwyther for her continued love and support. And to Justin Hoggan's for the impetus in writing this book. Even though it cost me many a lunch I remain grateful. And to our mutual friend David Crumpton, whose departing was such a loss and whom I still miss intolerably. A special thank you must go to Rowan Miller, for her integrity, honesty and steadfast belief in me over the years. Particular thanks to Jason Trevett, for always making me laugh and think in such large doses and in equal measure. And to Martin Shotbolt, for being such a strong and constant presence in my life. I remain eternally grateful to Jo Bush, Jules Hesketh and all the team at Training Exchange for making it appear as if I have a proper job. All the old LDAP team, Michael Czerkas, Geoff Williams, Tracey Derek, Sue Jacobs and Dee Parkin for trusting in me as much as you did. I am very proud of what we achieved. Here is to the US contingent of Bruce McDougal and Ellen Kalina. I know I do not write enough but you are not far from my thoughts and I am grateful too for all your enthusiasm and belief. And to Christopher Flook for remaining such a good friend for more years than either of us would dare to remember. Again, special mention must go to Geoffrey Mann and the good people of Russell House Publishing. Had this book taken any longer then you would have all qualified for canonisation on the grounds of patience. Thanks for your support, ideas and hard work in making this book happen. I am also grateful to the very talented artist, Racheal Nee, for the artwork on the cover of this book. I owe you a double Madame Geneva. A huge thank you must also go to the many clients that I have worked with. They have taught me so much over the last fifteen years and continue to do so. And finally, to the many students, training participants and supervisee's that have made me think about these experiences and encouraged me in articulating them to a wider audience.

About the author

Phil Harris is an independent writer who has worked in direct access drug services for over fifteen years. He has designed and delivered internationally recognised treatment programmes and accredited training courses throughout the UK and Europe. Having worked as a drugs treatment advisor to DSTs, Criminal Justice Services and Youth Services, he has also managed several organisations and implemented innovative, practical and effective approaches to addressing people's problems with misuse of drugs and alcohol. He continues to practice in the South West of England.

Introduction

An apology for the devil:
It must be remembered that we have heard
only one side of the case:
God has written all the books.

                    Samuel Butler

A supernatural rhetoric is reserved for those people who experience drug and alcohol problems. They are the folk devils in a post technological age. Politicians, the media and lay persons alike can speak without any embarrassment of the evil drug trade; the drugs menace; the demon drink; and demand the tireless crusade against them. No other social problem is understood in this way. Anyone can castigate, vilify or scapegoat the user without ever having to justify, evidence or qualify one's position. The very act of condemnation itself appears to entitle the speaker to occupy a higher moral ground. Such emotive depictions of intoxicants as a mindless evil has meant that no judgement is too extravagant, no budget is too small and no legislation too extreme in the moral charge that has reduced global policy to the status of medieval peasants at the castle gates.

It is difficult to assess where this tradition took root but superstition has always thrived on the edge of knowledge. Our medieval ancestors were in the habit of naming noxious plants after Lucifer and many of these were hallucinogenic. It may have begun in the temperance movement that first attempted to address alcoholism in the 18th century, where it was invariably assumed that God was on their side in the campaign to promote global prohibition (despite the bounty of psychoactive drugs that exists throughout all Creation). Perhaps the tradition is reflective of the complexities of the modern world. Social problems are sophisticated, multifaceted and interconnected. Their causes are obscure, the dimensions incalculable and their instigators remote. Poverty, promiscuity, prostitution, rioting, hatred of just government, family break down, mental health, physical illness, juvenile delinquency, acquisitive crime, educational underachievement, communism, moral decay and, more recently global terrorism, are not the result of esoteric domestic and foreign policies. All can be portrayed more simply as the outcome of the evil of drugs. In effect drugs and drug users have become an intellectual short cut for all things unquestionably bad. And anyone who questions this is guilty of a kind of apostasy that is to be *pro-drugs*. But, one simply does not have to be in favour of drugs to be in favour of understanding.

This theologising of the evils of drugs is more than an anachronism. It has been insidious in shaping our thinking with moral imperatives. Our historical approaches to substance misuse have been driven by what *ought* to be the case. What we *ought* to do about substances; what we *ought* to do with young people at risk; and what we *ought* to do with problem users. But there is a huge chasm between what *ought* to be the case and what *is*. This moral imperative has obscured the everyday experience. All too often we have taken the supposed right course of action at the sacrifice of the effective course of action. And our subsequent failure leaves us feeling that our best efforts ought to have made a bigger difference than they have.

It is only in the last few decades that science has broken with the moral tradition. Although its findings still generate apoplexy in the high minded, it has begun to illuminate the complexities of the addiction experience. In doing so it has unearthed one central finding: there are no neat explanations. There is no satanic DNA, psychological Faustian pact or sociological occultism that can lay claim to the instigation of problematic experience. Rather we have created our social folk devils precisely in our own image as the problematic user appears no different to any of us. As a result, research in the addiction field has led the way in understanding not 'addicts' but human change. Its findings and approaches have been adopted across the whole of the social welfare field: in offending, mental health, obesity, family work, homelessness, youth work, personality disorder and health, amongst others. Our emphasis has shifted from characterising people by the multiplicity of their problems towards considering the singularity of how people change their problems. This means that the ideas and approaches outlined in this book are directly transferable to a wide range of concerns, wherever they are based upon the idea of change.

As such, the central assumption of this book is that if we are to support those that experience problems we need to understand them as people first and foremost: what drives the inner experience of use of drugs and alcohol, what drives change and how people not only identify a different kind of life, but also how they sustain it in light of obstacles and set backs. This is not just about the individual, but also the relationships and environments that provide the contexts and reference points of their lives. In short this book will chart what it is that people actually do to recover and embraces the fullness of each individual life. This will provide the guidance for the kind of help they need from us, should they require it. What we shall see is that these struggles are no different from those that we all encounter in life. They only diverge in magnitude. Therefore optional exercises have been included to allow the reader to consider these internal and external pressures more deeply by relating them to their own experience.

The ideas, tools and interventions outlined in this book are wide ranging. They are designed to offer the reader a deep grounding in working with addictions, from the initiation of use to the establishment of the recovered life. This begins with the historical and cultural factors inherent in the drug using experience. Addiction is understood in relationship to these contexts. Consideration is then given to how we as helpers can form and maintain relationships strong enough to assist people. We then explore the assessment and management of what needs to change. The rest of the book then provides the means to see these changes through. This follows the initiation of motivation, planning change, implementation and sustaining it. Every chapter is heavily referenced to allow the reader to seek out compelling and intriguing research findings for themselves. So while the detailed overview will provide a comprehensive understanding of the field, it also hoped that it will provide the stimulation for further study.

The interventions described in this book were chosen due to the efficacy they have demonstrated in day to day practice as well as their goodness to fit with common challenges in each step of change. As such they are explored and developed here in the context of studies of self-changers in order to close the gap between theory and practice. This is with a caveat. Whilst the interventions contained in this book are mapped out in structured ways, they will only work when they fit the client's needs. Interventions should never simply be done, but only used when they relate to the person before us. We may then develop our ear for the common struggles that might trigger effective responses.

This is not to suggest that overcoming addictions or usefully assisting in that process is easy. Both the helper and helped must sustain a wilful effort in overcoming the challenge of reinventing a new kind of life, which very often has to be done in old environments. But the many advances in understanding of addictions give us reason to be optimistic. There are things we can do that assist change, even though the change horizon may be further away than we initially hope for. It is a new science. There will be further strides in unravelling the mysteries of addiction. Here we learn more about life at the extremes of existence. The exaggerated social forces and pressures of change become more visible. This will continue to offer a lens into the broader human experience. In short, the more we understand our devils, the more we understand ourselves.

Who is this book for?

Problematic substance misuse is no longer the preserve of street agencies and rehabs. These multifaceted problems are now being met by a multiplicity of support agencies. An armada of social policy has re-configured all services for both adults and young people to address substance use in some capacity. Services are now considered as either a referral route or support provider across the age range. It is no longer enough to be a good probation officer, prison officer, housing worker, social worker, youth worker or even teacher. In addition everyone has to be a good drugs worker. This book can help you respond to this expectation, by developing self-understanding, by helping to understand users and thereby open possibilities for helping make change occur.

Criminal justice system

The proliferation of Drug Testing and Treatment Orders, Restrictions on Bail, Drug Intervention Programmes, and Arrest Referral has made substance misusing offenders a new priority at pre- and post-arrest. Substance misuse is now being addressed in bail hostels, probation services and police stations across the country. Clients can move through these services quickly. This book provides brief interventions where the workers have to maximise the impact of only one session at most with involuntary clients. Why involuntary clients resist interventions is also explained in detail, and how to overcome this barrier to change.

Housing

In housing, the Rough Sleepers Initiative demands that the hostels recruit and retain the most chaotic problem users, regardless of their current use. The dismantling of psychiatric institutions and proposed changes to the Mental Health Act will shift mandatory treatment towards community based services. People with severe and enduring mental health problems are also at high risk of suffering from substance abuse, a circumstance that will demand even greater efforts to address this effectively. The tools outlined in this book are useful for the most unstable clients and can be easily adapted to encompass special needs. The chapter on motivation explains how crisis moments can be maximised to promote change. This book provides a unified assessment and user-friendly care planning model that is simple, relevant to the client's needs, allows for a hierarchy of goals to be set, and provides the means to sustain tenancies.

Social work

Social work, with its increasing focus on child welfare, is seeing expansion of auxiliary family and parenting units under the auspices of the Children's Trusts. Problematic drug use impacts on the lives of many families and a new generation of young carers of problem users is coming of age. However, this is far outstripped by the 'hidden' problems caused by alcohol use. The huge imbalance in funding that exists between drugs and alcohol often leaves the social workers not simply care planning but filling the gap. The chapters in this book offer clear guidance and skills in not only how to support concerned others but also how they can influence the behaviours of problem users. Particular skills are described in understanding how relationships augment change processes. Even the area of learning disability, for so long a conservative and insulated population, is seeing the emergence of increasing problems. A more independent generation of people in low-support independent living units are now confronting the same temptations as their peers. For those with mild learning disabilities the self same skills apply, and in some ways are more effective for this group.

The social work student must grasp the core understanding of these problems quickly before stepping into placements where they are destined to encounter problematic use first hand. Throughout each chapter, key concepts are defined, case studies provided and skills described. Each intervention is explained in the context of underpinning theory, with full referencing.

Young people

The fact that cannabis and alcohol have attained a common currency in some young people's minds, and serves as an impediment to their educational and social needs, has brought drugs onto the national curriculum and drugs workers into the classrooms. Whilst young people are maturing faster in an increasingly complex world, the burden of social education has fallen to youth work. This is often done in the informal relationships with little support or guidance. Ideas for effective education and early intervention are outlined based on the central drivers of use. The book also explores how to motivate young people so that Youth Intervention Programmes and Pupil Referral Units can compete with the gravitational pull of social exclusion. YOTS and CAMHS teams are at the vanguard of supporting the most disenfranchised young people and confronting drug use, anti-social behaviours and emotional disturbance at the most profound level. How to create and sustain relationships with difficult and erratic clients is described in detail and considerations given to the developmental delay that these young people can experience.

Substance misuse teams

Even substance misuse workers themselves are facing times of revision in practice as the discipline professionalizes. Drug and Alcohol National Occupational Standards is the framework of this change but it does not provide the means. As an NVQ it does not inform anyone on how to practice, but merely evaluates what people practice. The theory and research that inform practice will have to be more widely appreciated in the field. An antithetical attitude towards theory as a pejorative term is an anachronism in a discipline that in recent years has set new standards of understanding human relationships, behaviour and change. Many concepts in the field are confused, there is fierce debate over what approaches are effective and the treatment goal of recovery itself is vague and impenetrable. A central aim of this book is to provide clarity to substance misuse approaches. The 'what works' debate is reconciled and a democratic vision of treatment is offered. All the approaches discussed are client-directed and work towards a clear vision of recovery which draws on a wide range of research that all converges on the same central treatment outcomes.

This book's structure

Chapter 1: Provides an overview of the effects of drugs but places them in a social context. As such it includes an overview of the historical, cultural and economic forces that shape the drug using experience. Key concepts such as tolerance and withdrawal are defined and the contribution of both biological and cultural factors included.

Chapter 2: This chapter establishes a working definition of dependence and addiction. It clarifies the relationship between these two concepts which provides the ethos for the subsequent interventions. It explores how addictions evolve over time with particular emphasis on the cultural status of both the drug and the user. Based on clinical studies the chapter then reviews the ways in which people recover from addictions.

Chapter 3: The single most important factor in recovery is the worker's relationship with the client. This chapter explores the core elements in creating effective working alliances with problematic substance users.

Chapter 4: Assessment is a notoriously difficult element of practice. This chapter explains comprehensive assessment tools and the importance of assessing both dependence and the key indicators of addiction. Substitute prescribing is explored, as well as how the assessment is used as the basis of treatment planning. A simple planning tool is described that can be used in conjunction with the skills that follow.

Chapter 5: Motivation for change is described in both treatment and non-treatment groups. The stresses surrounding use often compel the need for change and the chapter explores how motivational interviewing maximises these forces. Detailed intervention techniques are described in supporting clients towards decision making and commitment to change.

Chapter 6: Preparation for change is a difficult process. Using tools from solution focused therapy this chapter describes key interventions in establishing meaningful goals and increasing the client's confidence in managing change.

Chapter 7: This chapter looks at the early recovery period and the unique challenges the client faces. Based on studies of non-treatment seekers it identifies the pitfalls and obstacles the client faces and describes the key techniques and interventions that will assist them through it. Particular emphasis is given to assessing the client's risk hierarchy and coping skills and lifestyle balance.

Chapter 8: A review of research identifies what the recovery process entails. Overcoming addictions is a process of re-building a more fulfilling and enriching life. Pragmatic interventions are explained in detail and are effective in assisting people to create more intimate and fulfilling relationships. How the concerned others and friends in the user's life can support this process is examined using community reinforcement and family interventions.

Chapter 1

On Intoxication

The Devil is most devilish when respectable.
Elizabeth Barrett Browning

Our modern understanding of intoxication is a portrait without a landscape. When trying to understand the action, effect and problems associated with intoxicants we have become fixated on two factors of the experience; the user and the substance. In a social vacuum the individual encounters the mysterious power of the drug as they bond at a cellular level in the deep recesses of the brain. The endurance of this union stems from some innate defect in the user, either metabolic or psychological, that is exploited by the molecular structure of the drug itself. Such assumptions shape the laws which seek to protect us and treatment which hopes to extract this all powerful longing. The problem is when we place drug use in context we see very little to support this view. This is because the context itself is not merely incidental to the experience but defines it. In this chapter, we will explore the missing landscape that shapes the present day experience of drug use. This begins with the historical role that intoxicants have played in human development. But history itself is not uniform. It is generated in the collective experience of defined peoples that forge their own culture. And culture is not merely the perspective of exotic others but is the medium of lives. Its manifestation in the laws, economics and politics of every society shape peoples' lives in physical ways. Substance use is no exception. In the light of these contexts we shall re-examine the individual experience of intoxicants to understand what determines their action.

Historical perspective

It would be impossible to do justice to the history of drugs use in brief because to do so would simply demand a history of mankind. The use of psychoactive drugs is as old as pre-history itself. Even when we view prehistoric cave paintings we can see white geometric shapes painted over these depictions of the natural world. This is believed to be the product of perhaps the oldest state of altered consciousness. When the human eye is deprived of light it stimulates nerve endings, generating an assortment of visual hallucinations. This includes shapes such as squares, dashes, grids and chevrons. In caves that are still dangerous to access, mankind discovered his propensity to experience the world differently. The fact that these states could be easily induced through certain plants became a short cut to this desire. The use of psychoactive substances can be dated back to at least the Palaeolithic period, where opium, cannabis seeds and the hallucinogenic fungus ergot have been found in cave dwellings. There is even evidence to suggest that opium poppies and cannabis were amongst the very first plants to be domesticated by Neolithic man and the use of the hallucinogenic fungus 'fly agaric' began 10,000 years ago at the end of the Ice Age.

In contrast to the longevity of cannabis and opium use, alcohol did not appear until 4,000 BC in Mesopotamia. It soon became central to the spiritual, social and economic life of this society (Rudgley, 1993). The first recipe ever found in history was for Sumerian beer and dates from

1,500 BC. The fermentation of alcohol demands fruits and grains rich in sugar which were not naturally available but had to be bred. As a result there is much debate whether the shift from the nomadic existence of early man to settled farmer was driven to produce grain not for bread but beer. Katz (Katz and Voigt, 1986; Katz and Maytag, 1991) suggests that these primitive four per cent beers fermented from whole grains were not merely intoxicating but offered a highly nutritious source of food. Whilst the desire for inebriation was the primary motive behind production, the unintentional consequences were an improved diet and the increasing cultivation of the land stimulating the growth of permanent settlements. Civilisation begins with alcohol.

Every society has made use of intoxicants and discovered its own alternatives to alcohol. It is estimated that there are over a thousand mood altering plants in Mother Nature's pharmacy. The North American Inuit chewed the ashes of a fungus which induced intoxication; the Australian Aborigine smoked the mild stimulant-hallucinogen root Pituri; the native American Indian made use of fungi and cannabis; the Mayans indulged in the excreted juices of the Bufo toad; whilst the chewing of coca in the Andean range is at least 2,000 years old. History also suggests that as soon as new drugs emerge they are rapidly disseminated and assimilated by other cultures. For example, the white slaver's shipments of New World tobacco reached the heart of central Africa long before any European did. Here it established itself not only as an intoxicant but as a currency (Gately, 2002). When reading social histories of drug use it is clear that every era has been characterised by the substances available for medical, social, recreational or spiritual purposes (Rudgely, 1993). But this blithe observation must also be met with the caveat that for as long as people have taken intoxicants, equally it appears that others have tried to stop them. Restrictions and laws on consumption appear as early as 1,720 BC with the discovery of a Hammurabic code that set the prices, and quality of beer and stipulated that criminals be excluded from Sumer taverns (Mandlebuam, 1965).

Drugs and modern history

The more recent history of drug use in the West is strikingly rich and dynamic. What is self-evident is that different drugs have come in and out of fashion with great alacrity (Daventport-Hines, 2001). Opiates and hashish were respectable in the 18th century. Tobacco smokers were imprisoned by the Inquisition on their return from the New World in the 15th century but later it became perceived as a health balm. Coffee users were held in suspicion for their mutinous political thinking in the 17th century but the very first parliamentary ballot box was placed in a coffee shop (Allen, 2001). Cocaine was given to children as a tonic in the late 19th century. It would almost appear that to make it into the annals of historical achievement you need a great idea, opportunistic circumstances and a drug of choice. The curriculum of history is replete with consumers of the *de rigueur* intoxicants of their time. But usage has never remained the preserve of elites for long. In her fascinating history of opium use, Berridge (1999) observed that the Victorian period was characterised by far higher drug consumption than our century. Opiates were used extensively as the muse of the romantic poets; a pain-killer to enable the labourers to hand dig the rail and canal systems of the industrial revolution; a form of child care for the women who worked in the factories; and was a major export to China where opium was a popular recreational substance. So in terms of culture, infrastructure, manufacturing and trade, it was opiates that made Britain great. The figurehead of this vast and sprawling Empire, Queen Victoria herself, regularly took cannabis for period pains.

Within this context we see that historically the concept of addiction as we understand it today is a relatively new phenomenon, despite extensive use. It first emerges in the 1700s in the form of alcoholism, notoriously in Georgian Britain. But it is not until 1795 that an inebriate, James Chalmers of Nassau, New Jersey, made the first recorded statement that alcohol had 'caused' him to lose control over consumption (Levine, 1979). Such testaments soon gained popularity as a recruiting gimmick for the Temperance movement who were the first to rally against problematic consumption. It was they who popularised the idea of consumption as a disease by the early 19th century.

The late emergence of alcoholism as a disease was somewhat in contradiction to the fact that the staple diet of fluids had been restricted to alcoholic beverages due to water contamination in many European countries for over a thousand years. An average European drank three litres of beer a day (this included men, women and children). The wealthy drank more, hence heavy alcohol consumption emerged as a status symbol and gave birth to the phrase 'as drunk as a lord'. The rise of alcoholism is often attributed to the development of distillery technology that increased the concentration of alcoholic beverages from five per cent ales to over 40 per cent spirits. The gin epidemic in Georgian Britain was predominantly confined to the transient ghetto populations of London and women who accounted for over 80 per cent of consumption (Dillon, 2002). However, research does not suggest that alcoholism is in anyway limited to the consumption of spirits alone. Problem users imbibe wine, beer, ales, or the street drinkers preserve, cider. All these beverages were widely available and consumed in pre-industrial Britain without alcoholism ensuing.

Even the word addiction is a recent incarnation of the many labels applied to high consumers of drugs and alcohol over the past 300 years. Derived from the Latin, *addicere*, its meaning is derived from *ad*-to 'belong to', and *dicere* meaning 'declare, adjudge or allot'. Its origins lie in a Roman practice whereby if an individual could not repay a debt to a borrower, they became their slave in the stakes instead. Thus the word originally referred to being formally bound to another. The word slips from history until Shakespeare's archbishop of Canterbury marvels at Henry V's grasp of theology when previously 'his addiction was to courses vain'. Shakespeare is the first recorded use of the word to mean a strong inclination, and is still used in this way today. By 1790, addiction was applied to morally questionable practices such as gluttony, lust and superstitious rituals. Though an isolated reference exists in regard to gin consumption and tobacco use in 1779, it is not until 1906 that addiction is explicitly used as a medical term. It was applied to narcotics, specifically opium, as a form of loss of control over consumption. Prior to this 'drunkard', 'habitual drunkard', 'inebriates' or 'morphinists' were popular alternatives. Despite its widespread usage in both a Shakespearian sense and as medical diagnosis, the concept of addiction has defied any coherent and accepted definition. Its use has also been subverted further through political correctness where, in reaction to its negative connotations, the term dependence is now preferred. Dependence tends to describe the physical syndromes attached to consumption without the moral judgement that addiction has come to imply.

Cultural perspectives

Reviewing the history of use juxtaposes our pejorative views of the drug user to such a degree it is hard to assimilate. It runs in contradiction to our current perception of drugs. We have to understand that our views are historically cited and are based upon our own cultural experience.

We make the assumption that this is typical. But what is most striking about the history of intoxication is not simply the diversity of different drugs used but the diversity of experiences of the same drug. For example, even amongst the kissing cousin societies of Europe, we still see an extreme diversity of experience in regards to alcohol. Whilst France has a high consumption rate of alcohol it does not boast the high levels of psychopathology found in the UK drinking populations.

Extensive studies have been conducted into the cross-cultural differences in alcohol consumption. Alcohol is an ideal drug for this as its use is well established and wide spread across global cultures. We see a huge spectrum of divergence in cultural responses to alcohol (Mandelbuam, 1965). Even within cultures the effects of alcohol have proven unpredictable. The Aztecs described their alcoholic beverage *pulque*, as 'centzonttotochtli'. This translates to 'four hundred rabbits' as a metaphor for alcohol's diverse and unpredictable effects (Marshall, 1983). MacAndrew and Edgerton's (1969) systematic study of ethnic patterns of alcohol consumptions demonstrated a wide spectrum of responses. Notable was the observation that anti-social behaviours under the influence only occurred in cultures which understood alcohol use as time out from everyday life. Other cultures see alcohol's function as to assist in work, to mark life transition points or to offer spiritual libations. As a result, in the UK, Scandinavia, the US and Australia alcohol is associated with violence and aggression whereas in the Latin countries it is associated with socialisation and integration with family and wider community. Any attempts Italians might make to excuse anti-social behaviour as the product of inebriation are simply met with derision (Marsh and Fox, 1993).

Crithlow (1986) also observed that societies who amplify the problems associated with alcohol use, predominantly protestant temperance cultures, also experience higher degrees of problems. For example, we can only justify anti-social behaviour to alcohol by attributing it with great power to control the actions of the individual. Whereas the Bolivian Camba have no concept of controlled drinking or alcoholism and frequently engage in bouts of heroic consumption to the point of chronic inebriation. Yet violence or other drink related problems are completely absent from their society (Heath, 1991a, 1991b).

Informal control of intoxication

Studies of alcohol use across cultures reveal the structures behind consumption. For example, where alcohol is consumed, cultures evolve prescribed laws governing it. These rules and rituals have a significant influence on consumption itself. The rules are pliable and open to change through the domination, influence or convergence with other cultures. For example, alcohol consumption amongst Spanish youth has moved from wine at the table with the family towards more Western European binge drinking. The greatest shared cultural taboo on alcohol is drinking alone. Even in societies where this is more permissible, drinking must be done in social environments such as bars. The Camba only drink in a social context, often sharing the same glass. This is an important social restraint on use. Research suggest that those who regulate their consumption through external measures, such as drinking only as much as everyone else, experience fewer problems (Apsler, 1979; Grund, 1993).

Alcohol is seen as a social act by nearly all cultures, and even in the images of ancient Egypt we see vessels containing alcohol also have several straws emanating from them. The ceremonies that surround intoxication appear to promote group cohesion, solidarity and bonding. Giving and receiving is important in these attachment experiences. This is through sharing both the alcohol and the rules of etiquette. Nearly every culture has evolved the toasting ceremony. This can range from brief salutations of cheers to elaborate speeches as signs of respect, which are sealed through the drinking ritual (Mars and Altman, 1987). These etiquettes extend into the permissible behaviours of the person inebriated. For example in Pearce's (1992) studies of Irish fisherman, to drink heavily was well-regarded amongst peers as long as they neither lost control of their judgment or behaviour. Likewise, Oshodin (1995) observed that Nigerian culture esteemed individuals who could drink heavily and remain sober. Only in cultures where disinhibition is permissible, do we see people act out on consumption.

As a result even the incidence of alcoholism varies dramatically from culture to culture. In Irish cultures it is very high, whilst in Italy, China and amongst the Jewish community rates are negligible. Each society has free access to alcohol, and yet we see huge disparity in consumption rates and behaviour. Whilst drug use is more localised we see similar examples. For example, many cultures do not associate substance misuse with mood state at all. The Biwat of Papa New Guinea chew the stimulant Betel but only as part of business negotiations (Watson, undated). Despite over production they show no incidence of addictions. Conversely, even the most innocuous drug in one society is devastating in another. The Sahal Bushmen of Niger experience delinquency, crime and social breakdown to procure the status symbols of their society, tea and sugar (Klein, 2001). The idea that intoxication, and by extension addictions, occurs solely in the user, immune to the wider cultural context in which they consume, is too simplistic. Both historical and cultural variables influence consumption, patterns of use and the subsequent behaviours. We see cultures immune to problems, we see cultures develop problems and we see cultures re-gain control over consumption. Addiction rates soar at particular moments in history and recede at others. It renders it impossible to project our present day concerns onto other cultures, historical or otherwise, without doing much violence to them.

Socio-economic perspective

Certainly, one of the most striking features of modern drug and alcohol consumption is the scale. Whilst the concept of addiction is new, so is the huge international infrastructure that supports it. Mass production and distribution have spread every drug to every corner of the world. The most obscure herb can cross any border and what is missing from the psychoactive periodictable can be produced in the laboratory. The economic, political and legal frameworks that facilitate this consumption are largely ignored. Our modern day preoccupation is diverted to the tragic particulars of individual cases with no consideration given to the wider forces that current use is embedded in. But just as one cannot expect to grasp mathematics by only looking at the 'equals' symbol and beyond, to understand drugs we must appreciate the political and economic variables so neglected in our calculations. We could do this with any drug but we shall take crack cocaine as an example. Try to answer as many questions as you can in Exercise 1.1.

The coca plant, of the *Erythroxylum* genus, grows on the Eastern slopes of the Andes. Whilst 250 species exist, four have commercial applications. Three are used for coca extraction, destined to be refined into cocaine, whilst the highly prized *Erythroxylum novograntese* variety *truxillense* has a different fate. Though high in coca yield it is very difficult to extract it from this particular plant. But it is cultivated for its strong flavoured leaves that are still used in the production of Coca-Cola. Plants reserved for cocaine production are rugged and produce high yields of coca when grown at altitude. The high demand, low maintenance coca plant is worth twenty times

---

Exercise 1.1: Cocaine

- Where does cocaine come from?
- Who grows it and why?
- Who buys it and refines it into cocaine?
- How much money do they make?
- Where does this money go?
- Why do Western powers not address production?
- Who transports the drug to UK?
- Who deals the drug in the UK?
- Who converts the drug into crack cocaine?
- Who uses crack cocaine?
- Where do they get their money from?
- Who is picking up this tab?

---

the value of cacao and six times the value of coffee per hectare. And unlike other fruit crops that are harvested once a year, coca can be harvested every two months. The principle reason for its popularity amongst farmers, predominantly in Colombia, Bolivia and Peru, is poverty. The collapse of national industries in the 1950s; drought conditions on weak soils; increasing third world debt; combined with the opening of their interiors to large, unskilled, urban populations created desperation. Coca is not merely a culturally accepted drug in the New World, it is survival.

In South America, national economic dependency on the drug compromises any ability to eradicate production without inflicting greater poverty. Drug production is the local farmers' only response to the crippling poverty. Ruthlessly savage gangsters are these farmers' greatest benefactors and international demands for coca eradication their greatest enemy. The poisoning of their land and families by US funded herbicide crop spraying does little to redress this balance.

The Colombians have seized control of the South American coca fields. In 1987 the most infamous drug baron and head of the Medellin Cartel, Pablo Escobar, was listed as the 14th richest man in the world, which he claimed was achieved through his bicycle repair workshops. This incredible wealth bought influence in every area of Colombian life. At one time Escobar had his own standing army of 3,000, was ordering 24 assassinations a day, and the impunity of his killing forced the country's judges to go on strike (Bowden, 2001). When threatened with extradition to the US, he offered to pay off the country's national debt. In a compromise deal he built his own luxury prison instead, where the inmates and prison guards worked for him and he could continue his business. The battalion of the Colombian army sent to re-house him also appeared to be on his payroll, allowing him to walk free and wage a self-financed war against his mother country. Such was his influence that the Colombian government, in concert with the CIA, US Special Forces and the DEA, could not bring him to justice. Instead they relied upon the 'unofficial' support of a vigilante organisation called Los Pepes – 'People Persecuted by Pablo Escobar'. They de-stabilised his power base by assassinating anyone with any connection to the drug lord. After his execution in 1989, it was revealed that Los Pepes was really the rival Cali cocaine cartel, who now increased international cocaine distribution unopposed, and diversified into heroin.

When the conquistadors invaded South American, the native populations knew of the Spanish approach as the hitherto unknown but virulent outbreaks of smallpox decimated their numbers, days before they arrived. In the same way corruption now heralds the way for cocaine that touches every aspect of social, political and economic life in the Andean range and beyond. Presidents, ministers, political parties, election campaigns, military coups, armies, navies, terrorists, revolutionaries, police, banks, trade unions and the civil services have all been lured by the cocaine dollar in scandals so frequent they are now mundane. Cocaine has created Narco-states. The rewards of trafficking are so incalculable that the central financial concern of drug barons is how to conceal it. Banks have been bankrupted when dealers have moved their money. Over a billion dollars of laundered drug money is invested in stock markets around the world every day. In 2000, the CIA cited the London Stock Exchange as the centre of drug money laundering (Davenport-Hines, 2001). Whilst banks and brokers are expected to report un-sourced money being invested, it is simply not in their interest to inform on lucrative clients and the commissions they bring.

The politics of cocaine

The hunt for Escobar was a high profile gesture of the war on drugs, and an electioneering platform for the staunchly anti-cocaine George Bush Snr. Traditionally, US foreign policy has not been antithetical to the cocaine trade. Ronald Reagan's determination to support the Contra rebels to overthrow the Sandinista government of Nicaragua led to a deep involvement between the CIA and the cocaine trade. The Sandinistas had seized power from a US sponsored tyrant that had bankrupted the nation. An unconvinced Congress was not so sympathetic towards the anti-communist Contra rebels, but $19 million was trafficked to them via El Salvador, which was also on the brink of turning communist. This bought aid of various kinds including weaponry. In return cocaine was imported to the US to increase finance for the war. A large scale cocaine dealer was arrested and it was discovered his bank account had been opened by Oliver North, answerable to the White House incumbents Ronald Reagan and Vice President George Bush Snr. North was destined to become the patsy for the whole operation. Only virulent amnesia saved Reagan.

Four companies used by the CIA to transit aid to the Contra rebels, and who received over $1 million in governmental financial support, were run by well-established international cocaine traffickers (Streatfeild, 2002). This is detailed in the CIA's own internal report available from their website (www.cia.com). Other indicted cocaine traffickers claimed they had charges dropped provided they make regular financial donations to the Contra rebels through CIA brokers. International drug markets are not necessarily profit making for Western powers, but undoubtedly they provide financial leverage to control foreign affairs and engineer and maintain governments sympathetic to US interests. US businesses can then exploit the mineral wealth at the sacrifice of the indigenous people's interests, compounding the cycle of poverty further.

Similar political forces are also what led to the CIA involvement in the global heroin market, financing the Mafia in return for destabilising communist states such as the post-war democratically elected government of Italy (see McCoy, 1972).

When cocaine's cost and distribution was limited to the wealthy there had been a lull in the concern voiced about the drug. When it hit the black sections of the communities, it fuelled hysteria. The influx of cheap Contra cocaine in the early 1980s was distributed in California at the time that crack, smokable cocaine, was coming into vogue. This fortuitous combination made dealers at the head of the hierarchy over a million dollars a day, as the drug descended from playboy to ghetto status. Control of the lucrative crack markets fuelled violence on an unheralded scale in the US, as those who traded a living in the shadow economies fought gang wars for the crumbs. Homicides, particularly black on black killings, soared as the most disadvantaged communities turned against themselves. Harsh sentencing of mandatory minimum sentences befell those busted in possession of the drug or dealing, doubling the prison population of America. Crack to the ghetto dealers was what coca is to the South American peasant. But contrary to the MTV hip-hop fantasies, street dealers risk the beatings, shootings and prison sentences for a pittance. The average street dealer earns a derisory $3.30 an hour, whilst others pay for the privilege to be street dealers in the hope of induction into the gang. For the most part, bad ass crack dealers still live with their mothers (Levitt and Dubner, 2005). In response Reagan, who was so instrumental in the creation of the crack-washed America, appointed a Drug Czar who advocated that all dealers face the death penalty without a hint of irony (Davenport-Hines, 2001).

Interestingly, those politicians who advocate the most stringent punishment for drug users reserve the right to exempt themselves. Schlosser (2003) details how in 1996 congressman Randy Cunningham attacked the Clinton administration for being soft on drugs, demanding ever more draconian measures to punish users and dealers. Four months later his son was busted by the DEA for smuggling cannabis, his father begged clemency and instead of the life sentence, he only received a sentence of two and half years. Had he not tested positive for cocaine three times whilst on parole it may have been shorter. The US Congress themselves have new laws to prevent young people prosecuted for drugs from receiving financial assistance in colleges and created a vast employment drug testing industry to identify drug users in the work place. Those identified can be fired, while alcohol use goes untouched, regardless of levels of use. At the same time any measure to introduce drug testing amongst the US government themselves has always been blocked.

Cocaine markets

Cocaine arrives in Britain through well established and often corrupt trade routes. In recent years attention has been drawn to the smaller scale, opportunist trafficking. Since 9/11 and increased airport traffic control in the US, Jamaican gangs brokering deals with the Colombians have diverted cocaine to Britain and Holland. Mules swallowing 'bullets' of cocaine powder wrapped in condoms or the fingers of latex gloves walk through airports and let nature do the rest. The typical payment of £2,000 is a lottery win for the poor who are easily recruited from the mass unemployed of the island. The major distribution centres of London, Bristol, Manchester and Birmingham have all seen increases in violence and gang feuds in the fight to control a market estimated up to £9 billion a year.

Once imported, the drug is distributed in a pyramid of local dealers. These markets can be 'open', where drugs are purchased from a stranger in a well-known market place; or 'closed', where the drug is distributed through those with the right contacts. Some dealers are merciless profiteers, others desperate users, and some are self-styled connoisseurs of intoxicants. But for most they are friends, family and associates in closed markets that are safer and a better guarantee of quality. They do not rip off their customers because they are associates. Dealers in closed markets tend to take pride in the quality of their product. Open market dealers are unlikely to see their punters again, disgruntled or otherwise. In these unpredictable markets it is the buyer who must beware, making themselves vulnerable to rip-offs, assaults, muggings or other crimes they can never report.

Cocaine is converted into crack as it trickles down the dealing strata and sold on the street for £25 a rock. The rush, described as a '20 minute orgasm', is self-evidently more-ish. £300 a day binges are not uncommon. A client of mine once spent £9,000 on it in less than three months. Crack has percolated every demographic drug using market. I once worked with a 67-year-old, white, respectable male who treated himself to a few rocks come pension day. He did not request help for his newly acquired habit, but got free condoms for his new friends in the sex industry. Whilst users may fund their habit through their own employment, and large numbers do, the poor is where the volume sales are to be had. These users resort to dealing themselves, crime, begging, benefits or prostitution. Exits out include public funded prison, probation and treatment centres. All this money is ultimately drawn from taxation, increased insurance premiums and the disposable income of the general population. So, even non-users cannot escape complicity in the global drug market that is estimated at $465 billion (8 per cent of world trade), rivalling both the petrol chemical and pharmaceutical industries for sheer scale. The only losers in this great chain of being are the farmers, the users and ultimately us, the tax payer. As such, the international drug trade can be understood as an indirect taxation on us all to pay for the US occupation of the third world.

Drugs: objective and subjective effects

In this brief overview we can see drug use is inexorably cradled in history, culture, politics, economics and society. Residing in the centre of this matrix are the individual users themselves. They are the actor whose script is shaped by these diffuse forces. Much is written on the effects of drugs and there is a powerful assumption that they are predictable. These experiences are considered pharmacologically driven and an inevitable product of the drugs' interaction on the brain. But there is much more to the experience than this. As we have seen, other cultures and historical periods have made use of the same drugs and had very divergent experiences of them. Whilst psychopharmacology has illuminated many areas of the actions of drug on the brain, it cannot account for this range of human experience. Even in the most highly controlled clinical settings, with the most attentive monitoring, managed by skilled experts, the effects of drugs remain defiantly unpredictable. For example, prescribing drugs for those with mental health problems is not an exact science. Initial attempts at medication rarely have the desired effects. Therapeutic drugs and doses are actually determined through monitoring and refinement. People with the same diagnosis can have radically divergent reactions to the same drug. Besides the drug working or not, their use can be accompanied by some, all, or none of the side effects. And the yellow card system allows for reporting new side-effects previously not noted in clinical trials.

An interesting experiment by Schachter and Singer (1962) offers a glimpse into what shapes a drug's effect. Primarily a study into the nature of emotion, a group of students were all given an injection of the stimulant adrenalin or placebo of salt water. They were not told what the drug was but rather given certain explanations of what they would experience. One group was told that it would have a stimulant effect; another was told that they would experience headaches and dizziness; and the third group were given no explanation at all. They were then asked to complete paperwork with other participants. Confederates, actors posing as research subjects, then acted out in extreme ways becoming either highly irritable or laughing. Those without an explanation of their experience adjusted their behaviour toward that of the confederates. Those who had an explanation of the drug's effect did not. Whilst the effect was short lived, it illuminates a telling reality.

The administration of a drug will cause a neurological disruption to brain functioning; however, there is nothing in the experience which reveals itself to the consciousness that it distorts. We do not 'feel' opiates bonding to receptors or 'know' that cannaboids are interfering with signals in our synaptic clefts. Each recipient of a drug must make sense of that internal experience. This demands both forging an interpretation of it and placing a value on what kind of experience they are having. They must also make separation between the effects of the drug and the context they take it in during this suspension of normal functioning. The reference point for these valuations is the pre-existent cultural norms of the user. The drug does not merely act on the individual; it is mediated by the expectations of the user who is located in a historical and cultural context.

Let us take a drug that most of us will be familiar with, alcohol. Consider the list of effects in Exercise 1. 2. Circle those effects which you feel are the product of the biological action of the drug.

Exercise 1.2: The effects of alcohol

What are the biological and what are the social expectancies of alcohol?

- slowing the nervous system
- depression
- dehydration
- dis-inhibition
- positive mood
- confidence
- increased libido
- decreased sexual arousal
- release enzyme
- aggression
- narrowing sense of time
- increased acidity of the blood
- slurred speech
- sociability
- hangovers
- interrupt neurological message
- increased aggression

Alcohol will slow the motor neurone system, slur speech, suppress sexual arousal in men and women, increase acidity in the blood (which breaks down nicotine quickly triggering more smoking), disrupt neurological thought processes, depress the nervous system and cause dehydration. The build up of enzymes to break this substance down will also cause that bilious hangover. But does anyone drink because they are seeking, and willing to pay for, these experiences?

Watching adverts for alcohol we see they are finely tuned to particular aspirations of identified social groups and that the biological effects of alcohol are conspicuously absent. They appeal to an individual identity, not neurology. Instead they depict alcohol as the source of positive mood states, sexual allure, heightened confidence and witticisms. Even though these are completely in contradiction to the actual effects of alcohol. Central to this narrative is one perennial fact: no one is ever drunk. They create, perpetuate and trade on the cultural myths, personifying the 'subjective' expectancies that are sought through alcohol consumption, none of which are pharmacological properties of the drug.

PET and CAT scanning have elucidated which specific areas of the brain are stimulated by each drug. But one area of the brain is central to them all and can never be divorced from these interactions: memory. Research by Goldman et al. (1993) has established a significant link between an individual's expectations of alcohol, their consumption and subsequent behaviour. The drug does not simply operate on certain sites in the brain but also spreads out in a web of associations about these kinds of experiences. Therefore, whilst we are clear about the effect of a drug like alcohol on the central nervous system, we cannot account for the behavioural, psychological and emotional responses to it in this way. This is a far more complex set of relationships and the drug using experience is a composite of both interactions. We cannot separate the objective biological actions of the drug from the subjective expectations which are culturally situated. MacAndrew and Edgerton (1969) suggested that disparate cultural experiences on alcohol are derived from the individual learning what drunkenness is from those around them, and acting upon this knowledge during consumption. This both confirms and conforms to the social teachings. As such, cultural regulation is not limited to the custom of when and how one drinks, but creates expectations of the drinking itself. The ways in which people behave on alcohol reveal more about their culture than it does alcohol. As Heath (1991b) observed, drinking is embedded in culture and culture is embedded in the consequences of drinking. As a result, every culture gets the drinkers that it deserves.

Expectancy

Expectancy theory in psychology identifies how early experience influences future behaviour. It explores the interplay between memory and cognitive thinking in an 'if'–'then' equation. Repeated perceptions of consumption and behaviour cultivate the belief that 'if' people consume this drug, 'then' they behave in this way. This memory serves as an expectation, that certain consequences are presumed to follow the ingestion of a drug. This does not demand direct experience to formulate these expectations but can be learned from others modelling these behaviours. Young people's expectations of alcohol can predict future behaviour even before they have experienced a drinking event. And those with positive expectations of alcohol, such as increased sociability and confidence, drink sooner and heavier. This means that when we enter into drinking situations we have a strong expectation of what alcohol consumption will to do us. We then drink and in amidst the ensuing events we must interpret the events that unfold. And we do this in accordance with our expectations (see Figure 1.1).

Whilst we may constantly iterate the need to get young people or heavier users to see the consequences of their behaviour, we never ask why they do not see the consequences in the first place. As we have seen, substances interfere with the brain processes, but it is the interpretations of this event that is critical. In one experiment (Darkes and Goldman, 1993) heavy drinking

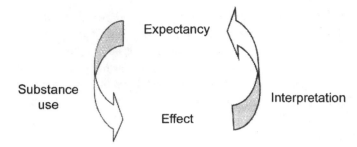

Figure 1.1   Expectation and consumption

engaging in a novel and risky behaviour and ascribe it to the drug. This experience can give way students were invited to a party. They were asked to judge which party goers had consumed alcohol. They scored no better than random chance. Behaviours which matched their expectations of alcohol were assumed to be alcohol induced. This can be a simple error where people mistake positive social interactions as the product of the drinking; whereas it is the product of the relationships people are having. As a result people may attempt to enhance these positive interactions by drinking more, as if double the alcohol is double the fun. But the heavier the consumption the more objective effects incapacitate the subjective experience that is sought. High levels of consumption of any drug tend to simply incapacitate the individual and leave them in a self-isolated introspective mood state. Less is often far more with consumption.

Challenging the expectancies can have a profound effect on consumption. In the 'party' experiment, high alcohol consuming students were subsequently assigned to either a controlled drinking programme; an expectancy group asked to explore the media portrayal of alcohol and compare it to the reality of use; and a third control group that did nothing. Consumption in the controlled drinkers went up having increased their confidence, whilst consumption was significantly reduced in the expectancy group, particularly amongst the heaviest users. This is a salutatory lesson for drug educators. Warning young people away from drug use because of their powerful effects only serves to cement expectation and subsequent 'uncontrolled' behaviour. Furthermore, it adds a prestige to high consumption as demonstrating the mastery of heroic dosages of potent intoxicants. Instead, the most effective treatment programmes (Lowinson et al., 1992) challenge the validity of young people's expectations and re-consider how much skill is involved in achieving high states of inebriation. More importantly, we should aim to break the deep Western assumption that mood state can be controlled by drugs. Whilst drugs appear to have many functions, their ability to be 'mood altering' is exaggerated within Western culture. For example, consider drinking alcohol in the following situations. If you have a wider experience of drug use, consider other substances in the same setting. Consider mood, feelings and behaviour in each of the settings described in Exercise 1.3 after consuming the equivalent of two pints of beer.

It is quite possible to experience mood states concurrent to drug consumption. For example, people can be depressed and drunk; they can grieve and be high on cocaine; they can be stressed and stoned on cannabis. We do not often identify the possibility of concurrent mood as we assume the drug using experience is all consuming. But it is not.

Equally drug using expectancies can vary considerably. First time cannabis users often report feeling nothing at all and appear to have to 'learn' how to be stoned. Other first time users

---

Exercise 1.3: Setting and consumption

- Stag do
- Business meeting
- In a hostile pub waiting for a late friend
- At home having received bad news
- At a dinner party

---

experience the 'giggles' when they first smoke the drug. They experience the excitement of engaging in a novel and risky behaviour and ascribe it to the drug. This experience can give way to more introspective mood states with longer term use. First time users of cocaine also report little to no effect from initial use. Hospital patients receiving high doses of pure opiates for chronic pain do not crave or resume use at the end of their treatment. Most are simply glad to complete the prescriptions and get on with their lives. Probably the most dramatic effect of expectancies is that of Koro. Male cannabis users may wish to skip the rest of this paragraph. Meaning 'turtle head', Koro is a culturally bound disorder, prevalent in China, Malaysia and Indonesia. It is an anxiety disorder that has become associated with the use of cannabis where the user fears that the penis is retracting into the body and will cause death. Panic stricken sufferers are liable to attach weights and other mechanical devices to stave off this fear. This condition has now spread to the US, but only in populations that have heard of it (Earlywine, 2001).

Placebo

The power of expectation is best illustrated in the placebo effect. A placebo is an inert substance given to the patient 'blind', so they do not know that it is an inactive substance. It is the patient's positive expectation in the pill as medicine which elicits a healing reaction in them. All new drugs, including those for mental health, are trialed against placebo in order to measure their 'objective' effectiveness beyond the subjective expectation of the patient. However, their potency is curbed as trials are designed to bias against the placebo, with measures to inform the clients of whether they are in a placebo group as opposed to the active treatment. Individuals susceptible to placebo effects are also removed from the test populations. In spite of the weakening of the placebo's influence, their effects can be so profound that subjects sometimes have to be removed from the research studies. Despite this we see very little difference in treatment outcomes between anti-depressants and placebos (Kirsh and Sapirstein, 1998). Research also demonstrates that the effect of placebo is greatly improved by the relationship that the patient has with the person prescribing it. Doctors tend to be more optimistic about new drugs, broadcasting this confidence to their patient enhancing its effect. As the old adage goes regarding new medicine, you are best getting it whilst it still works (Dixon and Sweeney, 2000).

Other people report improvement despite being informed that they are taking an inert substance or achieved different outcomes depending on the colour of the pill they were given (Evans, 2004). The subjective expectancies are so powerful they can induce adaptations in the human brain. Research shows that placebos can activate opiate networks in the brain, though more weakly than the opiates themselves (Petrovic et al., 2002). This might explain how placebos have been used on the battlefield to perform amputations. Placebos can also cause adaptations in the brain in the same way that medications can, though in different areas (Walach et al., 2003).

In terms of behaviour, blind placebo studies for drugs and alcohol are equally revealing. Violent drinkers given a placebo alcohol remained hostile, whilst disguised alcohol elicited no aggressive responses (Marlatt and Rohsenow, 1980). Opiate users often differentiate between methadone and heroin, however, in a Pepsi-cola style challenge, they can not discriminate between the two. In clinical practice, urine samples have shown that many drugs users do not test positive for the drugs they think they have taken and whose associated behaviours they are acting out, but do for a host of others. This is not to suggest that drugs have a purely placebo effect. Drugs do affect the neurology of the user, but it is the conscious categorisation of the experience that shapes it. For example, if placebos have some mild side effect, like a mild emetic, the effect is greatly enhanced as the physical sensation enforces the expectation that it is doing something. These objective effects provide the raw material which is shaped by the subjective expectations of the user. The subjective expectancies can be easily altered. If a patient in a clinical trial is informed that the ratio between placebo group and active medication is 1–16, placebo has a greater effect than in subjects who are told that it will be a 50–50 trial because people believe the odds of them having the active medication are greater (Walach, 2003). Expectancy theory does not provide a complete explanation of addiction. But expectations shape the experience as a cultural lens on the inner brain experience that does not reveal its own nature.

Self-correction

Expectations and their disruptions play an integral role in learning to manage intoxication. When we consider the evolution of our drinking patterns we often find that it is those 'never again' moments that amend our use. Here, overtly negative consequences force a reappraisal of positive expectations. Sometimes this self-correctional mechanism does not occur. This may arise because the user resides in a normative fallacy of use. Their group's behaviours is perceived as typical. This may insulate a person from shameful or negative punishments if everybody reacts in the same way. Therefore high and chaotic peer use normalises this behaviour. Conversely group norms can regulate people's use through negative social cues that shame deviants back into the fold. Recreational heroin use that seeps out of the weekend and into the week is adjudged junkie behaviour; sharp remarks about someone's alcohol consumption which falls between humour and judgement; the labelling of a cannabis smoker as a total 'head' may initiate negative feelings of self which amend behaviours in most people. All using populations will evolve their own code of practice and police it with negative punishment cues which can either insulate the user from problems or institutionalise them.

Numerous researchers have also consistently demonstrated that people do not attend to the negative consequences of their use, but are biased towards recalling only the positives. Some research has suggested that this may be the memory failing to process punishing events (Isbell et al., 1998). Other theories have suggested that memories are stored according to goals, and therefore subjective expectancies are recalled over the unsought realities of use (Wyer and Srull, 1986). Lazarus (1982) suggests that memories are stored in light of preceding expectation of whether events will be positive or negative, again causing a recall bias. But it may be simpler than brain function. Humans find shameful experience deeply uncomfortable, and when we act in ways which are in discord with our ideal of ourselves, we fortify ourselves against this kind of painful recollection. We may endlessly eulogise our reckless drinking behaviour as funny to sanitise discomfort and what cannot be salvaged as good humoured inebriation is simply kept secret. Certainly, in the later stages of problematic alcohol consumption, the brain damage caused through high drinking severely impairs memory. This cruel side-effect may retard this mechanism further.

When individual behaviour and consumption exceeds the tolerance of the group norms they must either change or become ostracised from the group. They may gravitate towards other high consumers who hold a higher watermark of acceptable intoxication. Settled in a comfort zone of acceptance, behaviour becomes normalised once again in context of the group. And heavy using groups can be very tolerant of the most anti-social behaviours. Alternatively, use may be conducted away in isolation from others, where there are no social limits, rituals and ceremonies to be adhered too. And therefore, no social brake is applied to consumption at all.

Biological problems

The diverse historical, cultural and psychological experience of intoxicants does not limit itself to the effects of drug but also to the problems associated with their use. The compulsive urge to take drugs is largely ascribed to the action of the drug on the human brain. Kitchen-sink scientific theories regarding the biological nature of compulsion had been popular since the 19th century. Early temperance reformists such as Benjamin Rush described chronic alcohol use as a disease of the will, whilst Thomas Trotter described alcohol use as a disease of the mind. Originally it was advocated that this disease could affect anybody. Such ideas became refined by the alcoholism movement of the early 20th century, when it became increasing apparent that not all drinkers developed problems. Instead, the concept of the 'allergy' was introduced, which was a biological sensitivity that afflicted a specific sub-population. This idea gained vast popularity, largely due to the 12 step movement's core assumptions and revival of temperance values as the treatment for problem users in the 1950s. These ideas were given credence by researchers at Yale University such as Jellinek, who conducted research on subjects active in the 12 step movement. Unsurprisingly, the findings of this research tended to support the exact same values of the treatment philosophy that the subjects advocated. Hence it lent scientific authority to the idea of a progressive biological illness that was characterised by uncontrollable consumption beyond the realms of an individual's own volition. However, it has been a point of continued scientific struggle and setbacks in identifying any biological mechanism that supports the idea of addiction as a biological disease.

One of the first modern biological models of addiction to gain broad popularity was proposed by Olds (1959). He discovered that electro-stimulation of the pleasure centres in the brain compelled rats to self-administer electrical charges. It is the powerful effect that drugs have on these pleasure centres in the brain that drive the compulsive experience. However, it soon became apparent that individuals may become addicted to drugs that do not induce pleasure (Hollister, 1998; Battegay, 2000). Instead, it was proposed that addictions were the result of the avoidance of aversive withdrawal and craving to drugs (Jellinek, 1960).

These theories, and the swathes of biological explanations which have followed, have defined addiction in context of these two key concepts: tolerance and withdrawal. Tolerance is defined as the need to take increasing doses of a substance in order to sustain the 'desired' effect. Tolerance originates in the brain needing to operate within a narrow biological window to sustain metabolic functions. As such it must make adjustment to any disruptions in functioning. So, when a depressant is taken that lowers brain functioning, the brain responds by working harder to counteract the sedation. When stimulants are taken, the brain must decrease metabolic processes to accommodate the artificial surge. Tolerance is not exponential but levels off with heavy use. Classic overdose is the body's inability to compensate to the effect of a drug which results in death.

Two forms of tolerance have been suggested (Julien, 1998). Metabolic tolerance results from increases in the production of enzymes which break down substances like alcohol far quicker. The more you drink, the more enzymes are produced and so the drug is metabolised more quickly. The second form of tolerance is cellular. It is not clear what causes cellular tolerance. One suggestion is that the attrition of drugs binding to the receptor sites in the brain damages them, creating an ever poorer 'fit' between the drug and the site, reducing efficiency. A second theory is that in reaction to the constant presence of a drug, the brain produces more receptor sites, diluting the concentration of the drug on the brain. Mechanisms of cellular adaptation probably relate specifically to the sites of each particular drug. Cross tolerance, higher tolerance to more than one drug, occurs when the two drugs operate on the same sites. As there has been no identifiable mechanism for addiction it is often construed as tolerance and these terms are sometimes used interchangeably. This is because it is believed that as tolerance increases it necessitates the user take escalating doses of the drug to sustain the desired effect, driving compulsivity.

Withdrawal is linked to tolerance as the readjustment of brain functioning when the drug wears off. As the drug's activity recedes, the brain carries on over-compensating for its effect for a short period. Therefore, as a depressant drug wears off the brain is left over-compensating; whilst stimulant use will leave the brain in a state of under-compensation for a while. This is known as the law of rebound and states the withdrawal of the drug is opposite to its effects. Depressants make you sleepy and sluggish and the withdrawal makes you anxious and restless. Stimulants increase energy levels and suppress appetite whilst the withdrawal crash leaves people lethargic and prone to binge eating.

These theories have been elaborated upon by subsequent researchers who are primarily concerned with the operations of the drug on human brain. There are a diverse range of competing biological theories. These models suggest an increased biological sensitivity to a drug, amplifys the effect of the intoxicant on the individual. For example Dole and Nyswander (1967) proposed a metabolic theory of addiction; where an inability to produce natural occurring brain transmitters would lead some people to experience a more powerful reaction to imbibed drugs. Increased exposure would then lead to the brain producing less of these naturally occurring neurotransmitters demanding increased drug use. Although elaborated upon, the biological sensitivity model still underpins much research (see Nutt, 1996) and the hunt continues for its primary genetic origins. The fact that these individuals are acutely sensitive to minute levels of variance in natural neurone transmission rates but wholly insensitive to the huge levels of imported narcotics which disrupt brain functions is not answered in these studies. Others have supposed a secondary genetic effect, based on the big five character traits which have been identified as the core of human personality. Cloninger (1987) suggests that those who inherit high degrees of traits of such impulsivity are more prone to engage in thrill seeking and risk taking behaviours. This would render addiction as a secondary genetic effect. But within this paradigm addiction cannot be considered a disease anymore than the introvert who becomes a librarian or the extrovert who becomes a traffic policeman.

Environmental tolerance

The problem with these theories is that biological exposure to drugs does not in itself create addiction. For example, animals in laboratory experiments will only self-administer drugs under very strict environmental conditions (See Harris, 2005). It has long been recognised that hospital patients receiving long term prescriptions of opiates do not experience use as euphoric but functional, and experience limited withdrawal. Woods' research (1990) estimates that the risks of developing an addiction from hospital treatment are less than 0.01 per cent.

Furthermore, the endless repetition of a pleasurable activity soon loses its gloss and becomes a mundane norm. In clinical practice, addictive behaviours are striking for their lack of any euphoric pay off for the relentless investment made. Clients simply do not present for treatment because they cannot tolerate any more fun. This suggests that constant exposure breeds an indifference to the euphoria of a drug, despite the same chemical interactions taking place in the brain. This can also be seen in retired drug users who may take a drug after many years of abstinence. They may not experience any euphoria in the once cherished experience and are just relieved to get through what now feels unpleasant.

What we also see is that the central concepts of tolerance and withdrawal are not simply conditioned by biological exposure. Environmental and psychological cues have been identified as critical factors in the development of tolerance (Harris, 2005). Alterations in the environment can alter tolerance. We may experience this personally as the 'dinner party effect'. At home at a dinner party you can consume large amounts of alcohol and not feel intoxicated, where as moderate drinking in a novel environment at a different time can induce high intoxication. Healy (2002) suggests an even more banal cause of tolerance. As he observes, the human brain is always drawn to the novel or threatening situation and disregards the irrelevant. He parallels this to living next to a train track, where the rushing trains are deafening to begin with but within days the brain discards the experience as an insignificant threat and it ceases to draw any attention. Repeated exposure to the drug normalises the experience as an everyday occurrence so is filtered out.

It is also notable that it is almost exclusively highly tolerant, long term opiate users who overdose on heroin. This may occur after a period of abstinence or the drug being taken in combination with other depressants which will increase the sedation of the nervous system. But many overdose on levels that were well tolerated only the day before. Without environmental and psychological cues there can be a failure of tolerance (see Kalant, 1987; Wolgin, 1989). Likewise, sensitisation to a drug is dependant upon environmental factors. For example, Post et al. (1987) describe that when animals are administered cocaine in novel environments they do not exhibit any changes in behaviour akin to the hyperactivity they demonstrate when given the drug standard environments.

Withdrawal

Even more problematic is the fact that not all drugs even produce tolerance or withdrawal. We can become tolerant to cocaine and LSD but experience no physical withdrawal. Other drugs like Prozac rarely promote tolerance but patients experience severe withdrawal. This has lead to the further distinction between physical dependence syndromes which do generate physical symptoms of withdrawal, and psychological dependence which invokes anxieties. However, even this distinction is not clear. In the very first study of morphine withdrawal conducted in the 1920s, researchers could not identify a uniform withdrawal condition. The heaviest withdrawal sufferers responded most vigorously to placebo injections of water, admonishment or engaging in strenuous work (Light and Torrance, 1929). Similar results have been found in animals. Symptoms of withdrawal from PCP were much reduced in monkeys who had to seek out food rather than those who passively received food (Carroll, 1993). In research cited by Davies (1993) rats were yoked together with intravenous catheters. When one rat self-administered morphine, a second rat received an equivalent dose whilst a third received a Ringer solution. Withdrawal was the severest in the self-administrating rats. Withdrawal is thus linked with motivation in ways which are currently not understood.

Even within street opiate using populations, expectations create unaccountable difference in experience. Most street users shun methadone as a more profound and protracted withdrawal syndrome than street heroin. However, when placed on blind reduction prescriptions, where the concentration of methadone is reduced but the volume of liquid remains the same, people are surprised when they discover they have been drinking pure formulae and have been opiate-free for weeks. What we may also see in withdrawal is the role of expectation playing its part, as it does in both the effects and development of tolerance. Expectancies have been identified as influencing catecholamine levels which drive the autonomic system, endogenous opiates in pain management and mediate the immune system (Bandura, 1992a). Cultural expectancies can have a direct physical impact on the body. And having completely detoxified from a drug it is difficult to see why people would return to use if they were purely motivated by avoidance of these terrible symptoms.

The handmaiden of withdrawal is cravings and we are yet to establish a clear biological basis for this searing 'want' to use but are believed to be the long term and defuse neurological adaptations from repeat exposure. People may experience cravings years after cessation from taking drugs such as nicotine or conversely not experience them at all. The experience of cravings is often cited as the biological cause of relapse. However Miller and Gold's (1994) research found that cravings could only account for seven per cent of relapses. In clinical practice, the most often cited reason for the resumption of heavy use is boredom.

These critiques of purely biological explanations of substance abuse are important for two reasons. Firstly, biological models are apolitical, ignoring the social and political context of use. Whilst science does not deal in ethics by its very nature, its limited focus on neurology dismisses social factors by default. The correlation between crack smoking and postcodes in poor urban communities is so predicable (Lillie-Blanton et al., 1993; Jones, 1992) it makes scientific ideas of genetic compulsion absurd. Likewise, the catastrophic effect of colonialism on indigenous peoples and the subsequent explosion of problematic consumptions in their otherwise regulated use cannot be accounted for by their own genetic make up. What we see in these brief critiques is that the cultural context of use is not merely an adjunct to the drug using experience but is an integral part. Secondly, it is important to recognise the limits of biology, not to decry science for its own sake, but to overcome an innate pessimism that deterministic models breed. Biology does have an important role in our understanding, but it is not the presiding factor. In clinical practice, the assumptions of addiction as innate in the very fabric of the problematic user create hopelessness. It does not simply serve to exonerate the user from their own behaviour but more importantly it instils a futility in their ability to change that behaviour. We need to understand what the biological and the cultural contribute if we are to help people overcome not only their addictions, but their self-defeating expectations.

Conclusion

Our understanding of addiction has limited our concerns to the biological compulsivity innate within the user. This preoccupation has served to obscure the true nature of use which appears inexorably entwined in historical, cultural, political and economic forces. Historically we have seen both shifting patterns of consumption and addiction. Duplicitous political forces have evolved around and direct the multi-billion dollar industry, and the economic wealth generated creates and sustains both geographic and political influence, often to the benefit of Western powers. Within this the dealer and the user represent the end products of these global forces, in a market economy of unmet desire for positive mood states. Culturally determined values shape the expectations of usage and their informal control and induct users into the anticipated effects. The expectations that drugs can enhance mood states may be only partially realised. Drugs do have an effect on the body and there are physical consequences to use. But these effects are always mediated, interpreted and evaluated by the user within the confines of their own cultural expectations. This experience cannot be reduced to snooker ball science of cause and effect in the manner in which it has been commonly established in the public imagination. And, as a result, our attempts to define addictions in purely biological terms are compromised by the interference of these psychological and cultural forces. However, understanding these relationships must be central to our ability to help people overcome the devastating consequences of their use.

Chapter 2

On Addiction

Hell is oneself:
Hell is alone, the figures in it
Merely projections, there is nothing to escape from
And nothing to escape to. One is always
Alone.

T.S. Elliot

A central problem in all the helping services is that they are dominated by ill-conceived concepts that are purely nominative. That is to say there may be little agreement on what is actually being talked about, and this may be expanded to include what is actually being treated and to what purpose. In this chapter we will work towards a concrete working definition of addiction which will provide the foundation for our response to it. As we have seen, culture and biology are both entwined in the process and we will make a clear demarcation between the contributions that both make to the evolution of problematic use. This demands we understand that drug and alcohol use exists on a spectrum and is driven by mutli-faceted problems that conspire insidiously on the user. Having established the descent into problematic use we will then consider the means by which people escape it. And we will identify the central factors which support it. The detail of this recovery process will then be examined in subsequent chapters to inform our practice. This will assist in the helping process by enhancing and accelerating the change process as it occurs based on pragmatic research.

What is addiction?

We are unable to establish a clearly defined diagnosis of addiction which is applicable across history and culture because the experience itself is locked into the diverse relationships within these cultures. An obvious example is the purely cultural artefact that the compulsion to drink alcohol is classified as a disease medically but the compulsive use of opiates is not. It is therefore assumed that heroin's powerful effect makes it compelling; whilst it is a deficiency in the user that makes alcoholics compulsive. Even the degree of consumption that might warrant the diagnosis varies from culture to culture, depending on the normative patterns of use. With the exception of alcohol consumption and liver cirrhosis, many problems associated with intoxicants are actually inversely proportional to the amount used. Consumptions can be a poor measure of addiction.

Certainly what is considered problematic consumption in one culture may vary a great deal from another. Any alcohol use in Islamic societies may cause far greater problems than consumption in Western cultures. Coca use in South America is normal compared to North America where it is a criminal offence. The reinforcing effects of drugs, their action on the brain and the discomfort experienced when sustained use is ceased are important factors. But we should not mistake the most obvious effects for the hidden cause.

Table 2.1   Comparative table of addiction criteria

Diagnostic and Statistical Manual-IV (APA 1995)	International Classification of Diseases (WHO 1992)
• Substances are taken in higher doses or over longer durations than intended. • There is a repeated desire to stop or reduce consumption without success. • A great deal of time is invested in procuring, using and recovering from the effects of the drug. • Important social, occupational or recreational activities are ended or reduced because of use. • Consumption continues despite awareness of psychological or physical problems. • Tolerance increases through either increasing dose or receiving less effect from regular doses. • Withdrawal is experienced and the drug (or similar drugs) are used to avoid withdrawals.	• Difficulties in controlling use in terms of onset, termination or dosage. • A strong desire to take the substance. • Neglecting other enriching experiences or interests in preference to using, and an increase in time spent using or recovering. • Persisting in use despite obvious problems, depression or impairment in thinking. • Tolerance develops reflected in increasing dosages. • Withdrawal is experienced and the drug (or similar drugs) are used to avoid withdrawals.

In the 1970s the World Health Organisation brought together a team of experts to define a conceptual framework for alcohol dependence. This definition has since been applied widely to all psychoactive substances. The definition, formulated by Edwards and Gross (1976) reconstituted alcoholism as a 'clinical impression' of a dependence syndrome which is difficult to integrate with a biological or psychological basis. Their criteria includes continued use regardless of the social context or mood state; use is a central priority in the individual's life; tolerance increases and the symptoms of withdrawal are present on cessation; individuals avoid withdrawal symptoms by continued use; there is self-awareness of a compulsion to use; and despite periods of abstinence, use is reinstated. This has been a highly influential model, in shaping both the US diagnosis (DSM-IV) of addiction and the European (ICD) (see Table 2.1).

What is often missed in these definitions is that they aimed to separate two kinds of drug related problems rather than assert one diagnosis. Edwards and Gross' definition was a purposeful attempt to delineate between the consequences of long term exposure to high levels of alcohol and the social complications that occur as a result of drinking (Edwards et al., 2003). It was recognised that whilst these problems may overlap they are distinctly different. Long term consumption of alcohol leads to a dramatic increase in tolerance that may be sustained over years. Tolerance then gives way to a profound withdrawal syndrome. This includes tremors, sweats and vomiting which make it difficult for the client to function without the eye opener in the morning. This first drink of the day becomes highly ritualised in the client's life. Eventually the high tolerance breaks giving way to gross and incapacitating intoxication, even on low levels of alcohol. Such lucid reactions are only developed over years of heavy, continual consumption. And despite the severity of these symptoms, the high tolerance levels may not debilitate people from wider commitments until the latter phase of dependence is achieved. Conversely, the social implications of drinking can impede social functioning. The use of the drug can interrupt the individual's ability to meet the demands of their social role. These problems are characterised by breakdowns in relationships, marriage, family life, employment and breaking of social and legal frameworks.

This is not necessarily the product of years of consumption or even heavy consumption. The binge drinker may have a low average consumption pattern, confined to erratic periods of heroic episodes of use. Whilst clinical dependence demands careful medical management of withdrawal, problem drinking does not. Where this model has been applied to other drugs, it must be remembered that the unique toxicology of alcohol does not always mean that these concepts translate well to other substances. Alcohol has a unique biological impact on the body. Many non-depressant drugs do not generate such clear concepts of tolerance and withdrawal or the collapse in tolerance experienced by the clinically dependent drinker.

The classical depiction of the clinically dependent user creates a deceptive cultural marker of problematic use. Augmented with disease and loss of control concepts, this may suggest to the socially problematic consumer that they do not have a problem because they do not fit this physical profile. This is particularly apparent with stimulant users who do not need to use daily but will struggle to go up to two weeks without binging. Likewise, young users and those who take culturally stigmatised drugs may experience huge social consequences but not perceive they have problems due to the lack of physical symptoms of use. We must recognise that problematic use is not simply about the biological tolerance, withdrawal and frequency of consumption. It occurs when the individual cannot meet their social responsibilities. This may be determined by the cultural threshold of acceptability rather than the impact of the consumption itself. It is important to separate out these concerns. Characterising use on a spectrum from abstinence, through recreational and onto problematic consumption will illustrate some stark differences in use. Let us consider this gradient in Exercise 2.1. Under each broad heading of non-users, recreational users and problem users, answer the following questions for each population (see over).

What we can see from this simple diagram is the values of non-using individuals insulate them from use. These may be cultural, spiritual, health or bad experiences of consumption that preclude use. For this group, their values foster negative expectations. Instead they pursue other activities available within the host culture in which they occupy. Individuals may vary in the choices they make from the menus of their culture and the degree they engage in these structures, but their life choices are similar to others because they share the same culture. This may include family, partnering, work, recreation and social lives with like minded others. These are the pro-social institutions of life that cohere people into family, social, labour, class and ethic groups. Individuals' choices within these structures are reflective of their own values excepting where discrimination or poverty obstructs or excludes them.

Our recreational users are typically entwined within these self-same frameworks of life. They are engaged in both purposeful activity of work as well as meaningful activities of recreation. This sustains relationships with family and friends to varying degrees. Their values may orient themselves to liberal beliefs about self-choice in their drug and alcohol use, which may be one recreational pursuit amongst many. They often use drugs not for specific pharmacological effects but because of what they represent. Drugs are symbolic lifestyle choices that express certain ethics about the user. LSD in the 1960s, ecstasy in the 1980s and cocaine in the present milieu are deeply entwined with the social trends, fashions and lifestyles of their respective eras. Heroin, once deemed the ultimate drug, is now seen as the preserve of the street homeless. As the negative social associations have increased, its popularity has declined, regardless of the drug's action. Even the type of alcoholic beverage we consume makes certain lifestyle statements about us. We prefer one brand over another not because of the effect, after all they are all alcohol. Our chosen brand has a taste we like and expresses something about us as individuals.

Exercise 2.1: The spectrum of use

- What kind of values might this group have?
- What might their expectations of drug and alcohol use be?
- What activities fill their day?
- What sources of satisfaction are available?
- Who they do this with?
- What is the drug using status of these individuals?
- What kind of relationships do they have?

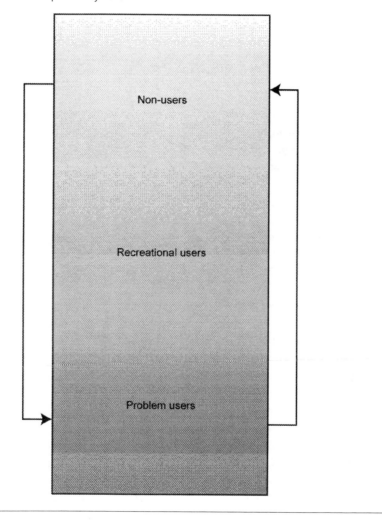

Drug and alcohol use amongst recreational users takes place with like minded others and occurs in clear ceremonies that demarcate and contain it. Going to a friend house to smoke hashish, dropping pills on the weekend or chopping lines of cocaine after a dinner party all occur in social groups which set limits on consumption and police permissible behaviours. Like the informal controls that evolve around alcohol consumption around the world, these boundaries of use prevent drugs seeping in to other areas of life. For example, we refrain from drinking alcohol in work because it is not socially acceptable rather than it is unlawful. Certainly people that use drugs and alcohol frequently will develop tolerance and withdrawal. But this does not interfere with their relationships in other aspects of their life.

As the user moves through the spectrum of use, increasing losses and pressures begin to inhibit and exclude them from meeting the demands of life. They are severed from cultural institutions such as family, peer groups, intimate relationships, and the receipt of wider sources of satisfaction. When viewing our problematic user, we see that they are disconnected from the social structures of life, relative to the culture they occupy. They are no longer attached to the established norms and obligations of their society or sub-culture and are left with nothing but the monomaniacal pursuit of drugs as the only purposeful activity available to them. This disintegration of cultural attachments orphans the individual into another way of life, along with others who suffer the same estrangement. In economic parlance we have the concept of the 'shadow economy', where undeclared money never percolates mainstream financial structures. The legal, cultural and psychological sanctions imposed on certain types of use exclude the problematic user from the mainstream social institutions of life. As such they dwell in the 'shadow society'. These are undeclared lives in the margins of society where the excluded are forced together by their poverty, isolation, criminalisation and broader social stigmatisation. Like any sub-culture, they develop their own ethics or ways of relating to others. The accepted rules of life are no longer applicable and give way to street etiquette, natural justice, rejection of pro-social values and where taboos become a badge of identity. These ethics create, sustain and deepen expectations which give rise to new strains of permissible behaviours that settle into new standards of normalisation. If everyone you know shoplifts it is rendered permissible. Within this, individuals become increasingly reliant on the drug as the architecture of their life, regardless of its pharmacology. Intoxication provides the only purposeful activity, locked into a cycle of raising money, scoring and using amongst a web of relationships of like-minded others. They will experience tolerance and withdrawal which may or may not be as extreme as the recreational user. But their life is now of a different order. They now experience addiction. Addiction is the global erosion of relationships in the pursuit of one source of satisfaction.

We must be careful not to reserve medical diagnosis for behaviours that we just do not like. If for example, a heroin user preserved quality relationships with family, friends and work, could they be considered as having a problem?

Some people say yes to this question whilst others say no. We tend to think of a drug like heroin as being problematic by its very nature. Let us consider this more carefully. The recreational heroin user will still be prone to dependence, characterised by increased tolerance and withdrawal but dependence is not the whole picture. Anyone who uses a drug with any frequency will develop tolerance and withdrawal but this in itself does not necessary incapacitate people from their wider social roles.

Addiction verses dependence

Working through this spectrum we can see that consumption occurs in certain patterns. Some consumption may be occasional. It is short lived episodes which are not protracted enough to develop tolerance. It may be recreational in that the drug is used at certain times of the week. Binge patterns can be sporadic consumption where the user can span a high bandwidth from low to high consumption. It can also be controlled where people use every day but sustain wider social function. And here, before the end point of addiction is achieved but many users sustain the position of the high functioning addict. The individual's life is strung between maintaining mainstream societal demands whilst staving off the erosion of relationships through consumption.

All points on this spectrum are possible for all drugs. For example, research by Warburton et al. (2005) identified 174 controlled heroin users. They controlled their daily use without any breakdown in wider social integration. These individuals showed early onset use, aged 20, and they had been using for up to ten years. Whilst we might expect that these individuals were on their way to problematic use, this research suggested that they had moved in the opposite direction. Many of these subjects reported past problematic use which they had since curtailed.

Key to controlling their use was being extremely selective who they used with. They avoided problematic users. Furthermore, they cultivated strict rules about how much they would use and at what frequency, and revised their expectations of the effects and risks of the drug. These controlled users did not consider themselves as addicts or that they were bonded to the drug. Also, aware of the stigma and judgements of others which could equally ostracise them, they kept their use secret. This suggests that users do not simply become more preoccupied with use over other relationships; but that these relationships may become estranged in reaction to use. Most important was that the controlled heroin user did not let their consumption interfere with their wider life structures. This included employment, family, accommodation and interaction with non-using others in wider recreational pursuits. A very high value was placed on these activities and commitments. The consensus amongst this group was that their use would be a problem *if it ever interfered with these other pursuits*. Harding (2000) reports the same findings in his controlled user groups. They too were far more likely to be employed, more able to resist use even when the drug was available and far less likely to have a limited peer group or be a loner. Undoubtedly, these controlled users were dependent; in that they experienced tolerance and withdrawal. The obligation to maintain and conceal their use must be demanding at times. But this is not the same addiction.

The erosion of relationships is important to understand in treatment of addiction because, as suggested earlier, we are working with a more complex set of problems than simply the individual biology. Both psycho-social and biological indicates agree on the definition of addiction in general terms (Vaillant, 1995). However, social indicators are stronger measures of treatment prognosis than biological ones. Success is often predicted by the degree of employability of the individual. Those with professional qualifications, who re-enter the market place, do much better than individuals with no employment prospects who are using drugs (O'Brian and McCellen, 1996). Let us take two fictional heroin users and make a comparison. We have a Dr Drake who has his own GP surgery, is involved in his family and undertakes a wide range of social activities. He has access to pure pharmaceutical heroin and has been using it for two years taking 2 grams a day. Joe has used for 10 years, has poor literacy, lives on the streets and begs to earn enough for 1 bag of heroin a day (approximately 0.1 gram.) Both enter into treatment. Who will do better and why?

Exercise 2.2: Addiction and Outcome

_____ will do better in treatment

because _____

What we find, all motivational measures being equal, is that our doctor will do better. Dr Drake has an economic ticket and skills to get back into the mainstream society, despite using twenty times more than Joe. This is because Joe's ability to integrate back into the mainstream is already significantly impeded regardless of his levels of his tolerance and withdrawal. Joe is addicted whilst Dr Drake is dependent. Research continually demonstrates that the outcomes of treatment are simply not predicted by the amount people use. The $36 million study of alcohol treatment, Project MATCH found that consumption levels, duration and frequency of use have little bearing on outcome. Those that did well were those who reintegrated back into pro-social groups (Project MATCH Group, 1997).

The problems associated with dependence are different to those associated with addiction. Problems with dependence tend to be primarily the medical consequences of repeated use. The multitude of diseases associated with socially acceptable drugs like alcohol or smoking tobacco stems from long term exposure. These are slow, long term and insidious. In contrast, health problems with addiction tend to be rapid and the product of social forces such as violence and crime, the results of unemployment and homelessness, blood borne disease from limited access to needles, poor injecting practice or overdose with polydrug use. Health problems with illicit drugs are dramatic, abrupt and entwined in these social forces. This effect is demonstrated in countries such as Finland where prohibition was repealed in 1932 in graded stages. During prohibition there was an increase in crime related deaths and dangerous adulteration. But on repeal, the number of drug related deaths actually increased as a result of the long term health consequences of use, such as liver cirrhosis (see Saunders, 1985). Debates regarding prohibition versus the legalisation of drugs is primarily a debate regarding what kind of problems a society wishes to contend with.

Addiction as a cultural threshold

Whilst individuals may differ biologically in their resilience to dependency, the threshold of addiction is culturally set. We must remember that use is a spectrum. The phrase 'high-functioning addict' is reserved for those users whose relationships with the wider social frameworks of family, work and recreation are in jeopardy of breaking, against the corrosive effects of their use which interferes with these attachments. In the West it is culturally, socially and legally permissible to be a high consumer of alcohol in a way that it is not acceptable to be a high consumer of heroin. The high consumer of heroin will be excluded from the social structures of life far quicker than the alcohol consumer. This means that people can engage in high consumption of culturally accepted drugs for far longer periods and are even esteemed for it. The illicit drug user will rapidly meet immediate judgment, disapproval and rejection. Research (Klingemann, 1992) demonstrates that problematic heroin users report higher incidences of social pressures than problematic alcohol users and this is significant in treatment and change.

Conversely in Islamic cultures, where alcohol is not tolerated, the consequences of alcohol use are much higher, even for ex-pat Westerners. Here alcohol consumption is met with social disapproval and legal implications. In the Emirates states any alcohol found in ones blood stream whilst driving will result in three months imprisonment. This will cost people their employment, create family tensions and elicit social estrangement from indigenous populations who have little regard for alcohol consumption. The social consequences of use are far more sensitive to very low levels of consumption. The threshold of addiction is much higher than in the West because of these cultural values enshrined in law.

Let us consider a thought experiment using the example of smoking nicotine. Currently because of the long term health consequences we are seeing policy shift to increasing legal sanctions against tobacco smokers who had previously only suffered dependence on nicotine. In Exercise 2.3, imagine that the European Union suddenly passed laws which would mean smokers faced prison sentences for use. They were not considered responsible enough to hold down employment and were the source of shame for family and friends. In light of these sanctions, what would happen to the following three groups of smokers?

Exercise 2.3: The context of addiction

A new law has been passed forbidding any use of nicotine. Users of this drug will face prison sentencing. They cannot be considered trustworthy to hold a position of responsibility. The shame and pain they cause their families and friends will leave them shunned. They will have no access to the drug other than the over priced black market, low quality supplies. What would happen to the following groups?

Those that quit?	Those who used irregularly?	Those that continue to smoke?

Here we see those that stopped smoking preserve the status quo of their lives, whilst those who dabble are at risk if they are discovered or exposed. Alternatively, those who choose to smoke regardless will be ostracised, excluded and gravitate towards other heavy smokers through criminalisation and poverty. This is exactly what we see in the evolution of heroin lifestyles once prohibition began to bite, where people resorted to selling junk metal to fund their habit (see Harris, 2005). We also see the same patterns for black cocaine users in the US at the turn of the century. Cocaine was once the ingredient in soft drinks. Individuals would have to buy their syrup separately and then go to a soda fountain shop to have the carbonated water added. Because of the American apartheid system, black people were forbidden to drink on the soda fountain premises and so would stand outside in groups talking. Newspaper reports soon emerged of black gangs high on cocaine on the rampage (Madge, 2001). Immediate measures were taken to quash them. Hence the cultural assumptions and their manifestation in law shape the experience of addiction in physical ways with profound consequences for users.

How does addiction occur?

Understanding how individuals shift from non-using to problematic use has evaded research. Every academic discipline has laboured in vain to identify a single causal factor in addiction. Needless to say that biology, genetics, sociology, psychology, psychotherapy and theology have all failed. In their wake they have left the husks of promising ideas which imprint themselves on the popular imagination but not on research findings. Single disciplines cannot fully account for the diversity of the drug using populations. In summary, we have no clear biological mechanism of addiction despite years of searching. Genetic research findings are modest or contradictory and are unable to escape the reach of cultural influences. Sociology's emphasis upon the impoverished fails to cast its net over the wealthy that are not immune from the compulsive experience. Addicts do not have overdeveloped psychological defence mechanism, whilst use is predicted by positive as well as negative mood states undermining a purely coping deficit. There is no evidence for a simple Pavalovian conditioning process of reward-seeking as initiation into drug use is often unpleasant. There is no evidence to support the notion of a distinctive 'addictive personality' forged in a trouble childhood. And whilst spiritual loss may have nebulous effects on society, not every atheist seeks out chemical salvation. The central problem with these models is that their research reduces human nature to the central concerns of the academic discipline studying them. Essentially they tell us more about the bureaucratic divides of universities than substance users.

Despite recovering addict's war stories, addiction does not occur spontaneously but evolves over time. What appears significant in this evolution is a constellation of events that cut across every domain of human interaction. This has lead to the development of multi-determined models which integrate findings from all disciplines (See Bry et al., 1982). These causal factors are then 'weighted' according to their relevant contribution. These findings suggest it is not the nature of the risk that the individual faces but the *number and range* of risks they are exposed to within a given period of time which promotes the addictive experience. In one study (Newcombe et al., 1987) 12 factors including educational performance, age of initiation, parent attachment, emotional distress and dissatisfaction of life accounted for 41 per cent variance in drug use amongst young people.

The weakness in these multi-causal models is the lack of agreement regarding what variables should be included, and how they should be weighted. There is no common agreement on the relative influences of biology over environmental influences. When we step outside biological confines we must account for everything else. We get the best of all disciplines in multi-causal models, but we also get the worst too, in having to compromise contradictory research findings from every discipline. However, they have shown greater predictability and capture the richness of the human experience which is so often obscured in reductive explanations.

It does nevertheless appear that the risk of developing problems is a stratified process. This is a cascade effect where every step forward in consumption always opens up the possibility of new threats and risk. There are factors that make people vulnerable to use but these demand initiation of consumption. Once people start to use drugs or alcohol, a new set of risk factors begin to support and maintain use. This increases the risk of escalation and opens the door to problematic use. The risk factors alter at the initiation, escalation, and problematic stages. Consider Exercise 2.4. What factors do you feel would be significant in promoting use at each stage?

Exercise 2.4: Risk factors of addiction

What factors may make individuals vulnerable to drug use?

What factors may initiate drug use?

What factors may sustain use?

What factors may escalate use?

What may convert use into problematic consumption?

Vulnerability factors are calculated to estimate the predisposition in the user. This is the degree to which the substance may resonate biologically. Research demonstrates that people's biological tolerance to drugs does vary but this does not account for the patterns of consumption that we witness. For example, Asian populations experience a condition called oriental flush. They lack an enzyme which means they find it hard to break down alcohol resulting in a high sensitivity to alcohol's effects and suffer violent hangovers. The Native American Indian and the Inuit both have this condition and suffer the highest rates of alcoholism in the US. Simultaneously Chinese and Japanese populations also have this genetic condition and show the lowest rates of alcoholism in the US. Cultural compatability of work ethics integrates the Chinese and Japanese into US culture whereas the values of the Native American and Inuit are discordant with it. Conversely Vaillant's (1995) research suggest it was not those with a high sensitively to alcohol that developed problems but those with high tolerance. Having a 'hollow leg' for alcohol, being able to tolerate frequent and high consumption, simply means the individual is less likely to experience the averse negative social consequences of use which intrude upon other commitments such as work. Whilst genetics give insight into tolerance and subsequently dependence, it does not appear to speak of addiction. Abnormal tolerance does not fate people to addictions just as average tolerance does not vaccinate people against it.

Certainly vulnerability factors cannot explain initiation into use. Our genes do not know drugs are out there. Initiation may be influenced by family and peer use. We have already seen how positive expectancies regarding use are strong predictors of the age of onset and levels of consumption. High consuming families tend to raise high consuming children who fail to learn about unacceptable thresholds of consumption and where overtly positive expectations of use are modelled. But equally, children who grow up in totally abstinent households are also at high risk where they learn no intoxication skills to prepare them for consumption in early independent life. A permissive attitude towards use in communities with transitory populations, where little ownership is invested in the environment is also a strong facilitator of initiation. As are a lack of alternative sources of satisfaction. Poor achievement in other areas of mainstream life such as school also figure highly. Trauma and difficulty with early relationships and life transitions can create difficulties in attachment as well as fear of future changes.

Sustaining factors may be determined by increasing enmeshment in drug using sub-cultures. Mood state, dissatisfaction or discomfit in pro-social roles may lead to disengagement with mainstream constructs. Drug use and the drug using peer group can become a surrogate identity for youth making difficult transitions into adulthood with little preparation for it. The problematic stage of use may be induced through increased cultural detachment, poor intoxication management skills, lack of susceptibility to social punishment cues, life events, breakdown or neglect in wider relationships and social functioning. In this way we see the function of use changes from mood enhancement to escaping mounting problems sourced in use itself. This interplay between substance use and further stresses was identified by Alexander and Hadaway (1996) who proposed use could operate as a positive feedback system. Stresses generated by consumption increase use as a coping strategy, which in turn generates increasing stresses that demand antidoting with ever more use.

This model underscores addiction as a complex web of cultural attachments, beliefs and contexts. The predictability of who is likely to experience drug and alcohol problems can be characterised by those who already have weak, or weakening, attachments across all social domains, that become increasingly eroded through continued use. As such, addiction cannot be understood as the result of exposure to a drug but as an adaptive set of responses to their environmental context. High usage may debilitate the individual's ability to manage increasing pressures and threaten social exclusion, but this is compensated for by the use of more drugs to distract themselves from such painful concerns, resulting in deepening problems ad infinitum.

Environmental volume

What is clear is that addiction grows in context to the environment which exerts powerful influences on consumption. Animal research consistently demonstrates that animals will only take drugs in impoverished environments (Harris, 2005). Avidity is the rate in which compulsivity is acquired. It can be easily promoted or delayed by the presence of alternative sources of satisfaction. For example, rats given access to sugar water in addition to cocaine (Carroll and Lac, 1992) develop avidity at very slow rates if at all. Falk (1981, 1983) demonstrated that through the manipulation of environmental factors he could control the consumption rates of alcohol in rats to high states of inebriation, a state that had never been invoked previously. The exact same processes are seen in human beings. Clinical studies of alcoholics drinking patterns in laboratory settings find little evidence of any loss of control over consumption. Mello and Mandleson (1965) observational studies of alcoholics drinking did not confirm the disease hypothesis. Despite free access to alcohol, subjects drank to sustain inebriation but neither lost control nor drank all the alcohol available to them. Furthermore, when individuals had to work increasingly harder to earn alcohol, they consumed less. Conversely, Cohen et al's. (1971) research on abstinence found it was possible to buy periods of sobriety from alcoholics with competing rewards of money, at a rate of between $7–27 a day. Even when these rewards were delayed or priming doses of alcohol were administered, abstinence was initially disrupted but then sustained. What these experiments demonstrate is that consumption is not conditioned simply by the individual's wants. Consumption patterns are very sensitive to the environment. Where preferred alternatives are available, or procurement is more difficult, consumption patterns decrease even in the most seasoned drinker.

What we see here is the environmental amplification of the dug using experience. For example, if your consumption of alcohol is one of many rewards available in your life, the role of alcohol may not be that significant. In contrast if alcohol is the only reward available to you its meaning is deeply amplified. Low incomes, unemployment, downward social drift and prison incarceration are powerful predictors of use (Bickel and Degrandpre, 1995). Poverty and discrimination limit the construction of meaningful lifestyles. It is not surprising that researchers have noted that postcode is a high single predictor of drug use (Newcomb, 1995). This variable contains within it impoverished communities characterised by high availability, low expectation and permissive attitudes to anti-social behaviour. Against this environmental backdrop, substance use as a source of satisfaction is unrivalled. Combined with losses incurred through active use, the environmental volume of economic, emotional and social scarcity can promote use in powerful ways. Consider how the meaning of attachments can change by shifts in the environmental context in Exercise 2.5.

Exercise 2.5: The environmental amplification of consumption

Think of the three most important things in your life. And number them 1–3.

1 _____

2 _____

3 _____

Now imagine a disaster was to happen, and due to some cruel trick of fate you were to lose numbers one and three. How would that leave you feeling?

How does this affect your relationship with number two?

Imagine now, that you were to lose number two as well. What would your life be like without any of these things in your life?

Problematic users can generate the same losses of meaningful relationships and attachments in their lives (1 and 3) leaving them only with the drug (2). These losses amplify the significance of what they do have, i.e. the drug. Consider having lost items 1 and 3 from your list, you are then forced to surrender what you have left, number 2. Imagine how your life would be in the next 6 months without these familiar structures? What would your life be like without any of these priorities left? Likewise when we ask problematic users to abandon the only thing that they have left they stare into a void that was their life. The hope of reconstruction of a new 1–2–3 may feel remote beyond belief. In the words of an old client, when it was a choice between hell or nothing he had always chosen hell. This is the central problem in changing addicted lifestyles. Symptoms of withdrawal are a pale distraction when you stare into the abyss of your life. But it is easier to articulate physical discomfort than voice the inexplicable fears of profound change.

The fact that the poor do not have a monopoly on addiction is cited as grounds for dismissing social-economic factors in addiction, and re-focusing on the biology not context. It is demonstrative of western cultures' deep assumption that materialism equates with happiness. But addiction prevalence cuts a 'U' shaped curve across the social strata. Whilst wealth may insulate the minority from the kinds of social pressures endured by the majority, it does not exonerate them wholly. It is easy to forget that impoverishment in the cultural landscape humans inhabit can take many forms. Significant wealth can preclude meaning in the same way poverty can exclude it. If one has no need to work in a work ethic society there is no outlet to express one's ethics or derive satisfaction. The acquisition of material objects as a social marker of progress has no significance against a backdrop of abundance. In short there is nothing to work for. Life may feel as empty as for those who have no access at all to these validations. It is perhaps no coincidence that one of the only purposeful pursuits available to the very rich is to preserve the family dynasty for its own sake; or, in other cases, to purposely deconstruct it.

Transition can also be as disruptive for the *self-made* as those who go in the opposite direction. Established relationships are changed dramatically with elevations in social standing which breed ingratiation or resentment. Increasing pressures of public life, over confidence of one's success or fear of public failure may conspire to disorientate individual's relationships to their social world. A professional bodyguard once told me the most difficult aspect of his job was managing the client not the crowd. Little wonder that so many from humble backgrounds who achieve celebrity also attain addiction and mental health problems in the same way in which those who lose social status do. It is less common, as such meteoric social trajectories are less common. But we only need to consider the glittering array of talented individuals who were broken on their own stardom to understand the impact of such repositioning. The poor and the wealthy face the same crises of a breakdown in meaning. And meaning is in the kind of relationships we forge.

Implications for interventions

Understanding the evolution of drug and alcohol problems is important too for interventions that aim to intercept their development. Both drugs prevention and harm reduction share this purpose though at opposite poles of the using spectrum. Both are knowledge-based interventions which aim to change behaviours. As yet we have no science of prevention. The outcomes of drug prevention programmes have been poor. This is due in no small part to the fact that their well intended messages have largely been moralistic. They have failed to understand drug use and misuse as it occurs in the lives of young people (see Harris, 2005). This failure has often made their attempts appear simplistic at best and patronising at worst. The overt focus on the dangers of use has failed on several levels. Firstly, as we saw in Chapter 1, the amplification of the power of drugs makes their use a challenge to be mastered and their users to be respected. Secondly, the physical health consequences of drug and alcohol use mean little to young people whose sense of mortality is latent. Thirdly, the emphasis on the long term consequences of use is too distant in both time and from their motivations for young people to relate to. No one sets out using drugs with the sole intent of experiencing profound deprivation.

Drug education's focus on intoxicants should debunk the experience rather than lionise it. This demands that we explore the expectations of use and support young people to untangle the many factors surrounding it. Within this it is important that we recognise what substances can and cannot do; what belongs to the drug; what belongs to our anticipation; and what belongs to the social environments that they are taken in. Whilst alcohol and cannabis are the most widely used drugs, it is worth contrasting the expectations of these drugs with the realities. Whilst drugs are accredited with the almost supernatural ability to transform moods, much of the time they merely promote an insular and self-obsessed mood. 'Drugs make you boring' is a more salient message to this than any other threat. In terms of risk education, it would be more effective to focus on short term problems rather than long term problems. In discussing this with young people one fear always strikes them first: getting off with the socially challenged under the influence. Damage to important relationships is a natural fear for young people who define themselves by these attachments. Making a fool of oneself in front of their peers is a source of profound suffering. Likewise, what they risk missing out on whilst they remain overly invested in use can be another important consideration. Certainly the success of Botvin's (1999) interventions have been built on skills programmes to support young people to access more rewarding opportunities and manage setbacks and negative mood states. This raises the concern of what forms of enrichment young people have access to and places a natural limit of class based education.

Certainly the idea of creating an intoxicant free generation is a fantasy. And an education that guides people to one conclusion is a contradiction in terms. What may be most important in drugs education is deferring the onset of use and the volume of early consumption. These two factors appear important in setting the pattern of using well into early adulthood (Pape and Hammer, 1996). The incorporation of expectancy theories could be a useful tool in this along with taking advantage of development psychology that would help target interventions to the appropriate maturational demands of young people. Certainly, appealing to the idealism and contradictory reactions of young people could easily be mobilized by exposing the duplicity of drug and alcohol policy. The fact is adults want young people to use them. For example, the UK government generates over £12 billion a year from an 80 per cent tax on tobacco sales. Smokers cost the National Health Service just under £2 billion a year. The government make more money than the tobacco industry itself. With the inconvenience of their customers dying new recruits must be found. The advertising budgets of the tobacco industry far outstrip any government anti-smoking campaigns.

Harm reduction is not naturally perceived as an extension of education but it shares the same basic assumptions and limitations. Harm reduction has been very successful in limiting blood borne viruses but has also been heavily criticised as merely enabling use. Whilst harm reduction has often claimed to reduce the consequences of use, in reality this has again focused exclusively on drug use itself. Improving injecting practice, needle exchanges, safer sex and methadone prescribing have an important role, but as we have seen, the development of addictions is more than biological and health problems. In reality, harm reduction has not made any progress in abating the wider social problems which people experience as an equal priority. This is a source of criticism from other treatment philosophies, educationalists and the wider community. As one street worker reflected, harm reduction is good for other people's children. Like drugs education, the narrowness of focus on drugs consumption and not the person weakens the potential of the approach in controlling use. Little to no attempt has been made to help individuals control their use, preserve their relationships or find competing sources of enrichment. The concerns of families and the wider communities have also remained peripheral to the harm reduction agenda which has often left it misunderstood and isolated. And all too often it has limited itself to changing using practices rather than lives.

Change

Changing addicted lifestyles is a formidable task. The magnitude of this endeavour demands re-configuring everything in life and never going back. Having worked with many different orders of problems it strikes me that two forms of change are sought. For some, the enormity of lifestyle revision may be too great to consider attempting. Furthermore, whilst no one wants to be stricken with difficulties, problems can sometimes serve useful purposes. Problematic use may not only create a life framework outside the mainstream cultural structures but can also provide a means of filtering out unappetising demands. Problems can provide the means to avoid challenges where there is a skill or confidence deficit without exposing one's limitations. For example, it may offer users a wider margin of tolerance, absolve responsibilities they find difficult to maintain or elicit support they might not otherwise receive. In this way problems can be too useful to give up.

As a result many individuals seek light change. They want to reduce the quality of their suffering *within* their existing relationships. As we have seen in the escalation of use, the losses and problems that consumption incurs is counter balanced by the relationships and purpose that substances can provide. People want to abate problems but preserve these connections. Harm reduction interventions such as needle exchange, methadone prescribing, attending low intensity treatment groups in lieu of prison sentences may reduce the stress that individuals are under. They may stop things from getting even worse but do not create any capacity to improve the quality of life of the individual.

Only when clients realise that the overall suffering can only be reduced to a limited degree, do they consider more global change. Deep change demands that the user breaks their existing relationships and reconstructs new ones. It is important to recognise the value and significance of both options in clients' lives. And I do not think this behaviour is at all specific to problematic drug users. How many people stay in unhappy marriages or jobs for years before making a more decisive break? When human beings confront the dilemma of life-course changing decisions, we tend to follow a line of least resistance. Rather than express conscious decisions we wait for life to make the decision for us by getting unbearable. Deep change may only occur when we have to.

Certainly, one of the central limits of many interventions is that they are issue specific rather than change specific. There is an assumption that knowing more about drugs, or mental illness or sexual abuse will change the client. Whilst this may be useful in finding a common ground, it does not change behaviour in itself. By understanding how people actually change we can get beside and augment the change process. Therefore we must grasp these change processes if we are to assist in enhancing them and focusing the tasks of helping others escape from their dissatisfaction with use.

Quantum change

Change processes appear to occur on two extreme poles: rapid transformations or gradual accumulation. The sudden, and often unexpected, change process has a long history in addiction work but is much neglected in current psychological research. At the turn of the last century William James (1902) cited case studies of those who were transformed instantaneously by a spiritual revelation. What struck him about these transformational moments was their permanence on the individuals who experienced them. The notion of a sudden, spiritual awakening was to form a central plank in the Twelve Step movement. Its co-founder Bill W, an inveterate alcoholic, claimed in a moment of desperation that he called to God to reveal himself. As a result he experienced a white light filling the room, and in a state of ecstasy, apprehended the presence of God. A new consciousness emerged in him and he knew in that moment he was forever changed. The Big Book, the Twelve Step bible, is dominated by similar experiences of transformational change, along with promise that adherence to the programme will spark similar events in those that follow this recovery path. Indeed, separation is still made in the fellowship between post revelation 'sobriety' and the pre-revelation 'dry drunk' who is yet to experience this permanent awakening. However, Bill W also suggested that the gradual change to a new consciousness was equally valid.

The inclination for contemporary psychology to pathologise spiritual beliefs may explain the field's reluctance to research this area. It is only within recent years that this phenomenon has acquired its own secular name – somewhat inappropriately – as Quantum Change (Miller and C'de Baca, 2001). This title is inadequate as 'quantum' refers to the very small and these events are anything but small. In a study by Miller and C'de Baca (1994), quantum changers were invited to come forward through newspaper advertisements and explain their experience. They were surprised at the sheer numbers presenting for interview, despite no inducement of payment. So, whilst this process is rare, it cannot be considered uncommon.

Miller and C'de Baca (1994) identified two distinct quantum change experiences. The first is the classic vision, like that of Saul's or Joan of Arc, where a sudden and unexpected ecstasy comes over the individual, and in a blaze of light, they experience the presence of an extremely benign Being that elates them. They report a deep sense of love and joy in this moment and a revelation of a new truth. The second type of experience is insight based. It runs deeper than mere realisation, breaking suddenly as a moment of heightened awareness that comprehends the totality of a more authentic underlying reality. It is a more Buddhist sense of the interconnectedness of all things. It is as potent and emotionally charged, but not as visual, as the mystical order of this experience. Certainly mystical revelations are not uncommon. They can be induced temporarily by charismatic speakers or through ritualised dance and drumming. Even helpers can induce 'crooked cure' insights in clients, where promising personal revelations fade quickly. However, the quantum experience is different in that it promotes an enduring and permanent change of self which sustains its lucidity over many decades (C'de Baca and Wilbourne, 2004).

Approximately half of the reported case studies occur in moments of deep personal crises and psychological distress. However, they may also occur outside of this context entirely. Certainly what changes for both these groups appears to be a global shift in values, ethics and identity. By default, this life revision appears more profound in the socially excluded. For those embedded in the shadow society, their dependence is assuaged instantaneously. Quantum changers that I have interviewed report a massive reduction in the symptoms of withdrawal post-conversion. Nearly all those studied report a benign effect on their lives, where they feel more secure and at peace at the world. And both groups saw themselves in a spiritual rather than an institutional religious sense, feeling no compunction to convince others of their new understanding, so deep is their surety.

Certainly the quantum change experience is difficult to understand within the context of current thinking in psychology. Several unconvincing theories have been suggested. Quantum change might be a dramatic maturational shift, where people experience a surge in 'older life' values. Another possible cause might be this experience is the sudden resolution of a contradictory sense of self in individuals. When a disparity exists between our idealised self and our actual behaviour, we encounter a deep sense of anxiety. This incongruence is profoundly uncomfortable and some insight that can reconcile contradictory aspects of our selves at a stroke might induce a profound release and incite a continued sense of inner calm. Both these mechanisms are important in changing addictive lifestyles and we will explore them in further detail. Alternatively, we should not rule out the possibility that these people are indeed touched by a divine Other. On this subject we may have to admit the limits of our understanding and let it dwell in the realm of only God knows.

Whilst every person supporting others through the arduous process of change would hanker for the sudden and enduring transformation, change for the majority appears to be achieved through gradual steps and self-corrective reappraisals. These incremental changes may be bracketed under convenient sub-headings but the reality is that they are probably deeply entwined. The first of these is the maturational process and the second is intentional change, when we make deliberate effort to attain a consciously desired goal.

Maturational change

Overarching all change is the maturational process itself (see Harris, 2005). Every epidemiological survey has demonstrated that drug and alcohol abuse follow clear trends within the life journey and that the vast majority of people simply quit use by 'aging out'. Aging out refers to the process where people abandon use and return to their normal life course. As such it might be considered akin to a narcotic menopause. Vaillant's (1995) longitudinal study of alcoholism across life course, which has followed university graduates and inner-city males since the 1930s identified clear trends. For the majority, alcoholism balloons in the thirties until the late fifties where high consumption begins to wane considerably. This is with the exception of a smaller population of early onset drinkers. In contrast, epidemiological studies demonstrate that drug use develops in the teens and tails off across the thirties for most users (Newcomb, 1995; Pape and Hamner, 1996). The earlier drug initiation commences the more problematic the use that follows. This suggests early social detachment is significant in the escalation of consumption across life course. And the more problematic the use, the more likely individuals will turn to total abstinence in later life.

Maturational models offer new insight into addiction treatment for those wanting deep change. However, life-span psychology is relatively new and, like multi-causal models of use, draws upon many disciplines. The notion of chronology of age itself may only offer limited insight. Consider and compare the age ranges in Exercise 2.6.

Exercise 2.6: Age

Consider yourself in the following questions:

- How old are you in calendar years?
- How old do you feel?
- How old do you look?
- How old do you act in work?
- How old do you act at home?

The richness of this field has produced many contradictory models that defy simple characterisation (Sugarman, 2001). However, there are perennial themes in competing life-span models. Most theorists draw on stage models. These chart the individual's development through prescribed cultural structures such as the mother, family, school, institutions of work (Kegan, 1982). Or through bands of psychological development (Erickson, 1995), such as sense of autonomy, evolving an identity, and integration with others. Research indicates periods of stability within these structures and moments of disequilibrium. This occurs when we shift into more complex cultural structures which place greater demands upon us (Levinson, 1978). The difficulty or ease of these transitions may be dependent on the individuals' willingness to separate from existing relationships as well as their preparedness for the more demanding cultural niche they must now occupy. Conflict has a critical role in severing the attachments to the old order and freeing us to enter into new ones. The greater these established attachments are, the greater the conflict necessary to break them. As such, the crisis moments of today are the gateway to more rewarding lives tomorrow. Not only are these transition periods fraught with difficulties but they are also ritualised with alcohol. In the West alcohol is the silent guest that accompanies us through our birth, christening, becoming an adult, getting married, retirement and our wake. It is little surprise that consumption often increases at important junctures of our lives.

Maturational preparedness can be considered as the individual's ability to meet the demands of their environment. It is the negotiation of tasks within these life structures, making life-style choices from a narrow cultural menu of accepted forms of living and the creation and resolution of relationships in this dynamic environment. Managing the demands of infancy, school life, or the wilderness years of early adulthood, family and career are all different and increasingly complex. We need rehearsal and preparation to master the basics of each stage prior to entry.

Age deviancy describes the social expectations on us to conform to expected life courses and complete the socially sanctioned tasks of life. We are corralled by others and we corral them in return into appropriate living. Where we fail to change we experience a life course drift as existential guilt. Guilt is the failure to live up to other people's expectations; existential guilt is the failure to live up to one's own. So both through the coercion of others and the disquiet of our own aspirations, we are forced to grow. This occurs within the infra-structure of modern western societies which house diffuse streams of class and ethnicity that overlap and distinguish themselves in their own ethics and foster their own life expectations. These structures are also historically malleable. For example, whilst we biologically grow much faster in the West we are committing to adult institutions far later. This generation's forty is last generation's thirty. However, the older we get, the less acceptable hedonism becomes. The party animal at 20 is loved in equal measure to the party animal at 40 is shunned.

Developmental delay

If we take the definition of addiction as cultural separation from these life structures we see that many of the problems drug and alcohol users face are deeply entwined in the developmental delay generated by this social exclusion. Those that become divorced from social structures through over-invested time in using, exclusion from school, family neglect, isolation from wider peer groups, unemployment or prison, miss out on these key rehearsals. They are truants from the classroom of life in that they are separated from the means to acquire the skills necessary to manage and operate in increasingly complex social structures. This may be more profound in young drug users who detach sooner from social structures, than alcohol users whose later onset will have offered them greater life skills prior to detachment.

It may also be particularly salient to Afro-Caribbean groups. Research shows a paradox in this ethnic group, where very low adolescent drug use contradicts high adult use. This paradox may be the result of young Afro-Caribbean drug experimenters being excluded from school (often the site of these studies), much sooner than their Caucasian counterparts (see Kandal, 1995). Furthermore, the length of active use is longer for Afro-Caribbean groups than that of white drug users. Discrimination excludes people from the social institutions of life. For the black drug user it presents additional obstacles to their recovery. They must overcome the social exclusion of addiction and the barrier of racism in order to reconnect with the prescribed life course.

Social exclusion appears important not simply for the type of help necessary to overcome problems but also in the time span of supported recovery. Time in itself is not a very crisp variable, because highly motivated clients often engage in treatment for longer, the intensity of the treatment varies and the wider time margin also allows for other variables to come into play, such as natural remission. Within these caveats, length of stay and treatment completion do offer an indication of treatment outcome. Treatments for drug addiction show better outcomes over longer time spans (see Unithan et al., 1992; De Leon, 1989; Simpson et al., 1997; Simpson and Sells, 1983). This may be determined by the earlier onset of the problem and the higher degree of social exclusion. People are removed from the social structures that provide the preparedness for adult life. The earlier the exclusion the greater distance people must catch up with in latert life. Intensity of treatment is a critical factor. Merely retaining people is not sufficient if this time is poorly directed at the development of change and life skills.

In drinking populations brief interventions of 1–3 sessions with an empathetic advisor appear to produce the same outcomes as those who enter into longer term therapy (Bein et al., 1993; Drummond and Ashton, 1999). The later onset of alcoholism means individuals have a higher baseline of skills and experience of adult life prior to the onset of the problems. As such they do not have to close the gap in the same way early onset drug users do. Instead they need to revive the existing skills base they already have as a means of reconnecting with the social structures of life. Whilst poly-drug and alcohol use has become a norm – we must remember it is not the substance but the age of the onset of exclusion that is important.

Life course and culture

This framework also links the individual to social and political changes. When cultural environments change rapidly we see increases in addiction rates. Addiction rates soared in the working classes during the industrial revolution of the 18th century and again at the industrial revolution's demise at the end of the 20th century. We see it in the legacy of imperialism whose devastating effects on the cultural, social order and practices of many indigenous peoples have given rise to such virulent strains of alcoholism that they border on genocide. And in more recent times, we see it in Eastern Europe. Since the Wall came down, consumption rates have soared in the former Soviet economies. Addictions do not simply occur because of the individual innate biological susceptibility. They occur when the environmental demands suddenly outpace a society's ability to meet them.

Georgian London in the 18th century was characterised by the immigration of rural labour into the uncertainties and poverty of a metropolis that promised much but delivered little. London demanded this influx as more died in its borders than were born. This age of 'betterment' was characterised by uncertainty and labour by the week. Unable to penetrate the guild system that demanded a seven year apprenticeship to enter a trade, people scraped a livelihood however they could. The poor lived in ghetto slums, found accommodation by the night and sanctuary in Madame Geneva, gin's original name. The parish system to help the poor was restricted to those born in the district. For the immigrant labour this meant that there was no safety net to utter penury. Likewise, in the UK across the 1980s, semi-skilled manufacturing industries were supplanted by financial and service industries. Life expectancies and opportunities were curtailed, heaping people upon meagre benefits with little hope of escape. The Native Americans and Aborigines were driven from their lands, their belief systems assaulted and the means to integrate denied through a clash of values where European materialism prevailed. The controlled economies of the Soviets that guaranteed work for life are now feudal market economies. All these populations had little preparedness for these environmental changes. These communities' expectations of the labour market became anachronistic; their values antithetical to the new cultural supremacy; and the means to acquire other sources of satisfaction curtailed. In short, addictions increase when the life course becomes blocked. The life journey is no longer a bridge to other roles but a pier leading out to nowhere. The drift into addictions becomes the only *habitus* on offer, as the cultural pool of opportunity evaporates. The shadow society is less demanding, less fulfilling but far more accepting of such cultural orphans.

Changing addicted lifestyles can almost be considered a social repositioning. Natural remitters, who quit addictions without treatment, stated that emergent intimate relationships, employment, family or other sources of satisfaction became more important than drugs (Erickson and Alexander, 1989; Labouvie, 1996). In other words, a cultural reintegration into the institutions of adult life shifted people's use. Other research has consistently identified a reappraisal of ethics and re-integration into pro-social groups as a core ingredient of successful change (Walters, 2000). As such, treatment outcomes have less to do with volumes of consumption or the substance's fanatical hold on our biology, and more to do with the individual's desire and ability to meet the demands of the mainstream cultural environment.

Intentional change

For the most part, drug and alcohol users age out of use with no recourse to treatment whatsoever. Indeed there are many people who are not conscious changers but just drift into other things. However, the maturing out process demands that people have opportunities and roles to grow into. For many users, who experience deep exclusion or do so through subsequent use, these opportunities are not available. Instead they have to consciously construct them. Intentional change describes the deliberate effort to amend an established behaviour. Research in this field has had a profound influence in shaping not just addiction treatment but social policy.

The most pervasive intentional change model has been developed by Prochaska et al., (1994). They began research into smoking behaviour but their results appeared to describe a more universal change process. Individuals were interviewed and studied regarding their smoking. This research identified that change was a series of key shifts in thinking and behaviour which appeared to occur as an invariant stage sequence. Initially smokers felt only the positive aspects of smoking and did not recognise any need to stop. They showed no awareness about the need to change and so were described as pre-contemplative. Once *consciousness* of the problem rose, it initiated other concerns such as *self-re-evaluation* and *emotional arousal*. At this point people began contemplating change. In high moments of concern, a *commitment* to change is made prompting preparation. This included *social liberation* away from other users towards non-users. These intentions are put into action and people stopped smoking. As a result they needed to make *environmental* changes in avoiding temptations and triggers. *Countering* old wants with new habits and *rewarding* oneself for successful abstinence. In sustaining these changes new pro-social support networks need to be built, hence *helpful relationships* figured heavily in these successful self-changers recovery. If people failed to sustain the changes they relapsed back into the old behaviour. Prochaska and DiClemente discovered that some individuals went through this process

5–7 times before achieving what they described as optimum recovery – hence the model becoming known in the field as the cycle of change. In the academic literature, the stages of change is the preferred name. There is also some evidence to suggest that initiation into drug and alcohol use and the development of problematic use follows the same sequence (DiClemente, 2003).

It is the grouping of nine mechanisms (highlighted in italics) which defines each stage of change. Reviewing the major counselling models available Prochaska and DiClemente (1992) found that most only contained 2–3 such mechanisms. Therefore, no one style of counselling was sophisticated enough to deal with the entirety of the human change process. This is what is meant by 'trans-theoretical model'. The stages of change transcends any one particular theory of counselling by providing a means to integrate all theories. This means that we must 'match' our interventions to the client's current stage in order to be most effective in supporting them through this process. The nine key mechanisms are defined in Table 2.2, along with examples of appropriate interventions. This also reflects the kinds of services that clients might find helpful as the change process unravels.

Reviewing Table 2.2 we can see both the key mechanisms along with relevant treatment responses. Relapse has been excluded from the table. This group has defied statistical analysis, and it was only their removal from the original data that statistical significance was achieved (Prochaska et al., 1994). Relapse is now considered an event rather than a stage as there are no mechanisms; the client simply passes through on their way back to either pre-contemplation (60 per cent) or contemplation (40 per cent). It appears strange that those who have attempted change should return to a pre-contemplative state. But we must remember that each stage is defined by clusters of mechanism not simply stated desire. So whilst some individuals re-evaluate, attempt to learn from the relapse and experience emotional arousal, others simply do not.

The stages of change model has had a profound effect on social policy in the UK, with the advent of Models of Care and Integrated Treatment Pathways. Models of Care stipulates the services that local government commissioners must purchase in every county of England. This ensures a broad range of services are provided to clients at every stage of readiness to change. Treatment Pathways defines how people will move through these layers of services. As such they identify clear entry and exit points in and out of every service. This means that there is a continuum of care for substance misuse, at every stage of the change process. These structures therefore attempt to unify helping services into a seamless range of support. Within this we see that treatment interventions intensify as the user moves up through these stages. Low intensity services engage with and support the client with harm reduction interventions as well as assist in the consideration of change. Referral is then made into a range of pathways according to the client's own individual needs and preferences. Pre-decisional group work and counselling may assist people to make decisions regarding change and help develop detoxification and after-care treatment. In-patient detoxification, structured day care, relapse prevention work and residential rehabilitation provide high support for those who quit use. This is without reference to the substance they are using. Essentially it remains focused on how people change. As such, the stages of change provide a whole population treatment approach which is able to meet the needs of those who are trying to manage, stabilise or change their use.

Table 2.2 Comparison of mechanism of change with service intervention

Mechanisms	Goals	Services
Pre-contemplation-contemplation: establish a relationship – harm reduction		
Consciousness raising	Increasing information about the behaviour through observation, interpretations, reading, recognising the nature of problems as well as how you can avoid pitfalls in changing them.	Needle exchange schemes Drop-in Detached work Advice and information Non-specialist services that may encounter problematic use such as probation services, social services, health services
Social liberation	Avoiding or controlling external factors that are not conducive to the old behaviour, such as non-smoking areas. Campaigning for rights as individuals which demand change in the social environment.	
Contemplation-preparation: motivational interviewing to elicit commitment		
Self-re-evaluation	Assessing feelings and thoughts about self with respect to the problem and the kind of life you want for yourself. What are the emotional or rational losses and gains in change or staying the same?	Semi-structured, rapid access services. Drop-in Needle exchange Outreach Assessments
Emotional arousal	Powerful and deep emotional experiences which raise an emotional awareness and catharsis regarding the problem. Often induced by crises or tragedies.	One-to-one sessions Low intensity group work for those considering change. Community prescribing services
Preparation-action: solution focussed therapy to develop goals		
Commitment	Once you have chosen to change, one's preparedness to make the private and then the public commitment to act. Increases pressure on oneself to succeed and achieve one's goals.	Assessment for after care Referral for intensive treatment interventions Aftercare planning
Action – maintenance: relapse prevention to remain drug free and restructure lifestyle		
Reward	Rewarding self or being rewarded by others for making change. This can include self-praise, gifts, access to alternative enrichment or other positive experiences. Punishments do not work well as rewards.	Community detoxification Symptom management detoxification In-patient detoxification Residential treatment Structured day care Housing
Environmental control	Deliberately avoiding triggers that elicit problem behaviours or removing the means to access them such as getting rid of drug paraphernalia, alcohol or avoiding other users.	Rebuilding social support Family Self-help groups Skills training Employment
Helping relationships	Enlisting the help of people that care for you. This may demand letting people know what we need from them. This may be from professionals but not necessarily.	Specialist no-drug specific services: (forensic psychiatry, Hep C, HIV, liver specialists.)
Countering	Substitute alternative behaviours for problem behaviours. When faced with cravings the user may use exercise as a means of detracting from them, smokers may chew gum instead or people with weight problems might eat fruit.	

Critiques of the stages of change

There are problems with the stages of change. Some of the criticism relates to the methodological problems of any research whilst other criticism relates to the stage structure. For example, the sequence is not necessarily invariant as users may opt back into use at any time (Budd and Rollnick, 1996). West (2005) also criticises the models for the preparation stage. Many users simply make the decision to change and act on it without planning, and indeed this was reflected in the early stage depictions. It must be remembered that this research was conducted on smokers. This culturally accepted drug does not activate the same levels of social disenfranchisement as illicit drugs. As such, the model retains its primary focus on the psychology and the behaviour of the user, and does not accommodate the significance of environmental contexts in which illicit users reside. These issues will be explored in more detail in subsequent chapters.

It appears difficult to identify crisp mechanisms of change too. This has led to the consideration that clients are in 'dominant' rather than 'absolute' stages (Conners et al., 2001). The human brain is capable of formulating goals and sub-goals which are simultaneous, contradictory and sometimes irrational. However, the stages of change does offer a conceptual model and common language for discussing change. So whilst refining our understanding we must also recognise it is not the only means of change nor necessarily complete in itself. As the treatment framework of our time it needs to be understood by practitioners within these caveats. Therefore we shall take a broadly trans-theoretical view of addiction treatment, it will also be enriched by research drawn from non-treatment populations who have successfully overcome addictions without interference of treatment philosophies.

Conclusion

It is important to recognise that addiction and dependence are different concepts and demand different treatment responses. Whereas treatment for dependence may be facilitated by prescribing, addiction is a breakdown between an individual and the social environment. This is beyond the ken of biology. Whilst dependence is determined by consumption, addiction is a multi-faceted and insidious process of erosion leading to social exclusion. The threshold of addiction is culturally set, dependent on factors such as societal values, norms and the law. When this exclusion occurs early in the life course it can compound the user's problems further by denying the means to rehearse and prepare for the increasing complexities of adulthood. The effects of social exclusion can further amplify the significance of the substance to the user as the only purposeful activity and source of satisfaction available to them. As a result, some users seek to alleviate the stresses within this shadow society, whilst others make purposeful attempts to escape it. Change processes can be profound quantum experiences, the maturational process driving them to seek out other sources of satisfaction drawn from the wider society they occupy or an intentional act of purposeful striving. Intentional change occurs as a sequence of stages which provides a framework for workers to apply salient interventions. But, in order to do this, the client must be willing to engage in the process with the practitioner. And this is wholly dependent on the therapeutic relationships that are created.

Chapter 3

On the Helping Relationship

Hell, madam, is to love no longer.
George Barnanos

If addiction is characterised by the breakdown of relationships it follows that the biggest impact on addressing it is the reconstruction of these broken bonds. This begins in the helping relationships and ends in the reconnection to others in the social structures of life. Research has consistently identified the therapeutic relationship as the most important single factor in producing positive outcomes *regardless* of the approach of the helper (Hovarth, 2001). This chapter will explore the core elements of effective helping relationships and how they impact on change. This is important because if relationships can promote change they can also impede it. Particular attention will be given to the establishment of the bond, the importance of goals and fostering the means to attain them. We will see why the helpful alliance needs to be established quickly and preserved against setbacks and tensions. This will inform all the interventions that follow.

Relationships and research

Whilst the relationship is the biggest factor in treatment outcomes, the exact degree of its influence is disputed. Lambert's (1992) research estimates that 30 per cent of all outcomes in counselling based approaches are driven by the relationship, whilst Wampold's (2001) research has suggested that it accounts for 54 per cent of outcomes. Random control trials are the means of testing the effectiveness of counselling models. In these studies, clients with comparative problems are randomly assigned to different counselling approaches. Workers on these studies are trained, supervised and monitored in their practice to ensure they deliver the exact stated intervention to a gold standard. In reviewing these studies, commentators such as Duncan et al. (2004) observed that outcomes remain remarkably similar across all treatment styles. As a result, they suggest outcomes do not stem from the particular intervention. The common factor of the relationship is the primary agent that generates change. In these clinical trials drop-out rates can be as high as 25–90 per cent. Therefore, special attention is given to relationship factors in these studies to ensure people stay in the programme long enough to retain a large enough sample to provide a statistically meaningful result. This is not translated into practice. In day to day work, outcomes may vary a great deal and little attention is given to retaining clients. Studies of outcomes in clinical practice do appear to show a hierarchy of treatment outcomes, with certain interventions outperforming others (See Miller et al., 1995). What is striking in this research is that interventions that emphasise the alliance in practice tend to do better.

Furthermore, research has failed to find any relationship between treatment outcomes and professional qualification, or indeed experience. Huge variance in outcomes can occur even between helpers delivering the exact same treatment (Lambert, 1989). These 'within programme' differences may be even larger than those delivering different interventions. Luborsky et al. (1985)

found a huge variance amongst counsellors, even when delivering manualised approaches. The difference amongst individual practitioners was so great that when they were all averaged out in the final analysis it equalised outcomes. This, they suggest, is why control trials tend to generate similar outcomes.

As such, we cannot evaluate the effectiveness of helpers on how well they deliver specific techniques. Instead, we have to understand that the individual person delivering these techniques is an active element of the process itself. The idiosyncratic aspects of each individual relationship can have both beneficial and damaging potential to the client. This is not as simple as saying that there are good and bad helpers. Orlinsky and Howard's (1980) research into individual practitioners' outcomes suggests that each helper has an optimum range. Most helpers could achieve some positive outcomes with clients with a broad range of problems. However, only a few workers can consistently achieve good outcomes, and can even do so with complex cases. This was regardless of the style that these helpers used. In conclusion, how the helper is appears more significant than what the helper does.

Within the realm of addiction work we see the same results. Connors et al. (1997) found that the strength of the client–worker relationship was the biggest single predictor of sobriety at one year follow up in the treatment of alcoholism. Again this was regardless of the approach used. Whilst two studies by Miller et al. (1983, 1993) found that it was possible to predict the future drinking levels of alcoholics after treatment, solely from the style of helper: the more confrontational the helper, the poorer the outcomes. Even in prescribing substitute drugs such as methadone, outcomes are determined by the relationships with the workers and not the drug itself (see McLellan et al., 1988; Woody et al., 1983; Chan et al., 1997). When reviewing the impact of treatment in more complex cases, we see that the role of the relationship is even more significant. Petry and Bickel (1999) identified that amongst dual diagnosis clients, the alliance was the strongest predictor of treatment completion amongst those with severe psychiatric symptoms. The categorical conclusion of this research is as obvious as it is neglected: the biggest difference to human beings is other human beings.

Therapeutic alliance

Whilst it has been long appreciated that the relationship is the central foundation of helping others, the vague representation of it has lead to problems within the field. Just because relationship factors are central to outcome does not imply *any* relationship is helpful. The lack of clear standards or guidance permits the assumption that we all have good working relationships with clients. Carl Rogers (1957, 2000) was one of the first to emphasise the importance of relationship in creating the environmental conditions for change. This was achieved solely by the client experiencing the helper's core conditions of empathy, congruence, positive regard (and warmth). Environments of acceptance allowed the client to experience their deepest thoughts, hopes and fears without distortion. As a result, clients become increasingly true to themselves and adjusted their lives according to these more sincere wants. Whilst these core conditions are important ingredients in helping they are not sufficient for change to occur. In order to build our understanding of what constitutes a helpful relationship we must look deeper into the research to understand what it is, how it operates and what this means for the practitioner.

Research into the nature of the helping relationship has bloomed in the last thirty years, stimulated by the work of Bordin (1979). He labelled this the therapeutic alliance, to demarcate it from ideas of the relationship in itself. Bordin observed that every kind of helping relationship demands an alliance must be formed between the client and the worker. The effectiveness of the helping relies primarily on this working alliance. The strength of the alliance was determined by the degree of agreement between three key areas. These are the goals of the intervention, the tasks that must be accomplished to achieve these goals and the bond between the helper and their client. These three basic concepts are inter-related and are not listed in any order of priority. For example, the greater the bond between the client and practitioner, the greater the trust in the tasks and the more likely the client will achieve their goal. Alternatively, the more helpful the tasks presented by the practitioner, the greater the bond will be become. However, for clarity, we will explore each of these concepts singularly and in depth.

Goals

Clients seek help to attain goals that do not feel obtainable to them in the normal course of their life. This is often motivated by their desire to alleviate internal distress or overcome external hostile environments. They may have vague or very clear ideas of 'what' they must do in order to overcome these difficulties. In contrast, the goals of the helper are implicit in the nature of the support they provide, whether this is formal treatment models or informal support. Implicit in all approaches is the assumption that although the client may feel overwhelmed or inhabit a difficult environment, they are none-the-less contributing to these difficulties in some way that they do not fully appreciate at the outset of counselling. The goal of the helping will be to make them aware of their contribution and foster insights or new behaviours to amend them.

Different styles of counselling are based on different models of human nature. As a result, they source the individual's contribution to their problems in different areas. For example, many psychodynamic therapies assume that the client's current problems are located in their feelings. Behaviour therapies would suggest that the client has developed powerful habits in acting in certain ways. Cognitive models assume that the client's problems are located in errors in their thought processes. Whilst the twelve step model assumes the client's problems are located in a unique biological allergy to intoxicants.

These examples are simplified, but we can see that each counselling model would suggest a different remedy to overcome these problems. Helping approaches dictate the goals by prescribing what the client must achieve to overcome their difficulties. Hence, the goal of psychodynamic therapies suggest that the client must resolve painful emotional conflicts; behavioural therapies would suggest the client must establish new patterns of behaviour; cognitive approaches demand that client masters new thinking styles; whilst the twelve step approach demands people to commit to life long abstinence. Each model has an implicit end point that it hopes to achieve with its clients. Treatment works well when the client shares the same goal as the help they are receiving. For example, psychodynamic models have shown poor outcomes for the treatment of alcoholism in general (Roth and Fonagy, 1996). Yet, for the sub-population of drinkers who believe their problems stem from past emotional trauma, the approach shows very good outcomes.

It is essential then that the client shares the same goals as the counselling model itself. The degree in which counsellors are willing to collaborate with what the client aspires to may vary dramatically across different styles. It is easy to confuse resistance to the kind of help being offered as a resistance to change. And clients who drop-out can be all too quickly labelled as unmotivated (Agosti et al., 1991), as opposed to the treatment approach being a poor match. In Kotter and

Carlson's (2003) fascinating interviews with leading therapists regarding their worst practice, problems occurred when helpers put the ideals of their counselling style before the experience of the client. For example, Norcross reports a case when a depressed client was dissuaded from anti-depressant medication by his counsellor. The counsellor interpreted the desire for medication as a pattern of emotional avoidance. As a result, the client's depression deepened and they experienced severe vegetation and were hospitalised. The imposition of goals by the helpers on vulnerable clients who place their trust in them always has the potential to become abusive.

It is therefore important that there is a good match between what the client believes they must achieve to improve their lives with what the helper believes they must do. Where there is disagreement, the helper is always wrong. Drug and alcohol services are notoriously bad at letting clients know what kind of support they are offering and how this will help them. If the client does not believe in, or understand, the rationale of the treatment they will not prosper. Without being clear we do not allow the client to make an informed choice as to whether the services will be of benefit to them from the outset. As such it is important that we collaborate with the client on the goal of helping. We cannot impose goals on them. Consider how much you love your own parents; but could you live the life that they wanted for you? We are cursed and blessed to identify what is important to us in life and this cannot be deferred to others. Treatment works at its best when the implicit goals of treatment match the explicit aspirations of the client. If the client cannot realise their goals with your service it is better that they find a service that does.

For the purposes of this book, the interventions described in this book share common features in that they focus explicitly on helping the client establish their own goals and support them to achieve this. The implicit assumption of these interventions is that clients are motivated to change by incentives. As such it departs from the idea that the client must attain the goals set by the helping process and instead focuses on the desired outcomes the client seeks. Nobody will put any effort into change in order to be worse off than they are, and the more desirable the outcome the harder they will work to achieve this. Incentives are not just the material tangibles and edibles of everyday life, but also include relationships, values and beliefs. These incentives can be divided into two categories. Positive reinforced change whereby the client is prepared to work towards more desirable alternatives to their current situation. And negatively reinforced change whereby the client seeks to alleviate undesirable aspects of their current situation. Substance misuse work needs to address these two key areas by setting two goals. The first is to establish what people want to do about their dependence in the short term to reduce the stress they are under. The second is to consider what they want to do about their addiction in not simply overcoming difficulties but in creating the kind of life they want for themselves. In this book, the ultimate goal of addictions work is assumed to be the reintegration of the individual back into pro-social structures of life that provide more enriching and fulfilling alternatives to use.

The tasks

Tasks are the activities that must be completed in order to achieve these goals. This is important in helping relationships. People seek help to achieve what otherwise feels unobtainable to them in the normal course of their life. The helpers role is provide the pathway to make this goal feel accessible. For example, formal counselling models prescribe set tasks, activities or techniques that the client must participate in to achieve their goal. In psychodynamic approaches tasks might include exploring the events of childhood, participate in free association or analyse transference.

Behavioural models focus on assessing coping, rehearsing new skills and practising them in different situations. In cognitive therapy the tasks are directed towards developing the client's awareness of logical errors through self-monitoring and thought correction. And the twelve step approach demands that clients work through a series of exercises based on the twelve edicts of the fellowship's name. This may also be expanded upon in care planning. For clients with entrenched and complex problems, their goals might only be achieved through several sources of support. This might demand a care plan that organises the client's goals and identifies who will support them to achieve each one. As such, each support provider will assist the client with their own set of micro-tasks. In this way every helping approach makes a demand on the client to do something which will help them achieve their goal.

Again, we see that different approaches use different techniques and make very different demands of the client. The 'goodness to fit' between what tasks the client believes will be helpful and the helper's approach is therefore essential for good outcomes (Carroll, 1997). What is most important is that the client believes these tasks to be relevant to achieving their goal and they are confident that they can perform them. And the more confident clients are the better they will perform. It is important to recognise that this is not about their actual ability but their *belief* in their ability to do so. Bandura (1997) refers to this as self-efficacy and it is defined as the client's perception of their ability to perform a task at a given level. As such, the success of resisting urges to use and implementing new patterns of behaviours are predictable by the client's self-efficacy belief that they can do so. The actual intervention, technique or skill may simply be a vehicle that fosters the clients belief that they have the means to overcome problems and achieve goals. What they actually do is not as important as the actual belief they can do something that helps them.

Understanding self belief is therefore vital. Our self-efficacy is specific to general domains of behaviour. So, your self-belief to do maths is very different from your self-belief to play football, but is closer to your grasp of physics. The higher your self-efficacy in performing a task, the greater the effort you invest in executing it and the more you will persist in its attainment. For example, in one experiment (cf. Bandura, 1992b) children of equal ability were asked to rank themselves in their self-confidence at maths. They were then given problems to solve. Children with the highest self-efficacy outperformed those with lower self-belief. They discarded faulty strategies more quickly, re-worked wrong answers and solved more problems. The highest performances were predicted by self-belief not ability. People's lack of confidence means they fail to maximise their resources because they focus on their doubts rather than the tasks and give up sooner. Whilst Western culture romanticises the notion of natural talent there is no evidence to support this concept. For example, child prodigies simply invest their time in practicing skills sooner than the counter-parts who invariably catch up with similar efforts eventually.

In fact, research into human performance warns against the dangers of such ideals as talent. Individuals who believe that their ability to perform a task is innate often suffer from higher stress, impaired functioning and lowering expectations in light of increasing demands. Whereas individuals who believe ability is acquired through experience, respond to more challenging demands positively, interpret the experience as a learning opportunity, and expect to make and improve upon mistakes. As a result their expectations increase whilst remaining emotional stable (Wood and Bandura, 1989).

As Albert Bandura (1997) warns, people wishing to change future realities have to manage a great deal of personal distress, as they struggle to cope with this attainment and the social reactions to their change efforts. They must overcome internal frustration, doubt and despair, as well as the external obstacles and resistance. And, as the outcome is far from certain, it does not take a great deal to knock people into the futility of their effort. We see exactly the same struggle for the problematic user who is trying to shape their future reality by turning their intentions into action. It is those that persevere that achieve. And understanding how we foster perseverance is an important part of the helping process.

According to Bandura (1992b) the primary source of self-belief is mastering experience. This is because it provides us with the most concrete feedback regarding the fit between our ability and the demands of any task. Successes at a task fosters an increasing sense of mastery whilst failures, particularly if encountered early on, undermine our self-efficacy. Those who easily achieve repeated successes are soon discouraged and de-motivated when they encounter failure. Difficulties provide important feedback on what skills the individual must refine to get back on track, and become increasingly resilient to set backs. Guided mastery of others, through teaching or modelling behaviour, can be useful in helping people to identify the salient features of the task in advance. This is enhanced if people are given objective feedback about performance and this is attributed to their own efforts.

Mastery and reading one's performance is not the only source of our self-efficacy. Another important area is social comparison to others. Others' ability to perform exerts a strong influence on our belief. For example, to see an individual who we assess as being good at a task fail may diminish our self-belief. Alternatively if we see someone we feel is not competent at a task do well it encourages our belief that we can do it too. This is particularly important during the development of skills. Persuasion is a common tool used to bolster self-belief but has limited value. Those who are affirmed in their ability to perform by others invest more effort over a greater time scale than those who are doubted. But this may set people up for failure, reducing self-belief and generating distrust towards the persuader. An evaluation of the motives of the persuaders is intrinsically important. Whether their agenda is to flatter, manipulate or exploit the situation in some way may generate a distrust which prevents the feedback from sticking.

Feedback from an individual who is highly competent in this area will have a much more profound effect. The way feedback is presented is also critical. For example, during the early state of skills development, persuading people that their progress is due to the effort they are putting in may be beneficial. But continuing this strategy may erode self-belief as high effort is often construed with low ability. Persuasive feedback appears more enhancing to self-belief when it suggests how well people are advancing towards a goal rather than outlining how far they are away from the goal. In the case of bad performance, feedback which highlights weakness is more damaging than that which offers guidance on how to perform more effectively. As a result it is much easier to instil negative expectations about an individual's performance than positive ones. This is because those with lower self-belief will avoid challenges, or give up sooner and thus fail to generate any disconfirming evidence as to their inability. Those with artificially high self-belief will enter into tasks, still struggle and confront the disparity between their performance and other people's appraisals.

The final area of self-belief is sourced in a closely related area of emotional and physical states. Some theorists (Schachter and Singer, 1962; Valins and Nisbett, 1972) have suggested that the symptoms of emotional states are too similar in themselves to be definitive. Therefore we have to interpret a general level of emotional arousal according to the context in which they occur and label them accordingly. Symptoms of high stress may indicate to some people impending failure whilst for other it may be the buzz of the challenge. The sense of imminent failure develops a certain kind of self-consciousness which can lower performance. The human brain finds it difficult to focus on more than one task at a time. We cannot focus on both the task at hand, such as public speaking, and our doubt about ability, scanning the audience for negative feedback. This can then conspire to decrease our performance. As our awareness of stress increases, our performance decreases, which in turn increases stress levels further. As a result, stress management skills appear to increase performance in all other areas as they allow people to focus on tasks with less distraction.

Self-belief that one can achieve is important. A goal does not need to be desirable; it must be realistically obtainable if we are to strive for it. Furthermore, the value of the goal itself can be an integral part of the motivational process. Challenging goals can influence motivation through the sense of self-satisfaction in progressing towards them. Self-assessment of achievement can bolster motivation as well as dissatisfaction with performance. If the individual believes that their sense of well-being is dependent on securing the desired outcome, this will demand that they intensify efforts to achieve things that are important to them in the light of failures.

Within this book, the interventions described provide the framework to assist the client to identify tasks that they believe will be useful. Rather than prescribing tasks the book assumes that the client has resources, experience and mastery to call upon to support them in their change process. Any gaps can be supported with skills. Testing these out in the real world then demands we titrate the level of these challenges to the confidence of the client. At all times these approaches aim to increase the client's self-belief in their ability to achieve change through identifying tasks that feel relevant and manageable to them. Where these skills and techniques do not feel appropriate to them, it is the helper who must make adjustment.

The bond

The bond between the client and the helper is the most mysterious element in therapy and it will be given deeper attention. But, any attempt to make this ineffable connection more concrete always runs the risk of clouding this issue further. However, in light of emergent research in both attachment and neurology, we are beginning to see how deep human bonds penetrate our lives and many hitherto hidden aspects of human relationships have been revealed. It had long been suspected that the maternal bond between mother and child was exceptionally important. In the 18th century, Fredrick the Great pondered on the innate language of human beings and so conducted a sadistic experiment. Infants were to be raised in all normal ways but not spoken to. He wanted to see what language they would spontaneously speak. Unfortunately all these infants died. Similarly, Spitz (1945) studied orphans and infants separated from imprisoned mothers, who were raised in foundling's homes. Once again these children were to be fed, clothed and kept warm but were not to be touched for fear of spreading infections. The mortality rates in these homes ran as high as 100 per cent for simple illnesses such as measles which most children shrug off.

The mystery of these infant deaths was not understood until a fortuitous accident occurred. Myron Hofer (1975) returned to his laboratory one day to find that a mother rat, a subject of his experiments, had escaped, leaving her pups behind. Examining these baby rats he noticed that their heart rate was half its normal level. Wondering whether this was the result of the removal of the mother's body temperature, he tested this idea. Using a heat lamp to recreate her body temperature he found it made no difference to heart rate but their activity levels increased. He set about isolating various aspects of rat mothering and stumbled across an incredible finding. Each mothering activity exerted an influence on one corresponding biological processes in the baby. Touch stimulated growth, milk set heart rate etc. (Hofer, 1987). These baby rats were not simply dependent on their mother for nurturance, they were unable to regulate their own biological functions, and without her orchestrating these processes, they fell into discord.

To understand this we must delve into the structure of the human brain. Developments in neurology have made impressive strides in understanding brain function and relationships. The brain of higher primates is a composite of three brains, each created in separate evolutionary waves. The central base of our brain is the proto-reptilian brain stem. And as its name suggests, it is the operating system of our most distant relatives, the reptile. It controls basic body function but little else, hence the eat, sleep, breed and die curriculum of a reptiles life. Reptiles lay eggs and their offspring fend for themselves in a world of predators including their own parents. Reptiles do not bond with their young as they do not have the emotional apparatus to do so. They live the one dimensional life of functioning without feeling. In humans, those medically diagnosed as 'brain dead', retain this basic level of functioning but nothing else.

Wrapped around this reptile motor is the limbic brain. This is the emotional brain that arrives with the evolution of mammals. Mammals give birth to live young. The limbic brain provides the apparatus to generate emotions. These emotions are then projected on to others and, as a result, bond with them. Mammals respond to whelps of fear in their young, engage in play, preening politics and rudimentary hierarchies of the herd. In this two dimensional world of consciousness they do not merely function but also feel. Whilst emotional capacity varies throughout mammals' species, depending on the size of the limbic region, the association of others with particular emotions is the seat of relationships. Our limbic brain is assessing mood, threat, allegiance and fear in every given situation at all times, filling our experience with feeling, though we are seldom consciously aware of it. Western culture elevates the rational brain, but the limbic intelligence is just as impressive. It also operates faster than our rational brain, making counselling highly impulsive people difficult as they tend to react emotionally before rationally engaging with a situation. Consider how the emotional reaction occurs for you in the following Exercise (3.1).

Exercise 3.1: Limbic processes

- Consider walking into a strange bar. What struck you about the place immediately?
- Think of a time when you told someone you loved how you felt about them. How adequately could you convey this in words?
- Think of a time that you have been out with your partners and they gave you a 'knowing' glance. Did you know exactly what they were referring too? How did you know?
- Think of a time when you got into conflict with someone, how did you know whether it was going to escalate or not? Who did you 'feel' was on your side?
- Think of a time when you were caught in a dangerous situation, where you had to react in an instant. Did you assess what action to take, or did you find yourself doing something?

Our limbic brain is constantly scanning the world around us and infers meaning in the small detail or tiniest gesture. As a result, the most significant body language of human beings is not the grandiose arm-crossing, back-stretching, angle-of-stance-gestures so beloved of popular psychology magazines. The most significant body language occurs in a milli-second. And your limbic brain detects it and replies, far faster than any behavioural expert can explain it. For example Condon's (1982) study of a four and a half second film of a family eating dinner found that in each every fame, the movements and pace of everyone were in perfect harmony. The minute gestures of one person sent a perfect ripple of movement in the others, in under 1/45 of second. This ripple was in perfect accord with the pace of the speaker's words too. When human beings come together we fall into a perfect dance that our conscious thought does not even comprehend. This makes emotion very contagious. In one study (Freidman et al., 1980) charismatic and less charismatic individuals were asked to assess their present mood. They were then paired up alone for two minutes where they were asked to remain silent. They then had their moods assessed again, and the less charismatic individuals moved towards the mood of their partners.

Even our speech will fall into perfect synchronicity with others, in both pace, rate and in the length of pause between words. Whilst our conscious minds listen and translate the information a speaker is relaying to us, words can denote many things. It is the limbic brain which colours and defines the meaning. In this sense, people who are attracted to each other, get the same jokes, like the same things about the same films are 'limbically' attuned to each other. They share the same mutual understanding of the detail that leaves others blank. Describing our attraction to another person as being on the same 'wavelength' may be more accurate than we think. Hence we understand sarcasm, irony, rhetorical questions yet respond badly to well meaning texts and email which are too clipped for our limbic brains to interpret. We need the smiley-miley or winking semi-colon to point us in the right emotional direction. Consider the problem outlined in Exercise 3.2.

Exercise 3.2: Rational and emotional interpretation

In order to minimise road rage incidents, it was once suggested that all cars should be fitted with an electronic screen on the rear window. This would allow the offending drivers to flash up the word 'SORRY' when they accidentally cut up another road user. But if someone cut you up in the road, how might you interpret this message?

Limbic regulation and relationships

It is the micro-gestures and our limbic brain's sensitivity towards them that influences not only our thoughts, but our biological self-regulation. Whist some biological systems in humans are closed and set their own self-contained rhythm, many are not. Several biological processes rely upon our relationships to others to maintain, adjust and fine tune them. This is known as limbic regulation and exerts control over heart rate, blood pressure, body temperature, immune systems and hormones amongst many others (Lewis et al., 2000). Essentially we cannot regulate our bodies as individuals but are inexplicable indebted to those around us to mediate our functioning, and we in turn influence theirs. Basking in the sunshine of love and the savage hurt of its demise is not simply psychological but reverberates into our biology. Hence we see that the chances of surviving serious illness are much enhanced amongst those with loving, stable partners; whilst the death of an elderly spouse may soon precipitate the death of their partner.

Geneticists who are apt to study addiction rates in those twins separated at birth to understand their predetermination for addiction, may only be measuring the echo of the separation which endures in higher primates lives, without the overcompensation of surrogate love (Kraemer, 1985). And the most striking feature of working with individuals at risk of committing suicide is often their deep sense of isolation and why the appeal to how their death would impact on others is a useful strategy in averting suicide (Williams, 2001). Loneliness and despair is the very same thing in the human brain. In fact the most corrosive emotion humans can experience is contempt. Contempt is the establishment of a hierarchy within a relationship, where one is less than another. As such, it is the emotion of exclusion. It is possible to predict the longevity of partnering relationships based on this emotion as well as the degree of physical illness on the scorned other (Carere and Gottman, 1999).

Brains, feeling and helping

Some researchers suggest that the bond with the helper operates as a metronome for the client. Their tone sets the mood and pace of reflection that can stabilise the metabolism and mood. The subtle transmission of feeling can be powerful. Although it is not a conscious feature of any helping relationship, this limbic exchange is an integral component. Indeed, this may also operate in the opposite direction, where the client shifts the mood of the counsellor. Rinks (1974) conducted a deep comparative analysis of a successful 'supershrink' therapist and unsuccessful 'pseudoshrink' therapist. They were both working with emotionally troubled young men using the same approach. Reviewing their case notes, we see the deepening negativity of the pseudoshrink, who became increasingly like his client group. Their desolation is echoed in his own clinical notes, he dreaded seeing the most difficult cases and fostered bleak expectations of their future prospects. In contrast, supershrink was more optimistic and helped these young men call upon their strengths and resources. At follow up in adulthood, 55 per cent of these young men experienced schizophrenia. But only 27 per cent of supershrink's case load received this diagnosis as opposed to 84 per cent of pseudoshrinks. The micro-gestures of the professional are extraordinarily powerful. For example, research shows that over 80 per cent of people in clinical trails can tell that they are on placebo from their doctors' body language (See Fisher and Greenberg, 1993). The lack of belief that the client can achieve their goals is easily transmitted. In experimental conditions, when the helper's expectation of the client's ability to change is altered it creates a self-fulfilling prophesy in outcome (Leake and King, 1977). This may explain why good personal adjustment in the help is important to outcomes (Luborsky et al., 1985)

The analysis of the world is reserved for the outer brain, the neocortex. In humans it is the sheer size of the necortex which gifts us our incredible facility to codify the world into logic, language and prediction that we can share with others. Reason is why we are so adaptive whereas other mammals are restricted to limited social communication, use only rudimentary tools and don't get card tricks. This is not without limit. The human neocortex can only process so much information. As result, we rely on collectivism to spread the burden of information. Research by Wegner (1991) has demonstrated that when humans come together in pairs and groups a joint memory emerges between the members. They not only take on certain roles but recall certain types of memories on behalf of the group. It means that we 'know' who to go to in the work place or among our families when we have a specific kind of problem because they take upon themselves to remember that kind of information. As such, memory is not so much in us, but in those that we are attached to. To lose someone you love is to lose part of your memory. Again research suggests that there is a capacity limit to relationships. Dunbar's (1992) research suggests that the size of the neocortex in mammals predicts their group size. In humans this suggests that we can only have 15 meaningful relationships at one time. This is because we not only have to process the relationship we have with each group member, but also the relationships that they have with each other.

The crowning achievement of the neocortex is not to be confused with the entirety of what we are. The inner voice we refer to as 'I' that hears itself think may display astonishing abstract complexity but it is not the air traffic control of consciousness. Rationality is not master of passions and appetites but rather runs parallel to them. As we have seen in Chapter 1, the brain does not have insight into itself when it comes to drugs' actions on these deeper parts of our conscious. Nor does it have access to the emotions that emerge from these depths. It must study the signals that emerge from these irrational zones to fathom out its patterns and motives and formulate an explanation of it. For example, when asking people why they are depressed they do not know. They may attribute it to certain events that they think ought to be relevant. Certain treatment models may suggest why they are depressed and if this rings true this model may be helpful. When working with people we have to accept that we are not purely rational beings but emotional beings too. Head and heart may pull in opposite directions in human neurology and common sense offers no advantage in this struggle. As a result knowledge does not change behaviour nor does the ventilation of feelings offer us insight to do anything differently next time.

The bond and motivation

The bond is also important to foster motivation of a different kind. We have seen the value of the goal and ready means to achieve it may increase motivation by use of incentives. But the willingness to comply with the help being offered is determined by the bond. As such, motivation as compliance to make change is not present or absent in the user but is dependent on their social environment. Consider a time when you have gone to see a professional such as a GP with a sensitive concern. We have all had good and bad experiences. In Exercise 3.3, consider how the negative experience compared to the positive in the following areas.

Exercise 3.3: Impact of relationships on motivation	
A negative experience	**A positive experience**
How did they behave towards you?	How did they behave towards you?
What was their body language like?	What was their body language like?
What was their emotional tone like?	What was their emotional tone like?

What was the power balance like?	What was the power balance like?
How did you end up feeling?	How did you end up feeling?
What happened to your motivation?	What happened to your motivation?

What we can see in the comparison of these two different experiences is that motivation is not an enduring quality that is innate in you. The quality of these encounters has a dramatic effect on it. The patronising, judgemental, contemptuous experience in the negative encounter diminishes your motivation. The warm, empathetic and considered approach of the positive experience enhances motivation. Motivation is not in the person, but in the relationship. It is the same when we look at addiction counsellors. Counsellors who retain clients share the common features of warmth, empathy and express a genuine desire to help. In this way we can understand motivation not simply as the client having an incentive to work towards but as a willingness to comply and engage in the process of treatment itself. As such the bond is essential in fostering compliance with the goals and tasks of the helping relationship. If we do not collaborate with the client in their change process, we lose them. As a result, treatment outcomes may say far more about the provider than the condition they treat.

The alliance in practice

The alliance is therefore more than the relationship. The personal qualities of the helper are good predictors of the alliance, especially when this is reciprocated by the client. But outcomes are still dependent on goals and tasks. For change to occur people still must apply purposeful effort to achieve goals that they value. Luborsky et al. (1985) suggest that the strong bond facilitates treatment more effectively by allowing the therapist to focus on establishing goals and tasks. In this way, interventions and techniques are deeply woven into the alliance itself. So whilst we need not be prescriptive about what goals the client must have or which tasks they must follow, they remain necessary. Clients tend to favour non-directive approaches, but they least like non-directive-ness itself (Toma, 2000). This means we must be able to establish a rapport with the client and provide the framework where salient goals can be agreed and helpful tasks negotiated. When reviewing natural remission studies (those who change addictions without seeking formal help), we see that many of these individuals simply felt that the help available to them did not offer what they needed. Each constructed their own 'programme' of recovery instead, many of which shared common features. This suggests that we need to be more democratic in the kind of help that we offer and trust in the client's own inclinations in terms of what they feel will help them.

Think of two clients that you have worked with, one that led to positive outcomes, and one which did not. Compare your answers to the following questions about the bond, goals and tasks in Exercise 3.4. Can they explain the success and failure of the process?

Exercise 3.4: Comparison of successful and unsuccessful alliance			
	Could you agree on goals of the relationship?	Could you agree the tasks in how they could be achieved?	Did you establish a bond of mutual respect?
Successful relationship			
Unsuccessful relationship			

Before the consideration of individual skills and techniques we must master two aspects of the helping relationship in order to be effective. Firstly, it is essential that we establish a positive alliance with the client, and secondly we must be able to sustain this alliance over the duration of the helping episode despite inevitable setbacks and ruptures between the helper and the client. The formation of this alliance needs to occur sooner rather than later if successful outcomes are to be achieved. Research that charts the effectiveness of the therapeutic dose over time consistently supports this maxim. Contrary to perceived wisdom, the majority of the clients' gains occur sooner rather than later, as illustrated in Figure 3.1 (see Howard et al., 1986; Barkham, 1990). Clients who do not experience any early improvement are unlikely to make any gains in this particular approach (Miller et al., 2005). This appears particularly relevant in the early stages of treatment where the client's satisfaction with the help they receive appears critical to retention. The curve also explains the doldrums of helping. Here the client who once made rapid gains now appears stuck and the focus drifts into the general traffic of their lives. This can be interpreted as the client moving backwards in some way, helping loses its momentum whilst outcomes become undermined. In reality they are reaching the critical shift in diminishing returns which is part of the process.

Secondly, it is essential that we learn to be vigilant for the tensions and fluxes in the relationship that may well be generated by our performance. The vast majority of treatment dropout occurs within the first month of treatment (Silbertfeld and Glaser, 1978). This is not simply a lack of client motivation as these individuals subsequently seek treatment elsewhere (Peterson et al., 1994). It is our responsibility as the professional to monitor the quality of the relationship and address any tensions before they lead to client drop-out. After all, treatment cannot be effective when the client is simply not there to receive it. If we are unable to address and heal ruptures as they emerge it will erode the outcomes (Foreman and Marmar, 1985; Coady 1985).

Outcome informed practice

In response to this research, Duncan et al. (2004) have dispensed with formal adherence to any particular theory or clinical model and have instead focused on the alliance and the outcomes.

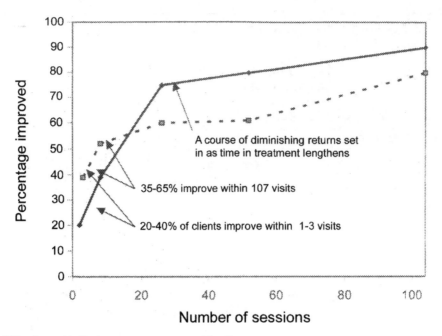

The bold line shows objective improvement, as measured by others.
The dotted line shows subjective improvements, as reported by the clients.

Figure 3.1   Representation of the Dose-Outcome Curve

They concur with wider research that suggests treatment outcomes are primarily driven by the alliance. They point out that diagnosis, severity of the problems, treatment theory and causality are simply not related to outcomes (Miller et al., 2005). Establishing the alliance and the experience of early benefits from treatment are the key to outcomes. This is important as helpers are not as adept as clients in picking up ruptures, disjuncture or drift in treatment process (Lambert et al., 2003). When the client and helper have access to this information it can make a considerable difference to treatment. As a result Duncan et al. (2004) have developed two simple outcome assessment forms; one to measure the client's progress and another to measure the helper's adherence to the alliance. (Available under licence from www.talkingcure.com)

The first, the Outcome Rating Scale, is used at the opening of each session. The client is asked to score themselves on four measures by placing a hash mark on four unnumbered scales. These four measures individually ask how the client feels they are progressing *personally* in themselves; *interpersonally* with intimate others; *socially* with their wider public relationship and *generally*. Each scale is then measured and this is then converted into a score from 0–10 and then added together, leaving a maximum score of 40. As we have seen, the client's subjective sense of improvement runs close to the objective measurements of improvement. So progress can be charted simply with a large degree of validity at the start of each session. This allows the client and helper to monitor progress. Clients who are not reporting any early progress can then revise their treatment plans with the helper sooner, abating drop out. Likewise for clients who feel they are deteriorating, this can be addressed before they drop-out of treatment. Where the worker cannot adjust or provide what the client is wanting, after a non-defensive discussion, the client can be referred to the services that are more appropriate to their needs. At the other end of the spectrum, clients who score over 24 equate with those who are not in treatment. Again, this provides a concrete cut off point for normal functioning. Clients who wish to continue in treatment above this point tend to fear relapse and so treatment can be tailored accordingly.

At the end of each session, the helper is then assessed on the Service Rating Scale. This tool asks the client to rate the session on four scales again. These are based on the therapeutic alliance and ask whether the client felt *respected* (bond), explored *topics* relevant to them (goals) and whether the helper's approach was a *good fit* (tasks). The fourth scale asks how the session went in general. These are then converted into a score of one to ten and added together for a total score of 40. If the therapist scores under 35, they explore what the helper missed in the session. This generates feedback on each session and provides a brake to ensure that therapeutic alliance is always maintained. Where the helper scores low, feedback is welcomed non-defensively and they make adjustment accordingly. If we are able to respond non-defensively and appropriately to tensions it only improves treatment outcomes (Duncan et al., 2004). Research shows that this is especially important in dealing with problems 'within' the helping relationship. This guarantees that we remain on course and deepens the alliance despite the set-backs and ruptures (Coady, 1991; Foreman and Marmar, 1985; Safran and Muran, 2000).

Clinical research shows that when the helper has access to in vivo feedback, it has a dramatic impact on outcomes. In a study (Miller et al., 2004) of several thousands of cases, feedback processes doubled the treatment outcomes whilst halving drop-out rates. Clients who did not have access to feedback processes were three-to-four times more likely to have a negative treatment outcome or for treatment to make no difference at all. This was achieved without the addition of any intensive training, specialist supervision, manualisation or any other means other than client feedback. The helpers were simply allowed to practice in their own way. Whilst these simple but effective tools have a powerful impact on treatment outcomes for clients, introducing them into clinical practice can have an equally powerful impact on practitioners. When asked to support agencies that are struggling, I always look at the workers' morale. When it is low, outcomes will be diminished, compounding the negative mood of the team. The ORS and SRS assessment tools offer concrete feedback to workers and teams that they are making a difference. It can increase work satisfaction and a sense of personal competence.

Case Study: The use of ORS and SRS outcome tools

Peter suffered from epilepsy and was drinking heavily when he presented for treatment. His alcohol consumption interfered with his medication making his epilepsy worse. His early ORS scores had shown improvement from the counselling that he was receiving but over time they began to drop. At the end of another session the counsellor asked him to complete the SRS for this session and the client scored him 27. In a non-defensive manner, the counsellor enquired what was amiss with the sessions? Peter said that the counsellor was spending the time discussing his drinking and his epilepsy. But he felt the real problem was in his relationship with his wife which they had completely neglected. The counsellor conceded that his concern about Peter's epilepsy had got in the way of the helping process. Instead they would focus on the issues in Peter's relationship. They followed through on this in subsequent sessions and the client ORS scores began to rise dramatically and, as the relationship with his wife improved, Peter's drinking decreased.

There is a paradox at work in these tools though. The abandonment of any formal theories or approaches, and instead matching treatment to the client's theory of change, demands that helpers are both competent and versatile in a range of approaches to accommodate this.

Creating the alliance

Forming alliances with problematic drug and alcohol users is not easy. Living in chaotic worlds, where the values of the shadow society normalise acting out behaviour, increase levels of impulsivity and repeated failures to change prompt pessimism. This can be exacerbated by previous unhelpful treatment experiences. These experiences militate against forming trusting and open relationships. When working with clients it is important that we are good at establishing the alliance with clients quickly. This is important as outcomes will occur sooner rather than later, and early improvement encourages retention.

Much is written about the style of the counsellor. Certainly, meeting the chaos and ambivalence with a confrontational or aggressive style is unhelpful. But within this, the most important quality that the helper can bring is authenticity. This is quite simply that the helper be themselves. Aping the ideals of counselling or 'performing' the role of the drugs worker will be transparent and unsustainable in the relationship. As we have seen, the idiosyncratic 'micro-behaviour' of the helper can be more important than the technique. Actively mirroring the client or taking up a posture of helping will be wooden and all too obvious to the client. If you are natural, the client can make more informed assessments of whether you are the kind of person they can work with. Within this it is important that the client recognises a sincere desire to help. Speaking honestly is essential in establishing the rapport, whilst at the same time acknowledging mixed feelings regarding change and the effort it demands to attain. Speaking down to the client, using jargon or getting into analysing them immediately blocks the rapport. Even if the therapeutic model you subscribe to is skills based or didactic it is better to let the client tell their story and demonstrate empathy before anything else. Focussing on their concerns and being both attentive and empathetic to their struggles is essential.

Selecting questions to ask is difficult for novice helpers. Uncertainty in what to ask creates hesitancy in practice which erodes the client's confidence. Likewise hopping about from one concern to another will be confusing. Short, open questions are important in the first meeting. Open questions are ones which the respondent cannot say a simple yes or no to. Who, when, what, where, how questions demand the client describe their situation and are easier to answer. We do not ask 'why' questions. This demands an explanation rather than a description. The shorter the question the harder the client must work themselves at exploring their understanding rather than selecting options offered by the helper. By asking the client open questions we get them to describe their situation first and foremost.

When working with a client it is important to remember that we are in the role of interviewer. And like all interviewers, our focus should primarily be on drawing out information from the person we are interviewing. Regardless of which counselling style we are using we wish to draw out the client's thoughts or feelings. If we think of our favourite chat shows, the guests are not invited on to the programme to listen to the interviewer's views on their latest books, films or news story. When working with people we are both the interviewer who frames the question and the audience who is interested in the answers offered. We must work hard at getting to the client's understanding rather than imposing ours on them. Consider the experience outlined in Exercise 3.5.

Exercise 3.5: Interviewing

Think of a concern or problem that you have at the moment. Do not choose a major life issue but a problem that has some gravity to it. Talk to a few friends about it one at a time. How do they respond? Do they explore your concerns? Do they tell you what you ought to do? In short, do they work hard to understand your problem or do they work hard at imparting their answers?

Which responses feel the best?

It was once thought that you could not teach helpers to be empathetic as it was a 'way of being' rather than a skill. But there are some rules to conversations which generate an atmosphere of empathetic understanding. Research by Matarazzo and Patterson (1986) identified several core principles. First we should never tread on the client's lines. We should resist all temptation to speak over the top of client, interrupt them or cut them short before they have finished their sentences. Even if we are speaking and the client steps in and interrupts us, we step aside and let them speak. In training session where I hear trainees do this I will stop them and ask their practice client to finish their statement. Inevitably the most salient point is made at the end of their speech which would have otherwise been completely missed.

Remember that we may be the metronome that controls the pace of the session. We need to pause before asking the next question or opening up the next set of concerns. It slows the pace, invites a contemplative mood and demonstrates to the client that you are working hard to understand and explore their concerns. Too many rapid-fire questions in quick succession usually invite short and unconsidered questions in the client. If you slow down and think before you ask a question, the client will slow down and think before they answer. This needs to be coupled with the accuracy of interpretation. Using frequent summaries or paraphrasing demonstrates that you are not just listening but understanding. The greater the accuracy of your interpretation the better the outcome will be. When you are wrong let the client refine you. In Exercise 3.6, read the following excerpts from helping relationships. What mistakes is the helper making here?

Exercise 3.6: Errors in listening skills

Listening exercise
Example 1
Client: I have been using for 10 years now and it is starting to get on top . . .
Helper: You feel you have got to stop now?
Client: . . . Em yes, things have got difficult. I am starting to realise that I can't go on with what I'm doing and must stop. I stopped before, I was 6 months clean, but I have been sliding back into and cannot face going back to prison and . . .
Helper: How long were you in last?
Client: . . . Oh, I did 18 months, for theft, I . . .
Helper: When was that?
Client: . . . I can't go back, I just . . .
Helper: Hold on, when were you inside?

Example 2

Helper: So you have been arguing with your mother a lot and that is getting to you even though you have put a lot of effort into changing, it's like she does not understand how hard you are working at this?

Client: Well, kind of.

Helper: Is it that she does not understand any of this stuff because she has not used before or things between you have just run their natural course?

Client: . . . I think that she does not understand because she has not been through this.

Helper: Is she not willing to learn and think about what she can do to help or she just does not know where to start?

Example 3

Helper: So that made you really angry. Not surprised, I only hear bad things about that agency.

Client: No, not really, I was just disappointed really that he would act that way.

Helper: Like he was punishing you for something.

Client: No, it was just a bit like they were going through the motions really. I was wanting help but at the drug agency it was like I was just another number. Not a person in my own right.

Helper: I know. They think that the same thing works for everyone.

Client: Perhaps, I do not know, I did not really stay for long enough to know what they thought. It was just their attitude.

Whilst these examples may look comical on the page, they happen more than we think. We see in the first example there is a battle for air time. We should not step on the client's words but let them think as well as speak freely. Sometimes when the client is working hard to formulate a response the worker can nip in with the next question. This usually occurs when the helper experiences silences as uncomfortable and intercedes, breaking the flow. Knowing when and when not to talk is important. A fear of silence in the session can compel novice helpers to fill this air time with the sound of their own voice. The session becomes driven by the helper and cuts out any thinking time for the client. The simple way to manage this is to watch the client's eyes when you ask a question. If they respond by looking up to the side, they are formulating their response. At other times, the clients eyes drop down, which usually indicates that they are considering feelings. Whilst they are looking away or down in this way manner the helper should remain silent – no matter how long it takes. When the client needs more from you they will look at you directly, as if to ask for more direction.

Our second example has the multiple choice style, where the client is corralled by the helper's options rather than identifying issues for themselves. This is a lawyer trick, where people are pinned down by opinions which are not of their own making. The function of the questions is to establish agreement rather than understanding. In the third example, the helper is inaccurate in their interpretations. Clients may refine us but if we continue to progress outside their experience the client will not feel understood, respected or listened to. Often it is when clients raise issues close to our own interests that we are most likely to reverse the flow and start transmitting our beliefs rather than understanding the clients'. Clients are not presenting for our judgments, but rather, first and foremost to understand their own.

What the client wants from you is also a priority in these first meetings. If the client is in the wrong service or you cannot meet this need it is better to establish this quickly. Along with this, acknowledging what the client feels about seeking help can be equally important. Do they have previous experience of treatment which was good or bad? Are they hopeful or pessimistic? Discussing these issues openly can help clarify what the client wants as well as what they may need from you as the helper. The client will be assessing you from the moment they meet you, so setting the tone from the first encounter is important. Likewise, any policy and protocols of confidentiality, what that means and in what circumstances it would be breached, are important in making the client feel as safe as possible and laying down the ground rules of the relationship.

The final element of establishing rapport with the client is to find an aspect of them that you like. Problematic users do not always make themselves endearing to others. But even within this there are facets of behaviour, personality or sheer bloody-mindedness that we need to appreciate or value. In every client we must find something to respond to, as they must in us. Whilst it is difficult to offer guidance on this mysterious bond, it is important to let clients gravitate to workers they can respond to. Certainly, it is has been a useful strategy in enhancing general retention rates (Chutuape et al., 1998). Difficulties only arise when workers are not operating to the same policy, which can create favouritism rather than therapeutic relationships.

Conclusion

If addiction is characterised by the erosion of relationships, the alliance represents their emergent reconstruction. However, we do not change people by being warm conversationalists. What is critical to outcomes is the alliance that forges the engagement of the bond with goals that are important to the client via tasks that feel manageable. Treatment works best when it makes sense to the client. We must remember that the aspirations of the client should never become subsidiary to the ways we chose to help. Within this gains occur sooner rather than later. That which helps, helps straight away. Where the client makes no progress, this should not be examined as their failure, but rather as a poor fit which needs to be re-addressed. And as treatment unfolds, the quality and direction of the alliance must be sustained as the curve of progress begins to tail-off and in light of setbacks. The helper that is attuned to the course of outcomes, has direct access to feedback and is prepared to acknowledge their own limits in this process, will retain clients through the difficult challenges of overcoming addictions. In some respects the quality of the alliance is the only important treatment outcome when working with those who suffer from chronic relapse problems. Because whilst use and adjunct behaviours fluctuate, it is whether the client returns that counts. Within this, both the client and the helper need to know what it is that needs to change, before using clear approaches to identifying how the change will happen.

Chapter 4

On Assessment and Care Planning

The Devil can cite scripture for his purpose
                    William Shakespeare

The central aim of all interventions can be understood as helping the client to find the means to achieve what otherwise feels unobtainable in their lives. As a result, successful outcomes stem from the compatibility between the client's aspirations with the helper's approach. Whilst the nature of the bond is both mysterious and unpredictable, goals and tasks should not be. The helper and client must identify the problem areas and negotiate the means to address them explicitly. This is difficult because, as we have seen, substance misuse problems occur across a complex set of biological and social problems. Dependency may demand medical intervention whilst the span of addiction means that we must reconcile the consequences of use across every facet of the individual's life. Assessing both the problems of dependency and addiction is important if we are to tailor our responses to the exact concerns of the client. As such this chapter will provide us with a framework for individually tailored treatment plans. It will describe how we map these multifaceted problems in as part of the comprehensive assessment that many services are expected to conduct, as well as brief assessments which can be very useful for non-specialists and can be equally as effective. Once we have identified the specific issues through the assessment we will then explore the key issues in addressing them through structured care plans. This means we can agree goals that address the client's concerns and orchestrate the most appropriate interventions that will achieve them. Wider consideration will also be given to atypical responses in assessment that may be indicative of more complex underlying problems as well as the inherent bias in disclosure itself.

Comprehensive assessment

There are many challenges in conducting assessments from both the client and the helper's point of view. Problematic users present with a diverse range of inter-related and multiple problems. This is compounded by long term histories of difficulties, poor treatment experiences and negative expectation of change. Clients may also be unaware of their wants. They can present with generalised goals that are often expressed in terms of what they no longer want rather than how they wish to be. As such, assessment is difficult to conduct where a lack of direction can mean that the morass of detail easily diverts attention into endless avenues of problems. This can leave the client feeling more hopeless about their situation than ever.

At the same time, new demands befall the worker in terms of assessment and care planning. Local authorities in the UK have implemented detailed comprehensive assessment forms and require that clients receiving structured help must also have detailed care plans. These assessment tools are usually home-grown hybrids constructed by local agencies that are all keen to have their concerns included. Extensive information is also required by government. This has led to the creation of huge assessment tools that are cumbersome, impracticable and often get in the way of creating any rapport with the client. As a result, assessment can be a protracted procedure that ranges from 45 minutes to several hours over the course of weeks. It must be remembered that overly complex assessment procedures simply increase drop-out rates (Gossop, 2003). There should be no need for any assessments which cannot be done in a session. This is especially important when assessing young people or those with dual diagnosis who may find it difficult to sustain their concentration as well as experience intolerable boredom.

If possible, it is advisable to conduct large scale assessments in the second session, once the rapport is created and the client expresses a desire for change. Sometimes it is not appropriate to do a deep assessment with clients who are uncertain whether they want to change. The skills of motivational interviewing and solution focused work described in the next chapters can be usefully deployed first, to identify the client's present concerns and fortify their commitment prior to the assessment that follows. Presented too soon, burdensome assessments that elicit a diverse range of personal information which has no obvious benefit to the client may just serve to alienate them immediately. Where this kind of detail must be taken in the first session, apologise from the outset.

In large scale assessment we also risk losing the purpose of the assessment in too much detail. This is important because the objective of the assessment is to establish clarity in two key areas. The first area we need to establish is the client's current level of dependence. This is deduced from profiling the substances that they are using, the frequency of use and administration route. This will indicate their current levels of tolerance and will inform us how the client might manage either stabilisation or withdrawal from the drug. Secondly, we need to assess addiction. These are the social problems that emerge from use that are maintaining the problem. We need to understand the magnitude of these problems in order to devise a plan that will negate, diminish or overcome them. If these are not addressed, then continued use will remain meaningful. In short, the assessment must provide the means to plan how the client will come off the drug and what will help them stay off.

Dependence and addiction must be teased apart and addressed accordingly. As such, the central discipline in assessing is not thoroughness. This can simply amass pages of details where the salient factors become lost. The key discipline of assessment is relevance. The question that must constantly nag at the assessor is what information is the client offering that is relevant to their use. This does not mean skimping, but rather seeing through the white-noise of the interview and identifying all the contributing factors that propel the client's consumption.

Preparing for assessment

It is essential that the helper is prepared for the assessment in advance. If they bring their own uncertainty into the assessment process they set a tone which is unprofessional, unguided and unsupportive for the client. Disorganised treatment providers tend to produce poor outcomes (Orford, 1999). Once a poor impression is inured in the helping relationship it is difficult to overcome and this tone is carried through the treatment journey. It befalls the practitioner to be clear about the policy and the process from the outset. Consider the following questions regarding the way assessments are conducted at your organisation. How do you meet the following criteria, and if there are gaps, how can you amend this with a clear and consistent policy across the agency? (see Exercise 4.1.)

Exercise 4.1: Planning for assessment

- Who is eligible for assessment at your service?

- Who is a priority for your service?

- What information do you check on previous assessment or other related assessments of the clients?

- Does the client have any particular needs that need to be taken into account during the assessment?

- How are the arrangements for the assessment recorded within the organisation?

- How do you confirm the arrangements for the assessment with the individual?

- Do you explain clearly to the individual the reason for delays between the request for an assessment and the assessment taking place?

- Do you give the individual any documentation that needs to be completed by them to allow them to consider it before assessment?

- Do you offer appropriate support to individuals who need assistance to complete documentation?

The interview

In terms of general etiquette, do not keep the client waiting prior to the interview, especially if it is their first time they have sought help. Be welcoming, introduce yourself, offer them a drink or whatever amenities that you have before the interview process begins. You might be conducting the formal assessment but the client will be conducting an equally important informal assessment of you. Setting a warm and engaged tone immediately is important. Even a hostile sounding voice has been found to dissuade clients from taking up support (Navjits and Weiss, 1994).

Comprehensive assessments are conducted via a semi-structured interview. Here the assessment form sets out an extremely broad range of open questions and the assessor must capture the detail within each heading and engage the client at the same time. This is very difficult to do well. The interview itself should take place in a comfortable and private surrounding. Whilst this sounds obvious, it is striking how often this does not occur. I recall one worker's frustration that no drug users admitted their use when being assessed in an open plan office. We would not be happy to consult with our GP in their busy waiting room and clients must also be afforded the same dignity. There is no excuse to deny clients privacy even if they do not request it.

Do not rush into the assessment. The client will usually have a somewhat rehearsed opening story. Remember the caveats in the previous chapter regarding creating the alliance. Before you begin, invite them to tell you what has been happening and what has led them to coming to the service. Letting the client ventilate pent up feeling will relieve stress and help them think more clearly as the assessment unfolds. Once the client has told their story introduce the assessment clearly. It is important that you have a clear rationale of the purpose of the assessment, how long it takes and why it is necessary. If the client understands why the assessment is useful to achieving their goals or even relieving their distress they will be more engaged in the process. And again, uncertainty in presenting the role of the assessment creates the impression that you are not clear.

It does not foster confidence that the service you are providing is capable of supporting someone who may be very vulnerable. Use the following prompts in Exercise 4.2 to frame your own description of the assessment process and use it before commencing any assessment.

Exercise 4.2: Setting the agenda for the assessment

Formulate an explanation for the following points that you will use at the start of your assessments.

- What is the purpose of your assessment?
- How long does it take?
- What is recorded and what is confidential?
- Why do you need this information?
- How will this help your client?

When assessing the client it is important that the form does not create a barrier between you. The worst assessment is when the helper uses the assessment form as the medium of communication, facing down, reading questions in a flat tone, waiting for a response and scribing the answer without even glancing up. The form should stay on the table where the client can see it. This is especially important with stimulant-using clients who may be very paranoid about what is being recorded. But equally, offenders, young people and those with dual diagnosis can be equally uncomfortable with a worker scribbling secretive notes. Tilting the assessment form at an angle where the client can see it can be helpful and invites them to participate. The helper should read each question out loud with some degree of interest and invite the client to respond. The helper must engage the client in discussing their current life situation in this domain. Eye contact must be maintained and the helper should listen and clarify the details.

Cultural sensitivity

Assessing the individual's functioning across these areas can identify the degree of separation that has occurred as a result of the addiction. And here lies a central problem with assessment and its sister procedure, diagnosis. Whilst it may be easy to identify the degree of drift that has occurred, we do not have a clinical baseline of normality itself. Society may be understood as a composite of slip-streams of sub-cultures and classes. This can be further divided by gender, sexuality and age. Each group operates with its own normative fallacy, believing its way of life is typical. Each may have their own baseline standards, beliefs, values, ethics and expectations that emphasise or underplay aspects of the wider aggregated cultural norms. Establishing degrees of separation is therefore difficult when baselines of functioning vary. For example, separation from extended family may not be experienced as severely for the white 'nuclear based family' European client as it is for the Asian client. This can bring obvious clashes in perspectives when an assessor views the client's world from their own social perspective. What is a priority concern or appears dysfunctional for the assessor maybe normative for the client.

We see this more clearly defined in psychiatric assessment, whereby the greater the social disparity between the diagnosed and the diagnostician, the more extreme the diagnosis. This does not mean that only like should work with demographically like, but it does demand a non-presumptuous attitude and sensitivity to the client's cultural perspective when assessing. Clients from diverse ethnic and socio-economic backgrounds tend to be bi-cultural, in having a clear understanding of their own culture as well as the dominant culture which surrounds them. This is not reciprocal for the dominant host culture which tends to only experience itself and not the sub-cultural niches within it. Acknowledging this at the outset is important, as it respects the client's awareness and the assessor's limitations. Without such sensitivity the assessment runs the risk of telling us more about the assessor than the client. It is important that throughout the assessment process we are sensitive to the client's language and work with them towards a mutual understanding of the problems that emerge.

Assessing dependence

The assessment of dependence is usually done as a drug and alcohol profile. This asks for the type, range, frequency and quantity of drugs and alcohol consumed over a recent period of time such as the last 30 days (see Table 4.1).

Table 4.1 Assessing dependency

Drug	Age of first use	How much per day (grams/units)	Prescribed? Yes/No	How many times in the last 30 days	Route
Heroin	21	0.4 g	No	30	Injected
Alcohol	14	4 units	No	15	Oral
Crack	26	3 g	No	7	Smoked

Assessing consumption is important for a variety of reasons. From a harm reduction perspective it is important to see if clients are experiencing problems as a result of their dependence itself. Whether poly drug use is placing them at risk by mixing drugs of similar types which may increase their risk of overdose or whether administration routes puts them at risk of communicable diseases such as HIV or hepatitis. This may be particularly salient for dual diagnosis clients, where the combinations of prescribed and illicit drugs can be lethal. The drug and alcohol profile may also be useful in determining what specific drug or alcohol use is problematic for the client. Whilst some treatment philosophies might suggest the use of all mind altering drugs is problematic, this does not appear to be true in either clinical practice or research. Some people may wish to change elements of their use but not all of it. This is an important area for discussion with the client at the outset.

Recording current use may also provide a baseline measure. As the client moves through their treatment journey, on-going reviews of current use can be compared to that at intake to identify and affirm what progress has been made. Recording reductions in drug and alcohol intake have become part of the outcome monitoring forms with which agencies can demonstrate their service effectiveness. However, these results are not always shared with the clients. Informative feedback of gains made can do a great deal to build client's self-efficacy belief when clear progress can be demonstrated. In this way, the bureaucratic demands placed on an organisation can be converted into useful therapeutic gains for the client.

The levels of current consumption are also important if people are looking to make change in their current use. Gauging the severity of tolerance is important when considering offering any substitute prescribing such as methadone for heroin dependence or detoxification from alcohol using benzodiazepines. Prescribing is a delicate affair, where too low a dose can be useless to the client with a high tolerance or, conversely, too high a dose may prove fatal for those with low tolerance. Therefore the prescribed substitute must match the current level of tolerance in order to stabilise the client effectively. The drug and alcohol profile can offer us a clear indication of the client's tolerance levels which should also be confirmed with a urine test.

Substitute prescribing

A number of prescribed substances are now available for opiate dependency. The principle substitute prescribed in the UK is still methadone that is administered orally. This synthetic opiate is carefully titrated to the equivalent dose of the client's heroin use. As a rule of thumb, 80mls of methadone are the equivalent of 1 gram of injected heroin. This must be reduced by 20 per cent if the heroin is smoked. This allows the user to cease using street heroin without the discomfort of withdrawal and frees the individual from the need to continually pursue funds for heroin. The drug has a 24 hour half-life meaning that it peaks and plateaus over this period of time making it suitable for daily prescribing. It has also been suggested that methadone occupies opiate receptors in the brain, satisfying urges for use whilst blocking the action of heroin, hence diminishing its effect.

Buprenorphine is increasingly being used as a replacement drug for opiate dependence. The drug has been widely used in France (Barrau et al., 2001) for opiate addiction since the 1980s but there has been little research on its efficacy. Mattrick et al. (1998) suggest that buprenorphine could be as effective as methadone in treating opiate dependence; whilst Kosten et al. (1992) believe that its reduced withdrawal effects could make it superior to methadone. Buprenorphine is only a partial agonist. This means that whilst opiates cap specific receptors in the brain and activates them, the partial agonist caps these receptors but only triggers some. In this way it simultaneously replaces opiates in the brain with limited action as well as blocking other opiates attaching to these sites. As a result patients report it has a less euphoric effect than methadone, and they feel 'normal' on the drug (Law et al., 1997). A benefit of buprenorphine's partial action is that it has a greatly reduced overdose potential (Auriacombe, 2001). As there is abuse potential with buprenorphine, it is often mixed with the opiate blocker Naltrexone. Taken orally the blocking agent is removed, but if injecting, the Naltrexone crosses through the blood brain barrier and induces abrupt withdrawal.

Another substitute drug that is not used often is LAAM (leva-alpha acetyl methadol). LAAM, sometimes referred to as long acting methadone, is a long acting opiate that only becomes active when metabolised by the body. Its half-life is 2.6 days (Rawson et al., 1998). This means that LAAM can be administered every other day. This frees up the client from daily pick up and drug agencies from intense daily management of dispensing. However, it takes many clients a long time to stabilise on it, up to two weeks, and its accumulative effect over long periods of time makes it an easy drug to overdose on. Despite its licence for dependence treatment in America, there has been little demand for the drug (Rawson et al., 1998).

In comparative clinical trials of methadone, buprenorphine and LAAM, we see the same generalised outcome. Substitute prescribing reduces illicit drug consumption, criminal behaviour associated with the drug and increased retention rates in services. Outcomes do vary between prescription regimes though. Johnson et al. (2000) randomly assigned 220 opiate using patients to high dose methadone, low dose methadone, buprenorphine or LAAM treatment groups. The least effective treatment was low dose methadone (20mls). Those receiving LAAM sustained the longest periods of continuous abstinence from street heroin. High dose methadone retained the highest group at 73 per cent, whilst only 58 per cent of the buprenorphine were retained and 53 per cent in the LAAM.

Other drugs used in the treatment of opiate dependence include clonidine and lofexidine. These are not opiate substitutes. Instead of binding to opiate receptors they bind to alpha–2 receptors. This has the effect of reducing the noradrenalin activity associated with withdrawal, decreasing many of the symptoms. This includes reductions in withdrawal distress (Gold et al., 1978). Clonidine can cause hypertension and therefore demands close medical supervision. Lofexidine is now used more widely as it operates in a similar way to clonidine but has less hypertension side effects. As these drugs reduce withdrawal severity, the client is essentially entering into abrupt withdrawal (cold turkey) with the discomfort dowsed. This means that people can withdrawal fairly quickly on these drugs. This has a range from between five days to four weeks (Bearn et al., 1998; Carnwath and Hardman, 1998). The central difference between lofexidine and methadone withdrawal is that the client experiences more withdrawal discomfort on starting on lofexidine, whilst methadone patients experience more discomfort at the end of their prescription. Lofexidine is often used in tandem with methadone, being introduced at the tail end of the reducing script. Clinical trials of clonidine and lofexidine have shown marked reductions in the client's symptoms (Gossop, 1988) and high success rates in treatment completion (Strang et al., 1999).

Besides opiates, many heavy-end drug consumers tend to be poly users. For example, research (Gossop, 1998) suggests that 33–43 per cent of problematic opiate users also use benzodiazepines. Because of the serious withdrawal symptoms associated with the cessation of their use, home withdrawal is not recommended. Treatment usually comprises of the gradual reduction of the drug with close monitoring. Alternatively people can be reduced on phenobarbitone as a substitute, because it has a long acting action as well low-toxicity on the liver, making it suitable for people with liver problems (Smith and Wesson, 1999). Whilst alcohol is chemically similar to benzodiazepines, substitute prescribing is not necessary for the majority of alcohol patients. Only individuals who experience the profound collapse of tolerance associated with alcohol dependence or have a history of fitting may require medical assistance. For this smaller drinking population, short courses of long acting benzodiazepines can be used to detox those with severe alcohol dependency (Edwards et al., 2003).

Regimes

Substitute prescribing usually occurs in one of two regimes. The first is a maintenance dose. This is where an equivalent dose of the replacement drug is prescribed and sustained at the same level as the client's current tolerance level. Alternatively individuals may receive reduction regimes. Here the client is stabilised on an equivalent dose of the replacement drug and then this level is reduced in short increments over a stated length of time. The rate of reduction is sometimes negotiated with the client but in some circumstance it is not. In inpatient detoxification settings the rapid reductions are conducted over a much shorter time. Although rapid reduction prescribing in the community tends to produce poor results (Gossop, et al., 1986; Dawe et al., 1991; Unnithan et al., 1992). However, in comparisons to methadone maintenance and reduction regimes at onset and over longer time periods, we see little clinical difference. For example, Strang et al. (1997) found the same levels of improvement in both methadone maintenance clients and methadone reduction clients in the first month of prescribing. Whilst Gossop et al. (2000) found that at 1 year follow up, treatment gains were similar for both maintenance and reduction clients.

The NTORS study highlighted a key problem in prescribing which has been identified in other research studies. In clinical practice this is known as the 'drift into maintenance'. This occurs when reduction programmes are mutually negotiated with the worker and the client, which tends to slow reduction rates creating a *default* maintenance programme. This also cuts the other way. Maintenance prescribing is not indefinite either. Reviews of methadone maintenance prescribing in the UK reveal huge differences in levels of methadone prescribed, adjunct treatment support and duration of prescribing (Stewart et al., 2000; Gossop and Grant, 1990). As such, a clear distinction cannot always be made between the two prescribing options. Instead, prescribing might be characterised by phases of stabilisation doses; followed by a period of maintenance; culminating in withdrawal management doses.

The finding that rapid reductions from the onset of prescribing tend to produce diminishing gains, suggests that these phases of prescribing should occur over a longer time period. However, Dawe et al. (1991) found that the longer the period of the withdrawal phase the less likely the client was to complete. This has been echoed in other studies (see Unnithan et al., 1992). Whilst negotiation of reduction is a popular idea in the field, it does not necessarily produce better outcomes or affect retention rates. This may suggest that reduction of methadone may need to occur over a definite time period, with a margin for negotiation.

Substitute prescribing treatment?

The term substitute prescribing treatment is misleading. The name supposes that the primary element of treatment is the substitute itself. Research confutes these simplistic explanations, as treatment demands a high proportion of psychosocial support in order to prove effective. In their historic review of the efficacy of methadone prescribing, Dole and Nyswander (1976), who pioneered methadone as a treatment for heroin addiction, surmised that methadone had been an effective intervention in supporting change with only 1 in 10 patients. Similarly, the NTORS research programme found a difference of 10 per cent between reduction client groups and maintenance groups (Ashton, 1999). Most of the gains we see on substitute prescribing are reductions in the problems associated with the using in the shadow society. As such they reduce illicit use because we give them the drug; reduce crime because we do not charge for the drug; and reduce negative health consequences because the type of drugs we give cannot be injected.

Prescribing reduces the stresses of consumption but it does not automatically confer any gains in the client's life. Overcoming the broken bonds of addiction and subsequent social exclusion is necessary to reduce the saliency of consumption. This demands the investment of high levels of personal support. For example, in a study by McLellan et al. (1993) clients were randomly assigned to one of three groups. This included a methadone only programme; a methadone and standard support programme; and a methadone and enhanced support programme. Amongst the methadone only patients some showed a little improvement. But the vast majority saw little to no gains at all. In fact, 69 per cent of the clients on the methadone only programme had to be transferred to the standard treatment programme within 3 months for their own protection. This group experienced continued problems associated with both heroin and cocaine use resulting in increasingly frequent medical emergencies. After being transferred to the standard support programme, the illicit use on top halved and the clients begin to make immediate positive lifestyle gains.

In contrast, clients in the standard support programme not only showed reduction in problems associated with heroin using lifestyles, but made positives gains in reducing all drug and alcohol consumption. They also demonstrated improved legal status and family and fewer psychiatric problems. They did not make many gains in the area of employment though. The enhanced treatment group saw further positive gains in significant decreases in wider drug and alcohol use, improvements in physical and mental health, legal issues and family relations and employment. The enhanced treatment demonstrated better outcomes than the standard treatment in 14 of the 21 measures used.

This highlights a common danger in the field when we mistake dependence for addiction. Addressing dependence does not result in overcoming the problems in the individual's life that make use meaningful. It is not uncommon to see that individuals who receive methadone begin to invest their newly acquired spare time on other drugs. Without the need to raise money and score heroin, alcohol and crack can fill the void that prescribing methadone has created in their lives. As a result between 20–50 per cent of methadone users also have actual or potential alcohol dependence (see Liebson et al., 1973; Stastny and Potter, 1991). Whilst this may predate prescriptions we do see clear trends in consumption. Generally, as opiate use increases the consumption of alcohol tends to decrease. This suggests that the revision of old drinking patterns or the establishment of new ones is closely linked to prescribing. And without significant lifestyle revision, the need to continue to use something will remain salient.

Assessing addiction

Overcoming physical dependence and overcoming addiction are two very different challenges. As any client will tell you, coming off is easier than staying off. Therefore assessment must also identify the factors that sustain use. This can be characterised by the individual's capacity to not only re-connect to the broken bonds of their social environment but to find alternative sources of satisfaction and enrichment in these relationships. As the corrosion of addiction spans all aspect of the individual's life, assessment must chart each and every domain too. There is no common agreement on the dimensions that should be included or excluded (Connors et al., 2001), but standard forms are generally based on what are termed as the 'great domains' of assessment. These include mental health, self-management, family relationships, offending, employment, education, housing, social and recreational life. Assessment could also include the much neglected area of spirituality. As we shall see, the development of values is a key feature of recovery. It is significant in outcomes for both addiction (see Miller, 1998) and other psychosocial problems (see Gilbert, 2003; Moss, 2005). These are the drivers that bring us to others in mainstream social structures and support relationships. However, this dimension is often wholly neglected in secularised treatment programmes.

Assessing the full spectrum of an individual's life places the helper in the difficult position of having to sift through each of these domains systematically. It is easy to get lost in a huge amount of current and historical detail. And there is no interpretative framework that can help us. We must remember assessment is primarily an exercise in relevance. We need to be able to identify the core issues in each domain that sustain the individual's use. These *key indicators* chart the breakdown in social functioning across the life of the individual. These may have preceded problematic use and contributed to its development or they be a direct consequence of use. The historic factors of relevance are those which precluded the individual from developing a social role for themselves. Certainly establishing the age of first use and the age in which use became a problem can give us insight into the treatment course. If social exclusion occurs prior to the establishment of a satisfactory and stable adult role, the treatment course will need to be longer. The answer to when (and in what way) use became a problem also indicates whether the client is driven to address their physical dependence or whether they are more orientated to preserve important relationships. This theme is important in the next chapter when considering the nature of motivation.

The present life situation of the client should identify the key indicators which maintain use. Substance use increases in a reciprocal relationship with problems in the social environment of the individual. As their interests narrow, other activities are neglected or rendered difficult to sustain and social rejection breaks the ties with a wider social life. As such, drug or alcohol use will remain salient as the only source of satisfaction in highly impoverished social environments. Therefore if we are to help people stay off drugs or alcohol we need to develop treatment plans that resolve difficulties and improve satisfaction in each aspect of the client's life. Each domain needs to be explored carefully. Asking broad opening questions allows the client to speak freely. But in complex inter-related problems it can be difficult to focus on specific issues. The assessor must listen out for discrete indicators in each domain and the relative significance. For example, street homelessness is a severe indicator that will seriously impede a person's chances of remaining drug free. Whilst living at home with one's parents may be a blessing for some and a nightmare for others. Weighting the severity of the indicator must be done with the client. A range of key indicators are outlined in Table 4.1. By no means exhaustive, it aims to offer examples of typical problems that may interfere with the client reconstructing a more fulfilling life post-use.

Again we may see a difference between the kinds of problems reported. Late onset alcohol users may be facing the destruction of the adult life they developed for themselves. In contrast, drug users may describe the failure to integrate into adult life successfully. Either way, within each milieu it is important that we identify the specific contributing factors that need to be addressed. This is not always easy. The client is unlikely to present their problems in neat medical or psychological terms. Furthermore, there may be issues the client is not divulging because they do not think it relevant or for other reasons. So follow up questions are needed to explore anything else that concerns them in greater depth. In Exercise 4.3, read the statement from an assessment interview and underline each key indicator of health issues.

Looking at the client's answer (Exercise 4.3) we see they clearly identify that Hep C, A and liver cirrhosis. The assessor should seek further clarity on each of these areas. Again we are looking for the facts of the situation; what, when, where and who else might be involved in this treatment is important in building a clear description of each indicator. But the client also hints at problems with circulation as a result of injecting. This could include DVT or abscesses. Checking more deeply with the client about what problems they have had and whether they have received treatment is important too. This would need further exploration by the assessor. We also see the client is engaged in high risk injecting practice and they hint at an undiagnosed depression. This would need to be separated out and explored in the mental health section.

Table 4.2 Typical key indicators identified at assessment

Domain	Key indicators
Employment	Heavy consumption can impair work performance and judgement. Social stigma may preclude people from wanting to report problems to employers or seek treatment that may identify them as problematic. This can lead to disciplinary problems and dismissal. Public shame and loss of status can have a particularly powerful effect on men. Certain forms of employment can also be conducive to high consumption. Low supervision work, like painting and decorating or those that involve considerable travel and overnight stays can remove the break of other scrutiny from consumption. Other professions, such as the building trade, may also have heavy drinking culture attached to the after hours work-social life. Long periods of employment, with no references can be a major obstacle back into employment, particularly for those with no work history at all. Disclosure of past problematic use may also stigmatise those seeking paid employment.
Housing	Deprived areas of poor quality accommodation with transient populations contribute significantly to drug use and alcohol problems. At one end of the spectrum present accommodation can fall into disrepair and disorder, contributing to the client feeling out of control. Problems with bills, rent, being disconnected from utilities can further compound problems. At the other end of the spectrum, temporary accommodation can further embed the heavy drinker or drug users with other high consumers.
Finances	Maintaining a drug or alcohol problem is expensive. Loss of earnings through incapacitation, sickness or unemployment can compound these problems. Access to cash through work or through significant others can prove a great temptation to some, as well as avoiding taxation or defrauding social security. Financial problems can mount and be hidden from family. This may generate even greater levels of stress, compounded further by use. Debt to dealers on other users can result in violence against the user or their families compounding guilt.
Homelessness	At the far end of the spectrum of drug and alcohol problems is the individual whose use has severed them wholly from their social ties. This can occur at the extreme end of clinical alcohol dependence or drug addiction or precipitate it. Young people that run away from home become a high risk for drug and alcohol problems. The hostile environment of living rough and the opportunistic lifestyle it fosters leads to complex poly-drug use, very often compounded with health problems, mental illness and multiple arrests. The background problems of those vulnerable to street homelessness include poverty, poor education, little employment history, and migration to urban inner city areas. Overcoming the extreme social exclusion feels hopeless for many on the streets, lowering expectations of possible change further.
Health	The health of the client may concern several areas such as; health problems prior to use, health problems as a result of use and problems as a consequence of the using lifestyle. Any long term health problems should be explored in relation to subsequent use. For example, whether these health problems prevent the individuals from engaging in wider social life. Problems associated with use may be dependent on the drug and the means of administration. For injectors this may include poor circulation, abscesses, blood borne viruses such as hepatitis and HIV. Smokers may encounter significant lung problems. Alcohol users can experience a profound range of physical ailments attached to high consumption. This can include heart problems, liver and stomach disorders, skeletal-muscular problems, endocrine disorders and metabolic disorders. Brain damage and cognitive impairment can also be significant. Physical consequences of the individual's lifestyle also means that they may have nutritional deficiencies, low weight and poor immune systems leaving them vulnerable to a host of other infectious diseases. The client should be encouraged to register with primary care and the impact of diagnosis on lifestyle needs to be taken into consideration. Psychological fears about illness can aggravate depression and hopelessness. Physical pain from long term illness can be

Table 4.2   *Continued*

Domain	Key indicators
	difficult to manage when the patient must refrain from opiate based pain killers due to their abuse potential and may bar them from accessing certain services such as residential rehabilitation.
Crime	The relationship between drugs/alcohol use and crime may be more profound than simple causality. Typically we believe that drug use causes crime in order to fund a habit beyond the user's financial means. Alcohol inebriation may lead to reckless behaviour. However, personality, background and culture also play a significant part in the equation. For example, is the anti-social behaviour and anti-social drug consumption a symptom of anti-social personality? People who are aggressive and violent may also choose to drink. Typically we do see more acquisitive crime associated with the use of class A drugs, and alcohol has a strong correlation with violent crime. Long term prison sentences may render the individual rootless from family and wider social connections and instead inhabit a criminal fraternity that normalises behaviour. People may become habituated to prison life and see it as a safe haven rather than as a punishment. Impending court appearances or court sanctions may prompt entry into treatment for reluctant clients. Motivation and engagement may be a central problem. Several previous coerced treatment attempts may make the client pessimistic as regards treatment. It may also make them well rehearsed in treatment which may inoculate them against the approach.
Mental illness	Mental illness and substance misuse have a complex relationship. Some individuals have primary mental health needs. Their symptoms pre-exist the onset of drug and alcohol use. These individuals tend to be less well connected in drug using networks and therefore have limited access to a wider range of substances. They tend to be isolated with limited peer groups and so use may provide them with the means to meet or socialise with others in public houses. Their use tends to be limited to cheap, easily available intoxicants such as alcohol and cannabis. A second group have primarily substance misuse needs, and mental illness has emerged as a consequence of their consumption. These individuals are well connected, have access to a wider range of intoxicants and are more likely to be poly-users. Knowing more about drugs they tend to be more suspicious of psychiatric prescribing. A final group may evolve mental illness alongside increasing consumption. Classically this is depression that coincides with social impoverishment. Whilst over 80 per cent of problem users have a measurable mental illness, it is only profound and enduring in a much smaller population. Certainly, any atypical symptoms which are not commonly associated with the clients stated drugs of choice may indicate underlying problems. Suicide attempts and significant self-harm should also be screened for. Paranoia, social stigma and poor previous treatment experience may make clients reticent to either disclose mental illness or build trusting relationships with professionals. 'Attributional creep' occurs when an individual increasingly conforms to their diagnosis, fostering negative expectations of change. Any diagnosis should be recorded and its impact on lifestyle taken into consideration.
Family	Family discord, violence and breakdown are common in the drug using experience. Families try many strategies which can range from ignoring the problem, over-reacting, protecting the individuals from consequences to anger and rejection. Problems can be even more complicated if other significant members of the family are also high users. The family of origin's expectations can erode self-esteem through a sense of failure, especially when compared to siblings' achievements. The desire to keep use secret can compound feelings of shame and guilt. Histories of sexual, physical and emotional abuse can alter an individual's boundaries, affecting their ability to manage intimacy with others. Subsequent symptoms tend to be more profound if the child is abused by a close family relative, has little social support at the time and

Table 4.2   *Continued*

Domain	Key indicators
	is not believed. Stockholm syndrome can occur, whereby they side with or identify with the abusers. Self-blame can lead to self-loathing. The continued need to expose oneself to further trauma can also occur as an attempt to master the situation 'this time' and restore a sense of control. Individuals may experience nightmares, flashbacks, disassociation or the desire to be someone else. Poor sleep, isolation and self-loathing may contribute to use. Alternatively there may be problems within the client's own nuclear family. Child protections issues, domestic violence or the strain of raising families on low incomes can all be major factors in driving consumption.
Social life	Clients at the high end of the using spectrum may have abandoned all other forms of social or recreational activities through use and are confined to contact with other high users. Reviewing past hobbies and interests can revive a desire for their old life, when things were more manageable. For those who are controlled or high functioning users, the identification of pro-social relationships and interests that have persevered through use can be built upon and expanded.

Exercise 4.3: Identify key indicators in semi-structured interviews

'My health is not too good. I have been using since I was 14, well 12 actually, if you include alcohol. Anyway, I did not start on the heroin till I was 17 and start injecting when I was 18. Anyway, I have been injecting for a long time, they say your chances of surviving go down every year. Anyway, when I was in prison for the first time, they just brought in random drug testing in 1998. I was wanting to stay off the gear and was just smoking the odd bit of cannabis. So then I got caught on a urine test. Everyone said to use gear as it stayed in the body for shorter time. So I was sharing a lot in prison and that is how I got the Hep C I think. I did not know at the time. It was not 'til a few years ago that I also got Hep A that I found out. I was really ill and rushed to hospital, but they did not keep me in long, they don't like junkies much. Anyway, they did some tests and found that there was a lot of damage to my liver. Caused by drinking on top. They said it is serious and that I need to get myself sorted or it could flare up again. I guess I panicked. I was really scared, thought I was going to die. I just gave up really. So I have been using heavily ever since. Just heroin. I have had a lot of trouble with my veins since then. I have not had it checked out. I have been injecting in the groin, I know it is dangerous but I had to use. Madness really.'

A sharp eye for indicators is important because of the sheer range of material that the semi-structured assessment can cover in so many domains. We will survey a person's whole life with all the richness that brings. And lives are rarely as neat as our assessment form. Furthermore, the complexity of the client's situation means that many of their problems are inter-related from many domains. For example, in one assessment a client reveals serious health concerns, mental health issues and marital problems. Understanding how one domain may link to other areas is also vital for understanding the interlocked forces that may drive consumption. It is difficult for any one worker to be expert in these three domains. Assisting the client to develop this insight into their own lives at the same time is equally important in itself. It demands that those conducting comprehensive assessments have a working knowledge of each domain they are assessing and the typical issues that problematic drug and alcohol users experience in these areas. Good assessment therefore demands a very wide range of experience and knowledge in the assessors, to evaluate all the potential problems that can emerge explicitly or implicitly in the interview. If in doubt we should always check with the client and ask for their view on whether this factor contributes to their use.

The art of assessment also demands the creation of a coherent picture of the client's situation. Any obvious discrepancies in this unified whole should be clarified. Inordinately high daily consumption achieved in a short period of time; contradictory reports of profound withdrawal on low doses; or high consumption with negligible impact on any other area of social functioning (usually suggested by those sat in custody suites) warrant further exploration. Whilst systematically charting the disintegration of their life is often incredibly painful for people, it can be a great motivating experience in itself, provided the means to change are available and manageable.

What to record

We must remember that the assessments that we carry out are legal documents. Other people within the organisation will have to read them, other professionals in other services may have to have access to them and they may, in light of a terrible event, end up being read to a court room. Consider assessments that you have conducted recently, how many would stand up to such broad scrutiny? While we have discussed the relevance of recorded information, it is essential to remember that first and foremost this is the client's assessment. Therefore, not only do we need to identify the key indicators but also summarise what the client is telling us succinctly. We need to include the client's 'voice' in the assessment too. The assessment is a picture of their life and their concerns. It is not an unravelling of the client for our own diagnostic talents. We must capture the voice of the client and how they understand their situation. Compare the following excerpts for two assessments in Exercise 4.4. What is different about them?

Exercise 4.4: Comparison of assessment responses

Section 1: Mental health: The client has a history of mental health and has been let down badly. They are obviously suffering from depression and yet no one has provided adequate help and as a result things have got worse and it is only a matter of time before they attempt suicide again. I think that they need counselling, as drugs don't work.

Section 2: Mental health: John feels that he does have needs around his mental health. He was hospitalised on two previous occasions. He was admitted to Epsom Hospital, Surrey in 1998 after a suicide attempt, where he was diagnosed with depression and was treated for approximately four months. More recently he was admitted to Barrow Hospital, Bristol, and diagnosed with bi-polar depression after a suicide attempt in 2003. He was treated for two months as an in-patient. On discharge he was prescribed lithium and offered out-patient treatment. He stopped attending these sessions and taking his medication which he felt was not helpful in Nov, 2004. His psychiatrist at Barrow was Dr Mallow and the key worker was Angela Black at the inner-city mental health team. Presently John reports his mental health is stable, but feels he does need support to help sustain it. He would like to be re-refered to the inner-city mental health team.

When reviewing the transcripts we see the first case study is largely concerned with the worker's own perceptions of why the client is experiencing problems. In the second, the worker is concerned with the who, when, where, how and what the client feels about their circumstances. The first is a subjective explanation; the second is an objective description of the client's situation. The evaluation, prognosis and diagnosis of workers as regards their client's problems and their hopes of overcoming them are extremely poor on the whole and serve no useful purpose. First and foremost we want a clear description of the client's concerns in their words. We summarize, check the meaning with them and then record this. Before recording anything the helper should summarise the client's answer and ask them if that sounds accurate. In others words, you seek tacit approval in recording.

Organisations may have priority groups and is important that everyone is clear what they are. Nothing is more disheartening than an hour assessment which is concluded by telling the client they are in the wrong place. Does the agency provide support for the homeless? Do they deal with mental illness? Do health issues such as HIV or pregnancy get priority? Is there any factor which makes the client unsuitable? The organisation should have agreed guidance on what key indicators the assessor needs to establish. Those working in agencies who are involved in deeper assessment should meet regularly to read each other's assessments and discuss common patterns and trends in the process. How does this team evaluate priority? Are they consistent in their evaluation? Do some workers stick with what they know and leave out areas they do not feel competent in? It may befall the team to establish a consensus. Sharing practice tends to support others' learning and inform our own work at the same time. This is important because if it is done well, assessment helps the client gain organised insight into their current situation and paves the way for them to consider what they feel they need to do about it.

Brief assessment tools

In drug services, care plans are becoming the expected norm for all clients engaging in any form of structured treatment. Only when we have a clear idea of the client's level of dependency and key indicators of addiction are we able to care plan effectively. In the triangulated conversation between your questions, the client's answers and the recording of information, it can be difficult to keep an overview of the whole picture being presented. Care planning can become difficult when conducted in tandem to comprehensive assessments. In order to overcome this, a means of summarising the client's situation can be done very simply by conducting a life audit (see Figure 4.1), such as the one developed on treatment programmes I have designed. It draws upon elements of several similar tools such as *Hassles Scales*, *Uplift Scales* (Kanner et al., 1981) and the *Happiness Scale* (Meyers and Smith, 1995). It has proved simple to administer in clinical settings and helpful in identifying strengths and areas that need to be addressed.

In addition, the life audit can be helpful as a starting point in its own right if you do no have prescribed assessment forms or are working with people that find comprehensive assessment forms difficult. Certain working environments such as detached work, outreach, or semi-structured environments such as drop-ins are not conducive to comprehensive assessment. The life audit can capture the most salient information quickly and simply, whilst weighting the client's concern in each domain. The client can prioritise what needs addressing as well getting a more cogent overview of the often disparate but interlinked variables that affect their life.

Each assessment domain is listed in the first column. These can be the great domains we have already considered. Alternatively they can be tailored to the particular comprehensive assessment

Domains	Satisfaction score		Frequency of problems in last month	Strengths/problems identified
	Not very	Very		
Drugs/alcohol	1 2 3 4 5 6 7 8 9 10			
Finances	1 2 3 4 5 6 7 8 9 10			
Marriage	1 2 3 4 5 6 7 8 9 10			
Family	1 2 3 4 5 6 7 8 9 10			
Social/recreation	1 2 3 4 5 6 7 8 9 10			
Housing/environment	1 2 3 4 5 6 7 8 9 10			
Employment/training	1 2 3 4 5 6 7 8 9 10			
Health	1 2 3 4 5 6 7 8 9 10			
Mental health	1 2 3 4 5 6 7 8 9 10			
Values and beliefs	1 2 3 4 5 6 7 8 9 10			

Figure 4.1 Life audit sheet (Harris, 2005)

tool that you are currently using or modified to match the specific priorities of your agency. For example, an amended format for dual diagnosis clients might include separate ratings for each diagnosis they have received as well as for prescribed medications. For young people in care or who are adopted, a column for biological family, adopted family or second families can be helpful.

At the completion of a comprehensive assessment, or as a stand alone assessment tool, the life audit can be used to summarise the client's current situation. Using the life audit, the client is asked to consider their current levels of satisfaction in each domain, rating it from one-to-ten. One represents complete dissatisfaction and ten represents complete satisfaction. The client should consider this carefully and base this score on how they feel at the moment of the assessment. The frequency of problems in each domain gives an indication of the severity of the problems and helps prioritise them. The strengths/problems column is used to qualify the client's rating. For example, if the client rates employment at three, we can ask what makes it three? This may highlight certain strengths that the client wants to build upon, as well as what is unfulfilling. For example, an individual working in retail may rate employment at three because whilst they may not like the pay, the conditions or derive little satisfaction from selling shoes, but they may enjoy the interaction with other people. This suggests where future career prospects lie in working with people. Every domain is rated in this way until it is complete.

The audit tool can thus simplify complex, multi-faced problems at a glance and provoke the client to reflect on their wants in every area of their life. Clients will often be able to make connections between problems in each domain. Dissatisfaction in a relationship for example may drive up certain scores, such as work as an avoidance strategy. Conversely they may drive down others. The client that rates their satisfaction with their drug and alcohol use as high but scores very low in every other domain can be gently provoked into reconsidering the impact of their use. The fact that the client quantifies each domain also means that the audit can become a useful baseline measurement of the client's functioning at intake. In subsequent review sessions using the audit, progress can once again be charted on the scales and the client can see their own gains. In this way the life audit can become an outcome measurement tool for the client. Unifying assessment tools with care plans and outcome measurement tools is an obvious necessity but rarely happens in practice. This simple measure would increase the relevance of assessment by linking it with the subsequent treatment response. It would also ensure that the outcome tools used measured exactly what was being done, rather than generalised areas. All too often assessment tools and care plans are bolted together with little thought of their coherence, and then an outcome measure is co-opted which does not measure any of the domains either assessed or addressed.

Care planning

Partnering life assessment with the goal setting is vital. Once the life audit is complete the client can then consider what they feel they need to do about improving their life in each of these domains. It is essential that we support the client to set goals that are important to them and identify tasks that will support their achievement. This may include formal interventions such as services within our organisation and the local community as well as the client's own strategies. Remember, the goals of treatment must be desirable for the client to invest effort in changing. The closer the goals address the concerns of the client the better the outcome will be. The result is a care plan uniquely tailored to the needs of each client.

Goals are set in each domain and should address the client's needs identified from the assessment (see Figure 4.2). Obviously, these domains need to match those in the assessment and life audit. The priority column indicates what needs to be targeted first, or what needs to be in place for subsequent interventions to follow. For example, a client wishing to attend rehab may have to demonstrate motivation by attending a structured community programme; whilst specialist prescribing services will require the client to be registered with a GP. We will explore different means of establishing goals through the subsequent chapters. But at this stage we should record the goal clearly and simply to avoid ambiguity. It should also be stated in the positive. This means it should describe what the client will do as opposed to what they will not do. The intervention column describes the tasks needed to achieve the goal. This should include other support providers as well as those in the client's social life that are relevant to the changes they are making. It is important that the responsibility for elements of the care plan are clearly established. This should be orchestrated by the care manager who has overall responsibility for the client. Finally, our measure column defines when or how frequently the client will engage in the tasks that help them towards their goal. Again this needs to be clear, so the client's progress can be assessed. If the client does not make any progress this can be reviewed, explored and more appropriate goals or tasks can be re-negotiated.

It is important to prioritise goals as the client may not be able to take changing their whole life in one sitting. Prioritising needs to take into account the clients readiness to change and imminent risk to themselves. For chaotic clients in contemplation it may be more apposite to set goals around use, health and mental health. For clients being fast tracked through the criminal justice services, offending behaviour may have to be a priority, alongside the other domains which sustain criminality. For example, it is very difficult to address offending behaviour prior to prescribing substitutes or addressing housing which makes the individual's life precarious. As the client stabilises, the wider domains of social relationships can be included. So depending on the degree of cultural separation, the most basic needs must be addressed first in a hierarchy of goals. What is important is that the stated goals are recorded, the means to achieve them are clearly negotiated and the client's progress is reviewed to see if they are being achieved. A small percentage of individuals do not respond to treatment. For example, research suggests that between 17–25 per cent of heroin using clients show no improvements on any measures in methadone treatment (see Gossop et al., 2000; Belding et al., 1998). Only when concrete goals

Problem	Priority	Goal	Intervention/service	Objective measure
Drugs/alcohol	1	(a) Reduce alcohol (b) Stop smoking grass	(a) Attend AA	(a) 3 meetings a week (b) Attend relapse prevention programme once a week (c) Stop smoking tobacco
Finances	3			
Marriage	1	(a) Spend time with my girlfriend	(a) Go to parents' caravan on weekends (b) Help around the house	(a) Once a month (b) Every weekend do housework. (c) Wash up every night
Family	2			
Social/recreation	3			
Housing/environment	4	(a) Change accommodation	(a) See housing adviser and request transfer	(a) Meeting on Tuesday 15/3
Employment/training	4	(a) Go to job club (b) Ask friends	(a) Get cv (b) Identify possible jobs	Wednesday mornings
Health	3			
Mental health	1	Monitor mental health	(a) Monitor paranoid feelings (b) Record anxiety attacks (c) Practice breathing exercises	(a) Weekly (b) Weekly (c) Every time I have an attack
Values and beliefs	3	(a) Have some quiet time to think	(a) Walk in the countryside	(a) Once every weekend

Figure 4.2   Specimen treatment plan

are agreed is it possible to evaluate progress, without which reviews become speculative and the higher support needs of some clients may be overlooked.

Once goals are agreed then the client can identify how they will be achieved through the development of tasks or appropriate services. In many instances, the client will have a straightforward idea of how to achieve them. For clients with complex needs, they may require help from a wide variety of specialist agencies to address the full spectrum of their needs. This demands that those doing comprehensive assessments must have a deep knowledge of the treatment landscape that their clients operate in, what services are provided at what stage of readiness and what these services will demand of the client. Mapping this out and keeping it up-to-date is difficult but essential if care planning is to work as a complete package. In reality it is rare for a client to be turned down for a treatment on the grounds of it not being appropriate at assessment. Not only does this reduce assessment to a formality but with high drop-out rates and waiting lists, it fails to target the services at those who do need it. It does not benefit anyone to send the client down dead ends or merely hold on to them because they presented at your service first. If the client's needs may be better met elsewhere it is important to discuss this with them and why. The service map described below (Table 4.3) is not intended to be exhaustive but provides an overview of what services *may* be appropriate at what level of presentation. Each area will vary in the availability of services. Where gaps appear but demand is high, this provides a good indicator of important areas of future service development.

Making referrals

Offering choice is important so that the client can select services that they feel are relevant to them and are based on informed decisions. Again, making the referral to a service when the client has no clear idea of what it is or how it will help them is a sure way of losing the client en route. Being clear about the reason for referral is important. Clients do not always know the services you are offering or why it is necessary. As such they may end up in the wrong service for them or have negative assumptions from the outset. In order to collaborate on the task we must be as explicit as possible from the outset. Consider your introduction to any referral carefully, whether it be an internal service or external one. Watch the client's reaction as their indirect feedback can be more important than what they say. If they look uncertain, check in with them using the following template in Exercise 4.5.

Exercise 4.5: Discussing referral

- What information does the client have about this service?
- What are the client's assumptions about the service that you are recommending?
- What is the service, what does it demand of them and how does this help?
- What does the client feel about it now?

If the client is still uncertain explore this with them. This may be due to other experiences which the client does not realise are being brought to bear on the current situation. Asking them what they are uncertain about may highlight a critical underlying block that prevents them from considering the idea. The question – *have you been in this situation before?*, often yields a deeper sub-conscious feeling. This usually precipitates the client's pessimism which is important to acknowledge and how it could be different this time.

It is also important to consider that adults and adolescents alike find it difficult to enter into pre-formed social groups. Clients often fear stepping over the threshold or making a commitment to a service that they have no experience of first hand. Discussing any concerns that the client has about the referral is important. If the service is not appropriate for specific reasons, such as bad previous experiences, then do not force the issue. On the other hand, if the client is reluctant to enter the service because of generalised fears or uncertainties you can always encourage the client to 'sample' the service without any commitment to engage. Attending the first visits with them can ease the anxiety of attendance, even with the most reluctant client.

Case Study: Reluctant clients and referral

Sam had been diagnosed with a psychotic disorder after protracted cocaine use. He presented in crisis, suicidal and delusional at a street drug agency. There his key worker supported him through lifestyle changes and worked in partnership with psychiatric

Table 4.3 Mapping the treatment

Domain	Pre-contemplation and relapse	Contemplation	Preparation	Action	Maintenance
Drugs/alcohol	Needle exchange schemes Drop-in Detached work Advice and information	Semi-structured, rapid access services. Outreach One-to-one sessions Low intensity group work Prescribing services	Assessment for aftercare Referral for intensive treatment interventions Aftercare planning	Community detoxification Symptom management detoxification In-patient detoxification	Residential treatment Structured day care Housing Rebuilding Social support Family self-help groups Skills training Employment specialist
Finances	Debt/benefits advice	Credit unions		Budgeting and bank accounts.	
Legal	Legal advice and representation	Probation or mandated community treatment	Treatment entry	Court reports	
Family/ marriage	CRAFT Al Anon Social services	Surestart/parenting groups		Couple counselling	
Social/ recreation		Diversionary activities	Separation from old using groups	Drug and alcohol free social venues	New pro-social groups
Housing/ environment	Benefits advice Emergency accommodation Homeless agencies	Hostel accommodation	Floating support schemes	Supported housing	Independence training
Employment/ training			Progress to work Voluntary work	Job clubs	Access courses, training and higher education, employment
Health	Community nursing teams Walk in centres A and E	Registering with GP Registering with dentist	Specialist assessment for detoxification	Inpatient detox services	Specialist medical support for illness such as Hep C and blood born virus etc.
Mental health	Voluntary drop-in centres Help lines Inner city mental health teams	Psychiatric assessment	Advocacy and support, self-help groups	Prescribing, community psychiatric nurse/inner city mental health teams	Specialist treatment groups for mental illness, day centres.

services to stabilise his condition and re-house him. Once through the crisis, Sam would still visit the project every day to see his worker, even when he had little to report or say. The key worker addressed this with him and it emerged that now he had stabilised he felt bored and alone in the day, with little else to do other than play video games alone or come to the project. The key worker suggested he find something more engaging to fill his time in the short term. Sam seemed interested. The key worker informed him that he had heard of a new day centre for people with mental health issues in the neighbourhood. 'I'm not a basket case!!' was the initial reaction. The social stigma of mental illness was hard for him to accept. The key worker listened patiently and then said. 'Well, I have been meaning to check it for myself. Maybe it is not your thing. Why don't we just go and have look together see what they are about and get a coffee after. No commitment lets just see.' Sam agreed cautiously and they made the appointment. At the centre a worker conducted a brief assessment asking Sam what he might want from the service and Sam shared his interests and concerns. The worker reiterated that it was entirely up to Sam what he did and if he wanted to engage in any of the therapeutic groups and at what level. 'OK' agreed Sam, 'But I am not talking in any groups.' Sam went on to make extensive use of the day service, particularly gardening and catering, which he went on to gain formal qualifications in. He also attended the group sessions, and became one of its most vociferous members.

Overcoming addictions demands a sustained and continued effort on many fronts. Clients must engineer greater enrichment across all the domains of their lives if they are to stay off. Too often drug counselling has limited itself to weekly sessions of self-introspection. But generic counselling models evolved to help people whose reactions to life stress were disproportionate. The reactions of those whose lives have been characterised by long term social impoverishment and exclusion may not be so disproportionate. If our best efforts are to be successful they must account for this environment too. As such, we must work collaboratively with the clients to create tangible improvements in their world. Fulfilling social and recreational lives, employment, housing and the re-connection with significant loved ones are all legitimate concerns that can make practical and sustained differences in people's lives. Research by Lambert (1992) suggests that up to 40 per cent of counselling outcomes are determined by extra-therapeutic factors. These are the benign events and circumstances that occur within the life course of the client. As such we should not be shy in breaking the fourth wall of the treatment room to try and improve these areas too.

Limits of assessment

We may only be working with the client's stated attitudes towards their problems but the translation of these beliefs is complex. Read any book on working with drug and alcohol users and you might wonder where the difficulty lies in helping them change. The magical formula is endlessly repeated. A thorough assessment is the foundation; identifying clear goals is essential; contracting exacting detoxification regimes is necessary; and negotiating after care treatment plans is intrinsic to guarantee treatment success. If we faithfully adhere to such guidance we must eventually confront the inevitable question of why does it never go to plan?

The endless debates regarding the structure of assessments, the effectiveness of counselling interventions and accuracy of outcome measurement neglects the most universal component of the interaction: the nature of stated attitudes itself. The way in which the client presents their 'story' is the very medium of helping and the conversion of these stated intentions into subsequent action the principle goal. We can change assessment tools, counselling styles or outcome monitoring forms but we cannot change the nature of disclosure. Ignoring the reality of how people present themselves condemns our most considered efforts to well intentioned failure. To grasp the hidden dimensions of disclosure, consider Exercise 4.6. This is the most important exercise in this book. So please complete it before moving on.

Exercise 4.6: Self disclosure

Think about your life, and the worst thing that you have ever done. The one that you have wished to keep buried deep inside of yourself all your days. Once you have it firmly in your mind, I would like you to decide on three people that you will tell this to within the next 7 days. One must be a member of your family, one must be a work colleague and one must be someone you have met very recently. List their names below, along with the time and date that you will tell them:

I will tell _____   I will tell them on _____

1 _____   _____

2 _____   _____

3 _____   _____

When you are confronted with this exercise, what feelings does it inspire in you? Who did you select and why? How would you explain this to someone? Would it differ according to your relationship? In what way might you tell this secret which minimises the impact that it might have on your self-image? What do you fear that people will think of you? Of course I am not expecting you to actually do this as an exercise. But I am expecting you to recognise that your disclosures could not be free from the contamination of very human concerns. How it affects people's view of you; how you would need to editorialise the story so as to receive a more sympathetic response; and who they might tell this story to in turn, are real concerns that have impact on the way you tell the story. When it comes to expressing any shameful or deviant behaviour, huge pressure befalls us all and shapes our disclosures in profound ways. This is particularly important in substance misuse where individuals are living not just on the edge of society but on the edge of social ethics.

Research into self-reported drug use demonstrates that whilst people's recall of events and consumption is generally good, it is always biased by these social concerns. For example, research suggests that light drinkers self-reporting past and current consumption showed limited bias whilst heavy drinkers overestimate their previous alcohol consumption and underestimate present consumption (Czarnecki et al., 1990). Research into the validity of self-reported drug use in wider populations demonstrates that the more socially unacceptable a drug is perceived to be, then the greater the degree of bias appears in self-reports of use (Harrison, 1995). Self-reports of cannabis use tend to be accurate but people under-report the use of drugs such as heroin. Furthermore, general lifetime use was more accurate than recent use, which again showed a higher degree of bias. Within high risk groups similar distortions are found in report. In their meta-analysis, where the results of many studies are merged, Magura and Kang (1996) found little correlation between what individuals reportedly used compared to what biologically testing them revealed. The average degree of bias in 24 independent studies demonstrated accuracy of self-report was as low as 42 per cent. Again in most studies, the socially acceptable drug cannabis was reported with high accuracy in adults, young people, offenders and non offenders. Whilst the less socially acceptable drug use such as cocaine were under reported in these groups. Within drug treatment populations, the accuracy of self disclosure varies immensely but, significantly, clients showed greater under-reporting bias after treatment than on treatment entry. As we shall see, this bias is not limited to mere consumption but demonstrates that all disclosures are distorted in the telling, prompted by a wide range of social factors.

Attribution: what is it?

It is a fundamental aspect of human consciousness to engage in trying to explain the world around us. It has been suggested that humans need to believe that the world and the people in it are both predictable and understandable and this consistency makes us feel safe. So, like an arm chair psychologist, we are constantly observing other people's behaviour, or considering our own, and we try to understand what 'causes' people to act in the way that they do. What caused you to read this book? What causes a person to take drugs? What causes you to try to help them? If you compared your answers to these questions with your partners, would they be the same? Our own and other people's motivation to act in certain ways is not apparent. We can describe what people are doing through observation, but we do not see 'why' they are doing it. Instead we must *infer* the cause. And, based on these inferences, we formulate explanations. Whether they are true or not is inconsequential, the fact that we believe them to be true and they are useful to us is what really matters. This area of social psychology is called attribution. It explores how we *attribute* everyday explanations to our own and others' social behaviour.

We can attribute the cause of people's behaviour as being driven by two different domains. People's actions may be internally driven by themselves, or they may be driven externally by circumstance. The difference between internal and external attribution is important. They are not merely different kinds of explanation. If we consider internal explanations of problematic use we might suggest causes such as; it is a lifestyle choice, they are anti-social people or they disregard others. External explanations suggest causes such as a disease which renders people biologically susceptible, they have a certain compulsive personality type, or they are victims of poverty or abusive histories. The internal causes suggest that the individual's behaviour is self-perpetrated whilst the external explanations exonerates them as a helpless victim. Cause can also change depending upon who we are talking to. In a fascinating experiment by Davies and Baker (1987) problematic drug users were interviewed by two different people. Initially they were interviewed by a fellow heavy user. At the end of the interview he asked participants if they would mind being interviewed by someone else from the university as part of another research study. The second interview was conducted by a man who presented formally in a suit. Comparing the results of both interviews, higher degrees of addicted-ness (external cause) were reported in the formal interviewer and greater degrees of self-control (internal cause) were disclosed to the other drug user.

The type of cause in these explanations locates blame or credit. They create a bias in explanations that enhance or protect one's sense of self from judgement. Hence we have a tendency to ascribe our 'good' behaviours as internally motivated and our 'bad' behaviours as the product of external circumstances. Our explanations are refined from these concerns and subsequently affect behaviours and future expectations. Kelly and Michela (1980) suggest that beliefs precede the explanations we attribute to our behaviour. Coggins and Davies (1988) tested this hypothesis with a small sample of drug users. They found that user's responses at the time of three interviews conducted over intervals of three months did not correlate with their usage at the time. Many of the self-labelled heavy users were actually using far less than those who deemed themselves light users. All users also characterised their own consumption as being driven by positive life events and that they stopped when they encountered difficulties. Whilst they all believed that other heroin users took the drug for negative reason and only came off when life was better. Habitual users ascribed their behaviour as 'addictive' whilst controlled users ascribed it to 'luck' that they did not become addicted. No-one admitted that they took the drug simply because they enjoyed it. To reiterate, these explanations of their behaviour were independent of the amount they actually used. The explanations they offered were functional rather than descriptive.

Explanations can protect people from blame. The concept of blame is very salient when considering behaviours that are culturally shameful or deviant but is rarely openly discussed in addiction. But shame is deeply entwined in the root assumptions of our thinking. In the West there is a powerful cultural value that suggests that if people are to blame for their problems then they do not deserve help. Ultimately, it is this deep seated cultural ethic of what constitutes deservedness that shapes the disclosures of those who may be seen to have brought problems on themselves. Hence people understate the use of anti-social drugs; users justify consumption as driven by external circumstance; whilst people in recovery overstate their prior use to make their current efforts more heroic. Genetic, disease and biological explanations of addiction are all attributions which emphasise the inherent inability of users to quit, absolving the individual from their own actions. As a result the medicalisation of addiction has made it culturally more palatable rather than physically more treatable. It has not been fully successful though, as research demonstrates that people believe addictions to be both diseases and simultaneously the result of weak willpower (Heather and Robertson 1989). But clients seeking help must create an explanation that makes them deserving of the support they will recieve.

Types of bias

This cultural judgement of worthiness generates an immediate bias in the disclosures of drug users. Self-presentations must serve a strategic function which protect from judgement rather than describe the causes of behaviours. So the problematic substance user presents as being the victim of external forces that they cannot control in order to qualify as a worthy object of our concern and assistance. This leads to a self-presentational style which is characterised by descriptions of how the individual is overcome by outside forces that they cannot manage. Research has demonstrated that there are higher degrees of externalisation in addicts in treatment, regardless of age, sex or social class (Haynes and Allcliffe, 1991). Such external explanations are also prevalent in depressed groups who often report feeling overwhelmed by the demands of their lives. It has also been associated with learned helplessness (Seligmen, 1975), the expectation that one is unable to control hostile circumstances of one's life. The endless presentation of debilitation may become increasingly self-defining. Besides the cultural judgement they face in their daily lives, people presenting for treatment must endlessly narrate their life as a struggle against terrible circumstances in order to receive services. So, whilst 'blame-free' explanations of addiction absolves personal responsibility they may do so at a price of undermining self-determination.

The nature of self-presentation may be further warped by stigmatisation. Research has shown that in stigmatised groups where the cause may be perceived to be self-inflicted, the emotional response of the helper is highly dependent on how the client responds to the problem. In substance misusers, empathetic responses and the intention to help is strongly related to the problematic users attempts to change (Schwarzer, 1992). This has an impact on self-disclosure of goals. The user must present as if they are committed to a deep change in order to gain access to the options that they want, which might be more akin to respite than change. The client may desire minimising the stresses they are under within their current relationships and lifestyle but intuitively recognise that this is not deemed legitimate within current treatment responses. For example, an opiate user presenting to a GP, stating that they really like using heroin but cannot be bothered to score it all the time, so would like a methadone prescription to tide them over and allow them to pick and choose when they used is not going to get a sympathetic hearing. A desperate plea that their life is out of control and they must stop at all costs is going to get a sympathetic hearing.

Again these attributions are significant. The repeated public commitment to an undesired goal inevitably ends in repeated public failure. Failures to adhere to an agreed regime must also be attributed to external factors. Using heroin on top of one's methadone prescription is thus caused by 'unmanageable' and 'unpredictable' events that they cannot control to exonerate blame. This introduces a second important concept in attribution theory, that of stability. When the cause of behaviour is 'stable' it suggests that the individual perceives the cause to be ever present. This is as opposed to unstable – where the cause may change. Thus individuals who fail to change must explain this situation and are likely to ascribe it to stable conditions beyond their control. Hence self-diagnosis of 'addict', 'junkie', or 'addictive personality' can take on a significance to the individual that does not meet the social expectation to change. All combined it generates a self-identity whereby the users equates consistent failures with an inability to change even though they never necessarily sought that as a goal. This may hamper future attempts by fostering a negative expectation of their capacity to change.

This is important, as the types of explanations that we offer for failure may affect future performance (Curry et al., 1987). For example, two heavy drinkers attempt to quit. Both of them fail. Drinker A offers the explanation that they failed because they did not manage circumstances well. Drinker B ascribes his failure to his genetic disposition. Who will do better in future change attempts? What we see here is that drinker A still feels in control because he can do things differently next time. Drinker B faces a formidable task that he cannot change. Already his expectation of change is limited, and this in turn will diminish his self-belief that he can change. Similarly this can cut the other way. Two crack users attempt change and both are successful. Crack user C attributes his success to the efforts that he has made. Crack user D believes that he has succeeded in changing because he had come across such a great counsellor. In such instances, crack user D may find it difficult to sustain these changes if the cause of their success, their counsellor, is removed.

As we have seen in Chapter 2, addiction is located in both the individual and the context they are embedded in. It is not either the individual or circumstances but both. People struggle to manage the demands of life. To some degree we must learn to shape our environment, and at other times, to adapt to the elements of life that cannot be controlled. None of us live a life free of poor decisions or difficult circumstances. We can manage good circumstances badly as much as we can manage difficult circumstances well. The criteria for offering help should not lie in the origins of people's troubles, but the fact that they want it regardless of cause. This demands that we as helpers challenge our own innate cultural assumptions in order to support others more effectively. It also means we must not assume clients are telling us what is in their hearts, but anticipate revisions of stated goals, explanations and commitment as treatment unfolds.

Atypical responses

Sometimes in the assessment process the client does not respond in the way we typically expect people to answer questions. Intoxication or mental health issues may become apparent through short interactions with people. Slurring or poor concentration may indicate whether people are intoxicated. People who are heavily under the influence will not engage in the assessment process to a useful degree. In this situation you should support the client, non-aggressively, to return when the assessment can be completed. The level of re-negotiation is more difficult with people under the influence of alcohol than other substances and it is easier to address this before entering into a private assessment room. Alternatively Berg and Ruess (1998) recommend the assessment be conducted stood up, which helps the intoxicated client remain more present. At other times the client may not have clear thought processes even though they are not intoxicated. There can be very obvious deviations in communication style which indicate that the person may be experiencing more profound problems. This may be accompanied by inappropriate emotional responses such as laughing for no apparent reason. It is important that we recognise when there may be deeper issues occurring. Consider the following responses in Table 4.4.

Communication style may be reflective of underlying and complex mental health issues. This is *not* to suggest that one can make a clear diagnosis of the client simply from the type of answers the client offers. But it could indicate the possibility that there may be more complex issues at work, especially if the client has not used prior to the visit. Check with them before leaping to conclusions. These communication styles, along with eccentric beliefs, suicidal ideas or inappropriate emotional reactions, are usually the first indicator that there may be more significant mental health problems. The client may themselves not be fully aware of these mental health problems or had any diagnosis. Very often it is the onset of mental health problems that motivates a concerned other to bring the drug or alcohol using client to a service, particularly if they receive no support from elsewhere. In this situation the concerned other can be a useful source of information. They can provide insight into whether there has been a marked shift in the client's mood or behaviour as well as their current drug and alcohol use.

In the case of poor thought process, simple messages will be necessary in order for the person to understand what you are telling them. Do not get into discussions in which people will be unable to reason easily. Keep it simple, polite and direct as you reiterate any necessary information to them. For those experiencing more profound and distressing symptoms of mental illness, referrals should be made to their GP. The GP should be informed of the client's symptoms, especially those which are not typically induced by their drug of choice. In crisis moments when the client is a threat to themselves or others the police should be contacted immediately.

Table 4.4 Thought processes (adapted from Elkin 1999)

Style	Example	Possible cause
Goal orientated thought or linear thought	Assessor: What made you decide to come to see me today? Client: I have not been feeling well, and after discussing it with my partner; I thought it would be good to speak to someone about it. Assessor: She noticed that you were having problems? Client: Yes, she noticed a while ago that I was very down and, after talking about it, we agreed that it would be helpful to see someone.	May indicate anxiety.
Circumstantiality: The client rambles and gives large amounts of information before returning to the answer the question.	Assessor: What brought you here today? Client: Well it's a long story, about two years ago, no two and a half years ago, I started feeling depressed. Well I am not sure if it was depression or just feeling low really. It was a difficult period in my life . . . Sorry, you asked me about this time. Things have been bad for some time and I started to feel that I could not go on anymore. That's when I decided to make and appointment and do something.	
Tangentially. Here the client's thoughts veer off into unrelated areas without reference to the idea or questions posed to them.	Assessor: What brought you to the hospital? Client: I have never been in a place like this before. So many people. Me, I have always worked as a car mechanic. Believe you me cars have got so much more advanced these days. It was very different when I started out 15 years ago . . .	May indicate anxiety, dementia or delirium.
Flight of ideas. Here the client rushes from one idea to the next, often speeding up as they go along, faster than their speech can manage.	Assessor: What brought you here today? Client: Hospitals are incredible places of social forces . . . the technology necessary to support life on our plant these days is colossal. Technology is doubling its power every 6 months . . . If my plan to connect the minds and computers together think what we will be able to achieve . . . people from here to Australia sharing one collective mind . . . Australia, there is a country . . . Assessor: I was asking about what brought you here? Client: . . . the wildlife and desert in Australia, so magical . . . did you know that Ayrs rock is a posting station for extraterrestrial life . . . they try to keep it a secret but I . . .	Common in bipolar or mania.

Table 4.4 *Continued*

Style	Example	Possible cause
Loose associations. The client shows a loss of logical connectedness between ideas. Whilst the client sees a logical progression the interviewer finds it difficult to detect any relationships.	Assessor: What brought you here today? Client: Vaccinating dogs won't stop car cancer Assessor: I am sorry, I don't understand? Client: . . . and then his eyes just bulged up.	Common in psychosis and delirium.
Thought blocking. Here the client stops in mid-sentence and is unable to complete the phrase.	Assessor: What brings you here today? Client: My mother brought me in the car and said. Assessor: And said what? Client: . . .	Sometimes seen in psychosis.
Concrete thinking. The client is unable to think in abstract thoughts, but instead, gives very blunt, literal answers.	Assessor: What brought you here today? Client: A car. Assessor: What was it that made you decide to come here today? Client: My wife.	Sometimes in dementia.
Perseveration: This term refers to repeated behaviours, thoughts or speech patterns.	Assessor: What brings you here today? Client: It's a global thing. It seems that way to me, global. You would have to understand the global picture. It's a global thing. It's a global thing.	Sometimes indicative of a central nervous damage.

If you are to assess people with mental health problems, keep it short, and gently paced. If they report hearing voices, acknowledge it and empathise with the person who is struggling to hear you over these internal distractions. The voices may be persecutory towards them as well as you. This is embarrassing for the client to admit but should be accepted. For clients with profound depression, anxiety or psychotic symptoms (or on medications), write down any follow up plans or action points for them to take away. The symptoms can cause problems with concentration and hence memory retention. Written notes are helpful prompts. But for practitioners who do not feel confident with mental health issues they should co-assess the client with a more experienced worker.

Conclusion

Good assessment is more than the form. It exists in the interplay between the assessor and the client who must transect both the key indicators of the dependence and the addiction. Where we confuse these two ideas at the assessment stage, subsequent treatment will fail. We cannot prescribe a more enriching life, and even stabilisation can rapidly equate with stagnation if the client has no means to change their environment. Addressing dependency will only reduce negative stresses in the user's life. To address addiction we must chart the corrosion of addiction and set goals that will address these broken bonds. Deciphering what is relevant in this is more art than science, and demands that the assessor's understanding is as expansive as the client's concerns. Once we have mapped the factors that sustain use we can cultivate plans to assail them. Again, we see the recurrent theme of the goodness to fit between the client's aspirations and the responses we offer. This is essential if we are to foster the client's engagement and motivate them to be more than the passive recipient of treatment but the driver of it. As a result, even brief assessments that identify the core concerns in each area can be as effective, and sometimes more so, than comprehensive ones when they capture the wants of the client simply. Within this we must recognise that the process of disclosure is dynamic. The unique social stigmatisation of addiction and the possible impact of substance on mental health can shape these processes in profound ways. This demands that we are not only flexible in developing plans but in reviewing them too.

Chapter 5

On Motivation

The mind is its own place, and in itself can make a
Heaven of Hell, and a Hell of Heaven.

John Milton

So far we have outlined the drug using experience, processes of dependency and addiction, the importance of the alliance and how to map the treatment course. This represents the helper's preparedness for the encounter. However, we must understand what motivates clients to change if we are to successfully build on this momentum. This chapter will explore the idea of motivation and change from the client's perspective first. People who seek formal help often adopt the language and concepts of their subsequent support programmes. To avoid this trap we shall explore remission studies where individuals make substantial change to their use without formal support. We will explore the competing forces that tip behaviour in the direction of use or change. This raw experience will be considered alongside wider research to establish what underpins these experiences. Once these mechanisms are established we shall see how interventions such as motivational interviewing address them directly to increase engagement and establish the commitment to change. This is important because our thinking has all too often been informed by folk wisdom rather than research.

Traditionally it was believed that problematic users were innately prone to high consumption. Disease concepts were supplemented by psychological theories to explain why people not only consumed intoxicants to excess but why they made no attempt to control this consumption. It was supposed that they had over-developed defence mechanisms such as denial, rationalisation, projection and regression (Fox, 1967). These psychological blocks were the central obstacle to recovery. As a result, traditional programmes insisted that the client needed to hit 'rock bottom' before change could begin. Only at the point of complete emotional, psychological and physical collapse could the individual experience a moment of lucidity and apprehend the magnitude of their situation and behaviour. Furthermore, this process of breaking denial had to be continued by any subsequent treatment through continued confrontation.

Extensive profiling of problematic users has consistently revealed that no addictive personality type appears to exist (Vaillant, 1995). Problematic users actually appear no different to any other sub-group in society (Loberg and Miller, 1986). Also, whilst some users do reach complete crisis before implementing change, other 'high-bottom' users halt their addictions prior to this point, even though they consume similar amounts over the same lengths of time. Rather than relying on the received wisdom it is important that we understand this tipping point of change in more detail.

Natural remission and change

Prochaska and DiClemente's (1992) study of smokers identified consciousness raising as the first mechanism of change. Whilst initial consumption is driven by positive expectations of use and often embedded in social relationships, the individual gradually becomes aware the consequence of their use. This awareness appears to reach a certain threshold before triggering more profound revisions of oneself and one's behaviour. This included mechanisms such as self-revaluation where the individual must consider whether these established behaviours are compatible with one's aspirations and values. The awareness of these stresses also elicits and drives heightened emotional arousal in light of problems, setbacks and the damage that use has caused.

Similar themes are broadly identified in the natural remission studies of untreated changers. Burman's (1997) interviews with 38 problem drinkers identified four core themes regarding the motivation to change. 'Having too much to lose' was the most common. This included damage to careers, relationships, status and sense of self-identity. Along with this, these drinkers reported experiencing 'terrifying fears' where bodily injury or death felt imminent as a result of chronic use. In comparison, more positive reasons for change emerged in wanting to be a role model for others, particularly loved ones such as children. Bargaining with God or a loved one to change in a crisis moment, not necessarily related to one's own use, but to the loss of another, also seem prevalent. Here people wanted to be alcohol free not for themselves but for important others. What is also significant in Burman's research was that many of her respondents felt compelled to change in light of the breakdown in areas of their lives that were important to them. This produced a deep conflict between their ideal self and their actual behaviour which become increasingly difficult to sustain. Van Kalmouth (1991) reports similar fears in his literature. Existential guilt that one has failed to reach one's potential along with the increasing awareness and concern on issues of mortality figured heavily in the transitional moment. Schaffer and Jones (1989) found the exact same responses in those who stopped problematic cocaine use. Feelings of humiliation, sickness and other powerful and noxious associations also operated as motivators for change and are also born out in other research studies by Tuchfield (1981) and Ludwig (1985).

Stall and Biernacki's (1986) natural remission model based on comprehensive reviews of research on smokers, drinkers, opiate users and those experiencing problems with food, identified a similar theme in all areas. The negative social stigma of the behaviour was a prime driver of change, which they sub-grouped further into the health problems, social sanctions, pressure from concerned loved ones and financial problems.

Klingemann's (1991) research of heroin and alcohol users suggests it is the psychological cost of having to address constant problems in health, social sanctions, relationship difficulties and financial debt that elicits motivation and the decision to quit. The 'naked lunch' experience was a common trigger for change. This shocking self-revelation had a dramatic impact on change. A number of interviewees reported that the brink of death experience that their use drove them to was the turning point. Other respondents relayed how changes in important relationships (both private and professional), psychological pressure and physical illness all drove them towards change. Many felt that they were at a crossroads in their lives, where their decisions now would irreversibly send them along two contrasting life paths: all consuming addiction or change.

We see some interesting differences between drug users and alcohol users in Klingemann's (1991) research. The social stressors appeared much higher on the heroin users than on the drinkers. They saw greater involvement in criminal justice as well as health concerns. As we saw in Chapter 2, alcohol's legitimate legal and cultural position assuaged the onset of these problems. High consumption was not met with such high social sanctions and therefore the drinker used for longer as they felt less pressure to change. The threshold of social acceptance controls the onset of the addiction for different substances.

Stresses and change

What is striking in the research is several themes. Firstly, the similarity in the clients' presenting stories, characterised by crises and social stresses. The discomfort of use, precipitated by events or protracted stress drives their change. The nature of these crises is interesting and correlates with our distinction between dependence and addiction. In these studies some individuals seemed more sensitive to problems in social relationships whilst others were more sensitive to the physical consequences of use. It may be that whilst some people respond to the affects of addiction, others are not as pressure sensitive and respond to dependence. It is not until they experience the physical consequence of prolonged exposure that change is activated. This needs to be considered when working with people regarding change. Health concerns will be salient to some individuals but others are driven to change because of relationships. For example, young people with a nascent sense of mortality will not respond to health warnings. Damage to relationships which are central to their lives and esteem will elicit greater reactions. Individuals who are sensitive to their own health may also use for longer, as the physical consequences of use tend to culminate over protracted time periods and may have no obvious visible symptoms until they become chronic.

Increased negative consequences did not seem the only motivator though. Klingemann (1991) also reported a gradualist change process where the problem user became increasingly preoccupied with other things in life and less interested in using. Erikson and Hadaway (1989) report similar trends in cocaine users. Many drift out of use over a relatively short period, leaving a very small minority who go on to sustained problem use. Once preoccupied with other demands, subjects give little attention or even awareness of the diminishment of their drug and alcohol use. Labouvie's (1996) research into populations that 'aged out' of use demonstrated that increased attachment into marriage, child rearing and work commitments decreased drug and alcohol use respectively across the life course. Other research demonstrates a significant decrease in drug consumption coincides with marriage (Kandal and Raevis, 1989). Such findings may give us some insight into cultural consumption patterns relative to the life course.

Young people in their twenties are the highest consumers of alcohol but rarely present for treatment. Binge drinking patterns have become a hotly debated issue in Britain and are often assumed to be driven by the low cost of alcohol. This situation may be more complex. Culturally we remain younger for longer, staving off entry into marriage until later in life. This extends the bout of youthful drinking identified in adolescence, which is intensified in early adulthood with an increase in disposable income. At the same time in the UK, young people are also excluded from investing resources in other rewarding assets. Prohibitively high house prices prevent these young adults from moving into the next stage of their expected life course. Saving and investing in home-making deflects income into more desired tangible assets than consumption. Binge drinking may be resistant to interventions because it may be more connected to the house market than psychological distress or physical dependence. Access to a better life may have a more curative effect in itself. This phenomena may have far reaching social consequences to society as a whole. Ledermann's (1956) curve demonstrates that problem drinking in any population is not confined to a sub-group of alcoholics. The severity of social problems with alcohol can be accurately predicted by the national average of consumption. Small increases in average consumption lead to disproportionately large increases in the problems caused by use. The future cost of current binge drinking is yet to be fully calculated.

Reinforcement

What appears critical in the initiation of change is a painful awareness of the impact that use is having on the individual or on their social environment. This conscious awareness of the need for change appears to be the product of competing forces. Whilst there are many complex and ornate theories of motivation, for simplicity we can strip these competing forces down to their most basic units. Drawing on operant conditioning theory as a model, we can determine that motivation takes distinct forms. *Operant* defines a behaviour that changes the environment that it acts upon. Procuring drugs are operant behaviours because they result in consumption which changes the user's (inner) environment. The consequences of these operant behaviours determine whether they will be repeated. People are motivated by the desirable or undesirable consequences that follow a given behaviour. Reinforcers are the consequences of actions that increase the behaviour that precedes use whilst punishing consequences decrease the behaviour that precedes it. Reinforcers and punishments are not standard but are unique to each individual. For example, if I give you a chocolate for every page you read and your rate of reading increases, then chocolate is a positive reinforcer for you. On the other hand if it decreases your rate of reading because you are on a diet then it is a punishment. Reinforcement can be achieved through a variety of means. They can be material, relational, value based or spiritual.

Reinforcement and punishments operate in two ways. They can be positive in adding to your environment or negative in removing something from your environment. For example, work is positively reinforced by bringing desirable rewards such as money, feelings of affirmation from making a difference and increasing self-worth. Motivation can also be negatively reinforced, when behaviours reduce undesirable aspects of our environment. Financial pressures to pay the bills, keep a roof over our heads, stay on top of our workload, fearing we will let our team down, all negatively reinforce work. Punishments can be positive or negative too. A positive punishment adds something undesirable to your environment like the pain of a hangover, whilst negative punishments remove something you desire, being fined for speeding costs you money that you could have spent on other things. Consider a behaviour that you are thinking about changing right now, and see if you can identify as many reinforcers and punishments as possible. Write them down in Exercise 5.1.

Whether behaviour is sustained or ceases is driven by the balance of rewards or costs that follow it. Whilst the reinforcement remains high and the punishments are low, the behaviour will be sustained. Once the punishments overtake the reinforcing rewards the behaviours begin to cease. The extinguishment burst occurs prior to the cessation of behaviour. For example, if a child always throws a tantrum in order to get their own way and the parent suddenly stops responding to this with the reward, the child will increase the tantrums before the behaviour breaks. Many parents yield before the breaking point believing that the tantrums will continue. Changes in behaviour are often preceded by intensified efforts to attain rewards.

Reinforcement and addictions

When we review initiation factors of addiction they included positive reinforcing effects such as the drugs pharmacological action, identity, bonding in using peer groups and esteem as a risk taker. However, over protracted periods of use, and in light of losses and stresses, the motivation

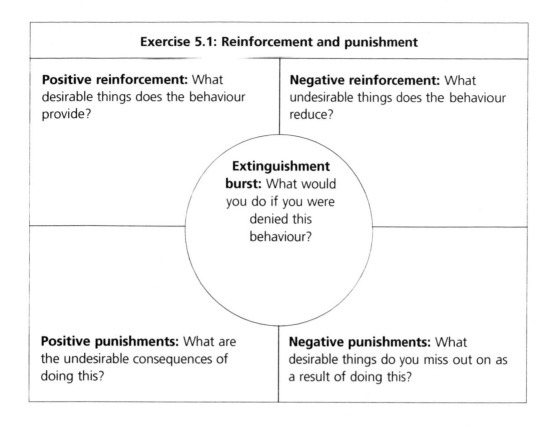

Exercise 5.1: Reinforcement and punishment

Positive reinforcement: What desirable things does the behaviour provide?

Negative reinforcement: What undesirable things does the behaviour reduce?

Extinguishment burst: What would you do if you were denied this behaviour?

Positive punishments: What are the undesirable consequences of doing this?

Negative punishments: What desirable things do you miss out on as a result of doing this?

shifts whereby consumption becomes negatively reinforced. The insidious shift into addiction emerges when people use drugs to sedate undesirable feelings. Breaking isolation, alleviating negative mood states, avoiding more painful concerns or escaping from problems or difficult relationships can be powerful motivators that drive consumption. Continued use also increases the positive punishments. This can be the come down and hangovers that follow use; the conflict with loved ones; the pain of breakdown in important relationships; the drama and assault of a chaotic life in the shadow society of use. The guilt that one is not living to one's potential negatively punishes use as it also excludes more rewarding lives, relationships or access to the pro-social groups. These are summarised in Table 5.1.

Reviewing literature about what motivates problem users to seek treatment we see that negative consequences drives it. People seek treatment to reduce the punishing stresses caused by use. Hence research identifies crises, around health, damage to important relationships, accidents, despair, guilt and feelings of shame, all generate undesirable mood states which people seek relief from. This is encapsulated in the popular maxim of recovering problem users. They report that they were sick and tired of feeling sick and tired. The pivotal moment of change thus becomes a decisional balance between the positive and negative rewards that reinforce use, versus the positive and negative punishments that drive change. In short, the negative consequences of use must outweigh any benefits for change to occur.

Table 5.1   Examples of reinforcement/punishment of problem use

Positive reinforcement of use	Negative reinforcement of use
The effect of the drug/alcohol.	Stress.
The taste/smell/sight of the drug.	Negative mood states.
Sensations induced by the administration of the drug (e.g. injecting, snorting, smoking).	Lack of alternative enrichment.
	Low job satisfaction.
People who also use.	Relationship problems/conflicts.
Places.	Isolation.
Identity.	Abates financial worries/debt
Expectations.	Poor social skills.
Self-esteem as a high consumer.	Low self-belief.
Knowledge about the drugs and their use.	Conflicts.
Ghetto stardom (dealing, fighting, the gang etc.)	Lack of pro-social identity.
	Emotional pain/trauma.
	Threats of legal actions.

Positive punishments of use	Negative punishments
Hangovers/comedowns.	Loss of self-esteem.
Domestic violence.	Loss of important relationships.
Assaults/conflicts when under the influence.	Loss of employment.
Conflict in peer groups.	Loss of money.
Impulsive aggression of others	Loss of personal freedom through criminal justice sanctions.
Being ripped off.	
Poor quality drugs.	Fines.
Family conflicts.	Rejection from friends and family.
Relationship break ups.	Deterioration in housing/environment.
Increased personal risk/accidents through usage.	Failing to reach ones potential
Shame or guilt from behaviour under the influence.	Feeling age deviant
Physical pain as a result of use e.g. liver damage, loss of limbs through injecting, nasal problems through snorting.	

Decisional balances

This decisional balance was originally identified by Janis and Mann (1977). They identified four key factors in this weighting process; instrumental gains and approval for self and others, and conversely, instrumental costs and disapproval for self and others. In terms of substance misuse work, the instrumental gains/cost are the biological action and withdrawal of dependency whilst the approval/disproval of others equates to the issues of addiction itself. Research (Velicer et al., 1985; Prochaska et al., 1994) has simplified this, suggesting that only the perception of the pros and cons of change need matter. Research demonstrates that the shift in balance between these two positions is both consistent and intrinsic to the change process (see Figure 5.1).

What we see is that the individual in precontemplation only perceives cons in change. The shift into contemplation is determined by the increased awareness of the pros of changing. The pros of change are driven by the awareness of increasing problems resulting from use. In the initiation of change we see a dramatic increase in the awareness of pros to change first, followed by a decrease in the cons of change. This increase in awareness of the benefits of change always

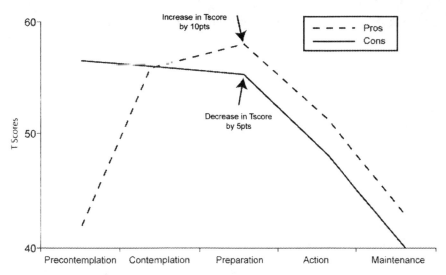

Figure 5.1   The relationship between stage and the decisional balance for an unhealthy behaviour (Velicer et al., 1998)

preceedes the reduction of cons, and always occurs in the same magnitude, regardless of the behaviour. As such it can be considered the only law of human behaviour ever discovered (see Figure 5.1.) What this means is we need twice as many pros to cons for change to commence.

The doubled-sided nature of change is articulated in studies of clients. Research with problem drinkers demonstrated that whilst they recognised gains from curtailing drinking they also recognised losses. This included loneliness, loss of sociability and boredom (Solomon and Annis, 1989; Rollnick and Heather, 1982; Burman, 1997). The emptiness felt in losing this structure is profound. Essentially we see that the contemplative client is locked in a struggle between competing forces of change and we define this psychological state as ambivalence. Ambivalence was originally termed by Bluer (1950) to describe contradictory feelings toward the same object. For him this was a conflict between two equally attractive but competing options. For the substance user this is nearly always the reverse. They are torn between two bitter choices. The substance that can alleviate stress at the price of dire consequences or change that increases stress but abates consequences. As such, the contemplator is caught between the unstoppable force of anxiety that drives the need to change and the unmovable obstacle of ambivalence which paralyses change.

Paradoxically, removing the negative consequences of use through substitute prescribing alleviates suffering but as a result also diminishes motivation for change. The build up of positive and negative punishments from prolonged use motivates people to seek help. As we saw in Chapter 4, substitute prescribing operates primarily by reducing the negative pressures individuals are under through their use by removing the pressure to score, reducing withdrawal and the chaos of life in the shadow society. Once the substitute drug reduces the stresses of use it removes the very motivation that brought them into services. This is exacerbated by the fact that the balance is not shifted in the other direction by increasing access to any positives of change. Hence substitute prescribing stabilises use but simultaneously paralyses the change process as the impetus to amend behaviours is lost. With no negative consequences pressurising them to change and no positive rewards to work towards, the prescribed individual now resides in a motivational limbo. They lose the previous structure offered by the addicted lifestyle and little replaces it. This leaves them open to boredom which is often abated by diversification into other drug markets, notably crack and alcohol. As a result, prescribing services attract large numbers of clients who then remain there for years.

To facilitate change we must increase the pros of cessation by providing more valuable and enriching experiences, whilst decreasing the cons of stopping. Once the differential between pros and cons is achieved, we need to maintain it through the establishment of environments that sustain this imbalance towards change. This was the situation describe by Burman's (1997) cohort of having 'too much to lose'. We shall see this basic principle run through all the subsequent interventions described in the following chapters. This does not always have to be achieved through the helping relationship. As we have seen, not all people change through seeking help and not all people change consciously. If we consider the drinker in their twenties who meets a new partner, settles down, sets up home and plans a family – high consumption interferes with these more rewarding life expectancies and so consumption is reduced. Here, the pros of change are increasing in their environment without them even being conscious that this shift is occurring and use is declining. For clients without naturally occurring betterment, the imposition of negative consequences may be all that can impel change.

Motivational interviewing

Motivational interviewing (Miller and Rollnick, 2002) was developed in the 1980s in response to research that challenged the convention wisdom of addiction work. Research by William Miller (1989) suggested that many of the assumptions of addiction had received little empirical evaluation. He saw the central problems in overcoming addictions were not defective character traits or denial but ambivalence regarding change. Instead of confronting, correcting and challenging the user, his research showed that a collaborative alliance that worked with the client to resolve mixed feelings regarding change was more effective. Working with ambivalence is difficult because it is easy to influence the decision the wrong way. Working collaboratively means we must take a basic position of neutrality towards the decision and be careful not to explicitly sell, promote or endorse change.

Forcing change on people is counter-productive. This is because it incurs the psychological process of reactance (Brehm and Brehm, 1981). Reactance occurs when people sense a loss of personal freedom or threat. In these conditions people tend to form opinions in contradiction to the source of this imposition as a means to self-protect. Not only this, but the more emphatically change is pressed upon us, the more vehemently we will resist. Consider a time when someone told you what you ought do or criticised you. How did you respond? (see Exercise 5.2)

Exercise 5.2: Reactance

When _____ told me to _____

I responded with _____

When _____ said I was _____

I responded with _____

Even when changes or feedback from others are in our interest, we will meet them with contradiction. It forces us to formulate counter-arguments to defend the very position that others want us to change. So, despite good intentions, confrontation reduces our openness to change (Cialdini and Petty, 1979). In addition to this, forewarning of another's persuasive intent will further enhance these counter-arguments, especially when the attitudes or behaviours others are attempting to modify are important to us (Petty and Cacioppo, 1979). This is central to the creation of stated opinion. We do not have ready made arguments on every subject already formulated in our heads, which we play at appropriate moments like a poker hand. Opinions are conjured in the moment. As such we learn our opinions as we hear our selves speak them. Think of a time when you had an argument with your partner or when management forced you to change your work practice. You would have had no opinion on this issue prior to it being raised, but as you instantly marshal your defence in reaction to these changes, a well formulated argument just emerged from you. And as you hear it unfold from your own lips you can marvel to yourself at just how cogent it appears to be. And once we have heard ourselves utter these arguments we must remain loyal to them. Our spoken words become our truth.

The net result is that ordering, persuading, lecturing or threatening ambivalent people with the need to change simply has the opposite effect. The more you push the client towards change the more they will resist. The response will be 'Yes . . . But . . .'. The client will have no recourse but to defend the opposite view, formulate counter-arguments why they should not change and in hearing themselves say it aloud they will only convince themselves of this position. Young people or those coerced onto treatment programmes will be highly sensitive to reactance. As such, resistance to change may not be endemic in the client's psychology but may be the product of the kinds of conversation that we are having with them. Motivational interviewing therefore considers resistance to change as feedback to the helper. They are doing something wrong in tilting the conversation too far in the direction of change, forcing a reverse in the client. These differences should not be underestimated as they are easily invoked. In an experiment by Patterson and Forgatch (1984) counsellors instructed to 'teach' and 'confront' clients generated far higher rates of resistance than when they were instructed to 'support' and 'facilitate'.

Working with ambivalence

When working with ambivalence we must not interpret it as the client being difficult. Ambivalence is to be expected in any life changing decisions, as reinforcers and punishments always compete in opposite directions. Instead we need to work through it. First, we ask the client to identify as many pros of change as they can. Then, we ask them to identify as many cons of change as possible. Once again we need to draw out of them as many as possible. To do this we continually use the prompt 'what else?' This will make the client work hard at identifying as many reasons as possible for change and not changing. We can camouflage this question a little to make it feel more natural. Consider an issue that you are thinking about changing. Answer the following questions in Exercise 5.3, doing the pros first and then the cons. Use the follow up question 'what else?' continually until you have completed an exhaustive list.

Exercise 5.3: Ambivalence

- What are the pros of changing?
- What else is there?
- And is there any more to this?
- What else is there?
- Are there any other pros?
- Is there any thing else in favour of change?

- What are the cons of change?
- What else is there?
- And is there any more to this?
- What else is there?
- Are there any other cons?
- Is there any thing else against change?

Continue until you have exhausted all pros and cons.

Working through this exercise you should observe the simplicity of the prompt 'what else?' It makes you dig deeper into your concerns. This puts the emphasis on the client to make sense of their own situation. Motivational interviewing provides a framework to make the client work hard at their decisions. It is not for us to judge whether the client's pros and cons are worthy ones, rather to understand that they are important to the client. Reviewing your pros and cons should reveal a pattern in the answers that you give. Initially clients tend to give symptoms relief statements about the benefits of change or rather shallow responses. But as the 'what else?' question digs further the nature of the answers change. They shift towards deeper concerns of values, beliefs, feelings and expectations. Such is the irrational stuff of the human mind. Rational reason for change may satisfy us on one level but, as seen in Chapter 3 we are not wholly rational. It is these deeper prised values and felt beliefs that are the foundation on which behaviours change. Our willingness to explore cons of change in equal depth emits a powerful signal of empathy and understanding (Grilo, 1993).

However, it is not simply the number of pros and cons, but the weight of these factors that we must consider. We do not simply want a list, but to understand what these things mean to the client, and for that we need to work with the underlying attitudes without provoking resistance. We need to be able to engage with the client to unpack the details – without trying to push the client into change because as soon as we do they will go in the opposite direction (even using too powerful a word in conversation will spark reactance and contradiction in them). Where the client has a balance of pros and cons it is important to raise their awareness of the positives of change by providing them with literature, information or general discussion, because change will not occur until that 2:1 ratio is achieved. Identifying the means where the client can increase their awareness of pros is important without pushing it upon them.

Case Study: Addressing ambivalence

Jason had a history of heavy cocaine use and psychosis. He was depressed, isolated and used cannabis heavily which his support worker thought was a problem for him. Jason resisted the idea but after discussing it he half-heartedly agreed to visit a drugs project to discuss it. In his discussion he revealed a deep pessimism about his mental health and capacity for change, feeling as though his label of mental illness would never leave him. He described himself as a 'nutter'. Exploring the past use and his symptoms he became aware that his mental health was connected to his cocaine using episodes. When the conversation came to his cannabis use, the worker noted some hesitancy in him. 'It seems like you have some mixed feelings about smoking grass, lets look at the pros and cons of it.' Jason listed his pros and cons and was surprised the worker was so accepting of his reasons to smoke. His list was well balanced, 50–50. 'Well' said the worker, 'Improving your mental health was something that you said was important. It would be interesting to see what effect cannabis has on the symptoms you described. I am not sure what effect they may have but would be interested to see more. How about we do some research on the internet and see what we can find out about it?' Jason agreed. They checked the internet and printed off various articles and reports. Going through the research the worker asked what Jason made of it all? Jason responded that he had not realised that grass could have such a negative impact on mental health, he had thought that as it was 'natural' it did not really cause any problems. On further consideration in the subsequent session he thought that it was not doing him any good and began to plan cutting down. Just as a trial.

Reflective listening

Motivational interviewing makes use of a distinct communication style called reflective listening. It can be a difficult technical skill to grasp because it is very much against the grain of how we are typically taught to listen. Many people in the field believe that they are good listeners when they are in fact good at asking questions. There is a big difference. Traditionally we are taught to ask the client open questions. As we saw in Chapter 3, these included questions which began with; what, who, when, where, how. What these questions demand is that the client describes their situation or feelings to us. As such, we can get a lot of surface detail but miss deeper evaluations. In reflective listening we work differently. We do not want more detail about the client's situation, instead we want to get at the meaning behind a client's statement. So for example, when we listen to a client talking about their concerns regarding their alcohol use, we do not want to know what they drink, when they drink or who they drink with. We want to know what drinking means to them. Read this short extract of reflective listening. Consider closely what the counsellor is doing in the reflective listening case study.

Case Study: Reflective listening

A client arrives at a drop in centre, in a badly beaten up state. They look tired, dishevelled and nervous. They have never been in a project before but after a recent fight whilst drinking they have come through the door for the first time.

Client: *Well I have been drinking heavily now for the last eight years. And my girlfriend is drinking heavily too, and last night, well, we had a fight.*
Helper: *Alcohol is causing problems in the relationship.*
Client: *Yeah, definitely. I have known it for a while now. I have wanted to do something about it for a long time but could not walk through the door. Then last night it all got crazy.*
Helper: *You could not ignore it anymore.*
Client: *No. After the fight last night I know we have a problem. We were just drinking a bottle of vodka and got into an argument over nothing. She just lost it – we both lost it – she attacked me. I went back to mine and smashed my own flat up. The police were called. They wanted to arrest me as they thought I had attacked her, because of the blood on me. I hadn't.*

Helper: *Drinking is causing you both to lose control.*
Client: *It's horrendous. I cannot believe we are doing this. It's awful.*
Helper: *You can't go on like this.*
Client: *I just don't know what to do.*
Helper: *You're not sure.*
Client: *No. I have to change – we have to change. She means so much to me. But it seems as though we are just destroying all we have by drinking. I do not know how we got into this situation.*
Helper: *Drinking is destroying everything you have together.*
Client: *Yes, I will lose everything but I can't seem to stop.*

The first thing to notice is that the helper does not offer any interpretations of the client's situation. Nor do they ask any open questions. Instead they work solely with the information presented by the client. The helper listens closely to what the client is saying, deduces the meaning of the statement and reflects it back. As such, the helper's responses are somewhere in-between an open question and a paraphrase. It is as if he is asking every time – is this what you mean? Even when the client states that they do not know what to do, the counsellor reflects back their uncertainty and the client answers. Other times, it is not the words but the power behind the words the counsellor reflects back. The words 'awful' and 'horrendous' appear in the same sentence suggesting powerful and significant emotions and so it is this feeling that charges the statement that is picked up on.

But notice too, that these are not phrased as questions. They are kept flat, much more like statements. This is important. We ask a question by applying a vocal inflection at the end. This invites speculation. However, when we keep it flat like a statement it remains very close to the clients intended meaning and reiterates it. Contrast the two examples in Figure 5.2.

---

1. *Client:* I don't know what to do really, I am not sure I can go on drinking like this.
Counsellor: You have to do something about it?

2. *Client:* I don't know what to do really, I am not sure I can go on drinking like this.
Counsellor: You have to do something about it.

Figure 5.2   Questions versus statements

In the first example, the counsellor's response posed as a question invites room for manoeuvre. The client can ponder this position and debate it internally before answering. The second example is very different. Instead it reinforces exactly what the client is saying. There is no room for speculation because it sounds more like agreement than exploration.

Framing reflective statements

Framing reflective statements is difficult, and so is explaining it on paper. On the page these short 'clipped' questions lack the emotional context our limbic brains need to understand nuance clearly. As a result, reflective listening can sound blunt, even sarcastic, on the written page. We must remember that the reflective statements are delivery-dependent. They are to be said in a warm and concerned way. The easiest way to build up to reflective listening is to begin with simple reflections. This can be done by listening to the client's answers and responding to the powerful words, the vague words or the emotionally charged inflections in the client's voice. Powerful words are rich in emotion, intensity or drama that needs to be unpacked. These might include words such as 'angry', 'hurt', 'terrible', 'hopeless', or 'desperate'. Vague words are general, non-specific or could mean different things to different people. Phrases such as 'Doing my head in', 'Its all coming on top', 'Things are different', or 'It's down to me' do not state the specific detail and need to be made more concrete. At other times it is striking when clients repeat the same words in a sentence, or apply specific emotional emphasis to them. This is when we reflect back the feeling in the statement. So, powerful words need exploring whilst vague words need firming up to achieve greater clarity. At other times, in emotionally charged sentences, we are more interested in the charge than the sentence (see Figure 5.3).

In this example, you can see that the counsellor uses an open question to initiate conversation, then follows the thread of the client's thinking through pure reflection. As such, in motivational interviewing you would use approximately five reflective statements to every one open question. The open question can move things on, but we do not want to move things on too quickly. Instead, we want to unpack each area first, otherwise we can acquire too much shallow detail. Consider the following client statements in Exercise 5.4, underline the powerful, vague or emotional intense phrases in the sentence, and then consider your response. How can you reflect this back in your own words?

Helper: How have things been since we last met?	*Open Question*
Client: Things have been tough. I had another **row** with my mother.	*Powerful word*
Helper: You have been arguing.	*Unpacking*
Client: Yes, she is on **my case again** about my using.	*Vague word.*
Helper: She is putting you under a lot of pressure.	*Firming up.*
Client: Yes, she still does **not believe** that I have stopped. She is always going through my things, calling me, asking where I am, **accusing me of this or that**.	*Powerful word* *Vague word*
Helper: She still does not trust you're clean and fears the worst.	*Captures both*
Client: Yes, even if I take the dog for a walk she wants to know who I have seen and why it took so long. I know that because of my using and the things I have done in the past she has no reason to trust me. But **I am working so hard** at this and she cannot **give me a break** or even see I am doing well.	*Powerful word* *Vague word*
Helper: Your achievement is unnoticed.	*Captures both*
Client: I'm **never** going to escape this. **Never.**	*Powerful word* *repeated twice*
Helper: Right now it feels really hopeless.	
	Reflects back the feeling not the phrase.

Figure 5.3   Basic reflective listening

Exercise 5.4: Reflective listening	
Client statements	**Reflection**
1. I have been using for 10 years now and I am sick of it.	
2. When I am drinking, I am blacking out. It scares me. I don't know what I have done.	
3. I know if I keep using they are going to take my kids. I could not bear to put them through that.	
4. I know I have to stop because of my health but I will miss using so much.	
5. I don't know what to do really.	
6. Ideally I would like to go back and live with my parents.	
7. My life is such a mess. Everything is so out of control. Its just a mess.	

In example 1, 'sick of it' is important as the client stress they cannot tolerate this anymore. In example 2 the 'blacking out' and fear is important, when they are drinking they lose control and are afraid that they might have done things they would find hard to live with. In example 3, 'take my kids' stresses guilt and pain. Example 4 demonstrates the client holding ambivalence feelings. 'Have to' and 'health' shows they have concrete concerns about the impact of their use whilst at the same time 'miss' suggests that they still find something desirable in continued use. They fear the risks but do not know if they can do anything about that. In example 5, 'don't know' is given the caveat of 'really', this suggests that they have vague ideas that they are not sure about. When clients are uncertain it is surprising how the reflection back of this uncertainty prompts not only a response but the answer to their problems. In example 6, the word 'ideally' suggests the client wants what they cannot have. And in the final example 7, it is the repetition of powerful feelings that is striking. 'Mess' and 'out of control' all suggest that their situation feels overwhelming. Reflection is the art of isolating these keys inferences and echoing them back to the client in a simple and concise way.

Deeper reflections

Reflective listening does not simply want to echo back the client's statements, but wants to reach the deeper underlying meaning. It is as if we are reflecting back the 'message within the message'. This is a delicate but important aspect of reflective listening. It is also difficult and entails listening to the nuance of the client's reply. It is sometimes likened to stating what is on the tip of the client's tongue or finishing off the end of their paragraph. Read the following example. Notation is included in order to colour the way in which the client delivers their lines and what the helper picks up on.

Case Study: Deeper reflective listening

Client: [Leaning forward with their head in their hands.] I have been using for years now and it's all coming on top.

Helper: It is a serious problem.

Client: Yeah, [tears in their eyes] I just can't go on living like this. My veins are shot, I am sick of doing the prison time, I am sick of chasing scores, I am sick of knocking myself out everyday and for what? I don't even get anything out of it anymore.

Helper: You're putting yourself through hell for nothing.

Client: It is all too much. It's not like it was you know. It was a laugh to start with, everyone was doing it. Didn't think anything of using. I did not think I would end up here. Got nothing, shot to fuck. [Fixes eye contact on the helper and swallows hard.] Seen a lot of mates go over.

Helper: And you are worried that you are next.

Client: [Takes a deep breath and sits back staring upward] Well, what is the average a junkie lives? Ten years? I am past that. I am lucky to be here now. My doctor can't believe it. He said I am one of the few that is left.

Helper: Even he thinks that you cannot sustain this much longer.

Client: Yes. [Begins to cry] I don't want this anymore. I don't. But I do not know if I can do anything. I do not know if I can.

Helper: You know you have got to change, but you are not sure you can.

Client: I have given up a few times, but always gone back. So stupid.

Helper: So the real problem is not stopping but staying off.

Client: Yes, I suppose so.

You can see in each response that the helper reflects back the message in the message. The thing the client is not quite saying but is inherent in-between the lines of their answers. To do this demands that we do not 'think' about the client's answers. Sometimes, as we are listening to the client, we can think 'Ah! I know what the problem is here.' And ask the client questions which are designed to steer them towards our hypothesis. In reflective listening we simply listen to the client's answers and instead 'feel' what the client is trying to tell us. As such it relies more heavily on the emotional intelligence that we described in Chapter 3. Reflective listening is more about following a thread of the client's concerns than generating shallow descriptions of the problem. We want to cast our nets deeper to capture those irrational thoughts, feelings and concerns. We do not second guess the client's feeling, but we intimate it from the words, tone and mood of their statements. In the subsequent unravelling of these statements the client enters into deeper reasons, feelings and importantly, beliefs. As such we use reflective listening heavily when the client talks about the need for change and equally when they talk about how they can change. In this way they hear themselves talk about the need for change. Motivational interviewing works best when there is a high ratio of client to counsellor talk, especially when focused on change. This is then echoed back and affirmed in our reflective responses. Within this there are lot of prompts that we can use to keep the client focused and expanding upon change (see Figure 5.4 below).

- In what way?
- Give me an example. When was the last time it happened?
- What else have you noticed or wondered about?
- What other concerns do you have?
- Can you tell me more about that?

Figure 5.4   Helpful prompts

Motivational interviewing requires the client and counsellor to work in close harmony together. The close proximity between the client's concerns and the helper's understanding is called consonance and represents the flow of the rapport. It is essential that the helper creates this flow to be effective in the delivery of the intervention. While at the same time, the helper gently keeps the client talking about the need for change so they hear it from their own mouth.

Structuring the session

When working with clients considering change we need to expect ambivalence. It can occur at any time and we resolve it in the same way by identifying pros and cons. Alongside this, we can use reflective listening to unpack each pro and con. This can provoke deeper, contemplative conversation regarding the need for change. Usually ambivalence surfaces quickly as the client tells their opening story. It is important to get the client's opening story and ask them what has happened and what has lead them to consider change. With this in mind, when clients present for services they are usually experiencing anxiety which drives the change process. Typically people present wanting to reduce stress in their lives first and foremost. Anxiety can therefore be considered as the engine of change. Client's can be highly emotionally charged at this juncture and we need to greet this with empathy and warmth but make no attempt to mollify the crises immediately. When we listen to this story we need to explore it with reflective listening. The classic mistake that people make in practice and in training sessions is that they attempt to resolve problems far too soon. The client has not yet finished outlining their concerns when the worker is already ruminating on the solution and edging the client in the 'right' direction. However, if the client does not understand the full magnitude of the problem, why do anything to address it?

By going deeper into the client's story with reflective listening we tend to cut through strategic presentation of stories into the underlying beliefs of the client. This reduces the attribution bias that we saw in Chapter 4. At the same time, we want the client to hear themselves talk about their situation as a problem. Here we ask questions which invite the client to describe their story as a problem. Think of these questions for yourself. Consider a problem that you are having right now and answer the following questions in Exercise 5.5.

Exercise 5.5: Problem recognition questions

- In what way is it a problem for you?
- How else is it a problem?
- What makes you feel you have to do something about this problem now?
- Are there any other reasons why you need to address this?

These questions will automatically lead the client into hearing themselves talk about the situation as a problem. We then use reflective listening to both endorse and unpack what they are saying. It is not uncommon for ambivalence to surface at this point. It could be signalled by those 'Yes ... but ...' statements; hesitancy in the clients answers; or when they state a contrary position 'I want this but I am doing that'. We must remain vigilant for and respond to ambivalence in a neutral way, exploring both the pros and the cons then sum up at them end.

Once the problem is established, we can ask questions which elicit greater concern. As we have seen, problematic users often have unrealistically positive expectations of use. Not only do they believe that positive intoxication or mood states may be induced by the drug (positive reinforcement), but that they can also sedate negative moods and stress with use (negative reinforcement). These powerful reinforcing aspects need to be reduced in order to diminish the cons of change and tip the scale of change further. The negatives of use can be surfaced and strengthened by the client themselves. Asking questions about extremes is a very powerful way of eclipsing these dominant expectations and inverting them. They knock the client into the heart of the consequences that will occur with continued use (see Figure 5.5).

- What concerns you the most about all this?
- What is the most difficult thing about all this?
- What hurts the most about all this?
- What will happen if you do not change?

Figure 5.5   Amplify concern

In practice, asking one of these types of questions and exploring it with reflective listening can suffice. But we need to mine deeply into these fears and concerns, to the point where it can almost feel that we are miring the client in their own predicament. Drug and alcohol using clients will respond to these questions in very powerful ways. This will be either the problems of dependency such as death, loss of limbs; or addiction-led in terms of the loss of family, destitution or prison. These are all realities that their continued use can incur. Using reflective listening to accentuate the client's awareness of these problems and to allow them to hear themselves say this is powerful. We may notice clients find it hard to articulate the realities they are under. They may hint at them or suggest them without stating them concretely. We must remember that reflective listening can pick up on the unsaid meaning and make it concrete. This makes it difficult for clients to avoid these painful realities.

As we saw at the beginning of this chapter, crises play an important part of the change process for many clients, particularly those who are deeply embedded in use or who lack opportunity to evolve into other ways of living. This is not to say that we are cold or indifferent to the client's struggle. The deeper a client goes emotionally the greater the empathy and warmth we need to demonstrate in order to contain this level of emotional arousal. What it does mean is that we let the client think through the consequences of their behaviour for themselves. If the client is heading for rock bottom, getting them to recognise this for themselves brings the immediacy of the crisis from some distant future into the present. If they encounter the full magnitude of that now, there is both time and reason to address it rather than let them career towards the cliff edge with our soothing words still ringing in their ears. In this way we can see that motivational interviewing is a highly challenging intervention, without being highly confrontational.

This aspect of motivational interviewing is underplayed and at times even apologetic, with Miller and Rollnick's (2002) allusions to the approach being akin to Roger's person-centred counselling. At other times Miller and Rollnick are more direct in their intentions and the fact that this approach does make the client uncomfortable (Miller, 1989). It may seem unethical to induce such states in a client as it cuts across the humanistic ethos of the field. However, we cannot generate anxiety in a client. If I ask you what concerns you the most about having a hole in your sock there is no consequence for you. So no matter how much I ask you about that sock you will not develop concern. On the other hand, if I ask you about your smoking it will liberate the concern that you already have. As we have seen in Chapter 2, conflict and anxiety play an important part in life development for all of us. Conflict serves a function in life, which is to enable us to separate from old environments that we are embedded in. They were once rewarding but can no longer satisfy. The anxiety and conflict of breaking from drug and alcohol use (and the incumbent relationships, values and lifestyle that goes with it), may be no different to the other great shifts we make in our lives such as leaving the parental home; leaving unsatisfying jobs; leaving loveless relationships. None of these things is easy. The status quo is the line of least resistance. If it were not for the unbearable conflicts and anxiety that force us to separate, we never would. As a result, our greatest growth occurs in the most difficult times because we have to. This idea does not have a wide currency in counselling. Our temptation is to sedate the crisis with substitute drugs or mollify it with empathy and reassurance. But if we subdue the anxiety, we may be simply holding the person on the wrong side of the crisis.

Devil's advocate

When the client experiences deep concern we may opt to use reverse psychology to elicit more motivational statements from the client (Miller, 1989). As we saw in reactance, people tend to form opinions in contradiction to others. When the client's concern is high we can play devil's advocate to suggest not changing, so the client contradicts. Some suggested questions for this are described in Figure 5.6.

- What makes you feel that you have to do something about this now?
- Well, you have to have very high motivation to complete this programme?
- Are you really ready for change?

Figure 5.6   Devil's advocate

Even though much of motivational interviewing is delivery dependent, these questions do not sound that empathetic. Instead, over-stating the role of the drug or alcohol use in the client's life can be more subtle – *Well, you have been using for a long time now; there must be something that you really like about it?* Projecting the historical period of use into the future can also be very powerful. But again, this technique tends to work only when the client is visibly concerned about their behaviour. Apply this technique at the wrong time and it can backfire horribly.

Case Study: Adapting devil's advocate

Working in a busy needle exchange, a long term heroin user came in with their returns, sat down and looking at the worker sighed – 'Been using for seven years. I ought to think about stopping up really.' The worker remained neutral but interested.

'Can you see yourself using for another seven years?'
After a long silence he looked up and said. 'God that would be a nightmare.' They began discussing change.

Intention and optimism

Using reflective listening to chart the dimension of the problem is essential. Both self-revaluation and emotional catharsis are important in cementing the need for change. This may surface deep concerns in the client as they hear themselves talking about the need for change which generates an uncomfortable state (Miller, 1989). They can only respond to this concern in one of two ways. They can go for a risk reducing strategy of changing the behaviour to reduce the associated pressures. Or they can go for a fear reducing strategy, using more drugs and alcohol to sedate these concerns. The way to tip the anxiety towards change and not more use is the availability of a means to stop which feels manageable to the client. As such, we do not simply create negative expectations of use, but also deepen the client's opinion that they can change. Here we wish to strengthen the pros of change. Again we use reflective listening to develop the client's intention and belief that they can do this. Questions about intention, fortified with their optimism, are important. And we use reflective listening to now mire the client in their belief in the capacity to change (see Figure 5.7).

Intention

- What makes you think you can keep doing this?
- What makes you think you should stop?
- If you were 100% successful in stopping, what would be different?

Optimism

- If you decided to change what makes you think that you could do it?
- What encourages you that you can change?

Figure 5.7   Building confidence in change

Discrepancy or dissonance?

A key strategy recommended by Miller and Rollnick (2002) is the development of discrepancy in the client. This idea runs closely to the concepts of cognitive dissonance. However, Miller and Rollnick state that these ideas are different, causing some confusion in their writing. Cognitive dissonance theory was pioneered by Festinger (1957) who identified certain attitudes or behaviour change that occurred after an individual realised they were holding two contradictory thoughts. We have a basic drive towards internal consistency, so to hold certain opinions and act in contradiction to them generates acute discomfort. In Festinger's (1959) early experiments, students were invited to take part in monotonous research tests, and then paid to try and persuade another candidate (actually a stooge) that the test was interesting and worth participating in. Half were paid $1, the other half were paid $20 for doing so. Asked afterwards whether the experiment was in fact interesting those that accepted $20 dollars said it was not, those accepting a $1 said it was. Those who had accepted the high fee for lying could attribute their lying as done for the money, but those who lied for a paltry dollar could not. Therefore the research had to be interesting to make sense of their subsequent action and for them to remain internally consistent.

There are rival theories to explain this displacement, but what we see here is that the candidates shifted their opinion to match their actions. We are much more likely to do this when we have had free choice to express a contradictory opinion. In another experiment by Elkin and Lieppe (cf. Zimbardo and Leippe, 1991), students *asked* to write essays in favour of student parking fees experienced the greatest degree of attitudinal change than those that were *forced* to present a case for a change that was not in their own interest. Those that acted against their own interests voluntarily adjusted their ideals to accommodate their actual behaviour. By ideals, I mean the deeper values, beliefs and the self concepts that the client holds dear to their identity.

Miller and Rollnick's (2002) work draws upon similar discrepancy but in reverse. In dissonance research the candidates amended ideals to fit the contradictory behaviour. In motivational interviewing we elicit a disparity to change the client's behaviour to accommodate their ideals. This may operate in reverse in drug and alcohol using clients because we operate on a far more profound and global scale than the discrete and self-limited actions induced in experiments that the research subjects actually cared little about. As we have seen, existential guilt at having failed to achieve one's potential; the slow seduction into a shadow society of anti-social ethics; the realisation that use takes priority over more precious relationships; or the realisation that they are destroying a life they want to live, presents a profound contradiction between the individual's perception of themselves (their ideals) and their actions (their behaviour). When the ideals are so central to a sense of self, they may have the gravitational lure to pull behaviours in their direction, rather than vice versa. Asking questions which invite these comparisons in problem users can open up this chasm between ideal and actual behaviour, which may generate a similar experience of dissonance. In such a position, clients can only respond in a limited number of ways. Consider a time when you suddenly realised that you had neglected an important issue; semi-intentionally let someone down; or told a lie to escape an onerous task. Answer the following questions in Exercise 5.6 to identify the feeling of dissonance that we all experience at times.

The wider the discrepancy between our ideal sense of self and our actual behaviour the greater the discomfort we experience. This discomfort is physical, with symptoms that include increased heart rate, sweat, palpations, sickness and sleeplessness. The physical effects can be so acute that the dissonance can be detected on lie-detectors because it changes the way the skin conducts electricity. Research suggests that the discomfort of internal inconsistence can last from a few minutes (Losch and Cacioppo, 1990) to enduring over a period of up to two weeks (Higgins et al., 1979). It appears to be very easy to reinstate, even after a long period of time. For example, you might have felt some of that old feeling return as you completed the questionnaire.

This state is so uncomfortable that we must respond to it and try to close down these feelings. One way is to strengthen the belief that what we did was in fact ideal. Here we torture our logic to justify this position. Misattributing the cause, blaming others or circumstances may also diminish our sense of responsibility. Another way of reducing this discomfort is to minimise what we have done through trivialising the event. This entails minimising its impact; underplaying consequences; or normalising our behaviour as the same as everybody else's. This may reduce the discomfort because if the impact of actual behaviour is insignificant it can feel less disparate. Finally, to change our behaviour involves having to face others in telling the truth, apologise or make recompense.

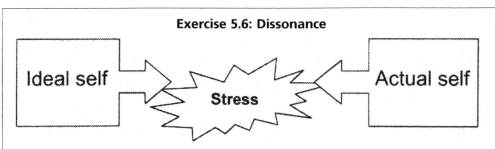

Exercise 5.6: Dissonance

- What physical sensations do you get when you recall the event?
- What kind of things could you say to yourself to strengthen the belief that what you did was actually right all along?
- What might you say to yourself to minimise what you did as not that important?
- What might you have to do to move closer to your ideal?

This demands we confront a negative or unpalatable aspect of ourselves. It is a psychological blow to our self-concept. It makes us feel the very vulnerability that our rationalising and minimising is trying to protect us from. However, of all the means to reduce this dissonance, behavioural change is probably the most effective but, at the same time, is the hardest.

In the early writings, Miller and Rollnick (1991) suggested using stark comparisons between ideal and actual behaviours to elicit the discrepancy. For example, clients who have managed to engineer their use without their life collapsing often lack the crises to impel them towards change. These high functioning addicts hover between heavy use and a life of diminished quality rather than chaos. This situation is more common in social accepted use such as alcohol, prescribed drugs and tobacco smokers. Here direct comparisons may be useful to maximise the psychological discomfort to compensate for their environmental comfort. In this it is essential to elicit their values and ideals and contrast it with their actual behaviour (see Figure 5.8).

• What is the real you like?	• What is the using you like?
• What is important to you?	• What is important when you are using?
• Who are the most important people in your life?	• Who is affected by your using?

Figure 5.8   Developing discrepancy

This comparison often makes apparent a deeper sub-conscious feeling of ill-ease which is difficult to articulate. It can also separate different aspects of the self, which allows the client to distance themselves from the unpalatable persona that no longer feels 'them'. This can occur as the life course progresses. What is Byronic in a twenty-something is boorish in a thirty-something. Age deviancy and cultural conformity legislate against such behaviours.

Case Study: Developing Dissonance

Ray had been using crack for 11 years, lived in a bare flat, his relationships broke down and he felt life was passing him by. In session he began to talk about the training he had in ornamental and architectural building work that he now neglected. Ray had wanted his own studio, saw himself as an artist and hoped one day to put his talent to use. The counsellor explored this and then asked about who he was when using. He said he turned up, did casual labouring, took the cash, disappeared for a few days on a binge and felt like he had it stamped on his forehead. He could not face anyone. He was like a selfish teenager. The counsellor then asked what he was like just after the binging. He gave people his time, money, worked for free, and accepted other people's bad behaviour without comment because of what he done. Resentment and anger would build up. He got frustrated and so would end up using again. The counsellor kept teasing apart these different characters and asked which one was really him? Ray said that were a lot of things he needed to do for himself, he wanted to achieve his full potential. Having spent a session exploring these factors the client returned the next week. 'I have gone legit, I have signed off and am declaring my earnings. I have cut off the teenager's pocket money! I meet with the architects next week about a new job.'

What we also see in this case study is an aspect of dissonance which is often over-looked in addictions work. Clients often find themselves responding to this discomfort by over-compensation rather than recognition. Many clients who report guilt and shame about their use will take on a supra-ideal self to make recompense to those that they hurt or feel they have let down. Many carers or partners report in clinical practice that when their using loved ones stop they are wonderful. This is often an attempt to reduce dissonant states, where overt and extravagant self-sacrifice for others is necessary to demonstrate one's worthiness (see Figure 5.9).

This supra-self is unsustainable. It leaves the user empty, tired, resentful and opens the way for more use and another cycle of over-compensation. We may also see this in other areas such as domestic violence, where aggression is converted into extravagant holidays or purchases to recompense the hurt caused. Again, mapping this out with a client can be helpful to them in seeing the vicious cycle that they may be trapped in. But as advised before, this may not be useful

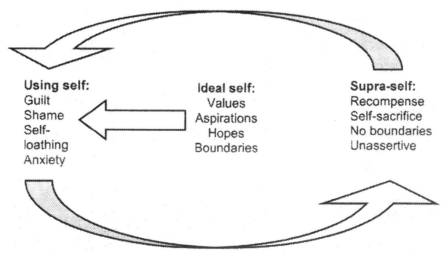

Figure 5.9 Dissonance and over-compensation

with clients with very low self-belief in their ability to change. There remains a 'comfort the afflicted and afflict the comfortable' sub-text to working on motivation, and it falls to the judgement of helper to consider how deep one can take this disparity, whilst preserving the client's perception that change is not simply necessary but possible. Miller and Rollnick (2002) recognise that this 'behaviour gap' can feel so wide that the client believes change would be so formidable that it is impossible to close.

Miller and Rollnick (2002) also advocate more subtle techniques in developing discrepancy which may be easier on the client. Here they clarify what is important to the client and then state:

> *Here we compare two possible visions of the future in direct comparison to the client's values; one in which the client has implemented the change and one where the change is not made. Again, we make no attempt to tip the client towards change. Instead we let the client gravitate towards the option that best matches, or least disrupts, cherished values and beliefs. In this way we can augment the need for change. Remember, incentive is important to change and not all incentives are material. They can be ethical or relational too.*

- What is the most important to you in this area?
- How will these things be affected by changing? Explore with reflective listening.
- How will they be affected by not changing? Explore with reflective listening.

Figure 5.10   Questions that invite discrepancy

Resistance

As we have seen, clients experiencing the discrepancy between ideal and actual behaviour undergo discomfort. The ways they can close this down are limited. These include the rationalisations and minimising that we have already seen. Furthermore the client may attempt to undermine the helper. Because if the helper is wrong in their understanding of the discrepancy, there might be no chasm that the client is impelled to cross. Resistance strategies are not the product of a denial of their reality. It is the client who sees the behaviour gap all too clearly that sparks defensive resistance. As such, we might afford denial a little more sympathy as it can be seen to have a self-protective function. A wide host of defence mechanisms have been identified (Blackman, 2004), but we must recognise that such resistance to change is not innate in the user's psychology but is a very human response to the magnitude of change. The denial ridden client often perceives the need for change, but this can feel beyond their means. Therefore, if we can work creatively with this resistance, we bring people towards change.

In motivational interviewing it is important not to confront resistance as this breeds deeper contradictions. Instead we must recognise resistance and roll with it. Whilst Miller and Rollnick (2002) have drawn upon eight key strategies to address resistance, for the novice practitioner these can be a little cumbersome to retain. Instead we can simplify dealing with resistant clients in three more basic ways. The first way is to check ourselves; are we the cause of the resistance because we are pushing change? If we are at loggerheads with the client we must back off and acknowledge our part. When having slipped into a power struggle, I have never known a client respond other than well to hearing: 'You are right, you know what you need more than I do. I am sorry. Tell me what you think needs to happen next . . .'

The second basic technique is to simply go with the client's story. If you give a little, you can get a lot more. Empathise with the resistance. Understand the value of the position to the client before bridging them out.

Case Study: Rolling with resistance

A client reached a point in the session where they suddenly backtracked on changing their use of cocaine. 'Well,' he said, 'I might lose everything. But I could get it all back. I have got a lot of skills. I am always in demand. I might lose the house, even the wife. But I could get it back again.' He looked at he counsellor with a satisfied confidence. 'You are right.' The counsellor replied. 'You could. With your background you are always going to find work.'

'Yes,' said the client, sounding a little less sure. 'There are very few people that can do what I can. And I am very well connected.'

Nodding the counsellor continued to agreed, 'It will always be there for you.' The client sat quietly. After a pause the counsellor asked. 'But tell me, is that the life you want for yourself?' The client remained very quiet.

'No. I am 48 now. I cannot keep doing this. I am too old. I can't keep going back to square one.'

'It's getting tougher to keep starting from scratch.'

'Yes, and my daughter would never forgive me . . .'

The third way of working with resistance is to stay with the reflective listening skills. Resistance statements are often wholly irrational. This means that by using this technique we can reflect back the essence of the resistance, often illuminating the limits of the thinking. We can use our reverse psychology to over-emphasise the point, prompting contradiction (see Figure 5.11).

I cannot stop using right now; I am under too much pressure.
Heroin use is making life manageable.

I cannot stop using right now; I am under too much pressure.
Heroin use is making life much more manageable.

Figure 5.11   Reflective listening and resistance

When working with resistant clients it is essential to stay with the skills. Too often, when the client makes a negative comment about the helper, it paralyses the process. Suddenly the counsellor feels that their actions are not helping and this falls short of their own ideals of being effective. This induces dissonance. The practitioner is suddenly focusing on themselves, and cannot simultaneously focus on the client and the whole process is interrupted. Staying with the skills, remaining open and responsive to the feedback of the client or just working through the client's attitude before flipping it back towards change can be a simple but effective means of keeping the client on the change track.

The decision

Once we have established an empathetic relationship, resolved ambivalence and used reflective listening to elicit and expand on concerns, we can then move to the critical moment of decision making. We pull together the relevant background detail from the assessment, summarise both the pros and cons of change and include any self-motivational statements by the client. When summing up pros and cons it is important that we use the word 'and' not 'but' as the conjunctive. When we use 'but' it tends to over rule what ever preceded it – 'On the one hand you feel this . . . but you think you should change because . . .' We want to keep it balanced, though we are tipping towards change in more subtle ways.

Case Study: Summarising and the decision to change

Marcus was a long term amphetamine using client that presented to a session reporting that he no longer wanted to stop anymore. If he could just have a big sack of amphetamine by his bed, life would be great. He could just use when he wanted and time it so that it did not disrupt his life. The counsellor agreed, and shared the fantasy with the client but wanted to test out this decision at the same time. Once they had talked it through the counsellor asked 'So, considering that you are not going to have a sack of amphetamine by your bed, how will it be then?' The ensuing session closed with the following summary.

'So, you have been using speed now for the last 15 years, and injecting it for the last four years. It played an important part in your life, lead you to meet your wife but has impacted on your mental health and ultimately led to divorce, which is really hard for you to accept even now. You said that speed gave you confidence to socialise, to get involved with bands and play live, which was important to you and at the same time it has made it increasingly difficult to manage these commitments and they always broke down leaving you feeling frustrated and depressed. You said yourself that you were sick of the old crew, the speed was poor and your parents could not support you financially anymore. You don't want to shoplift because the idea of prison scares you. So, considering all this, what do you think you are going to do about your use?' After a long pause the client replied – 'I have got to get clean.'

Asking about specific goals about use is important. It is essential that we target the drug using behaviour and the client sets a goal that they feel is relevant to them. In terms of use, there is a spectrum of goals the client can set for themselves. Whilst some treatment advocates abstinence as the only legitimate treatment strategy, there are other options. Consider the following treatment goals and what the pros and cons of each one are.

• Total abstinence	• Tapering towards abstinence
• Trial abstinence	• Trial moderation

Figure 5.12   Treatment goals

Total abstinence reduces the risks of use but it is the most formidable task to achieve. Clients may not feel ready or able for this initially. Rather than getting locked into resistance breeding conflict, working with clients' goals is important. As we saw in Chapter 3, we simply cannot impose goals that the client does not want. And, ultimately many clients may want to reduce the stresses they are under rather than make deep lifestyle change. We should consider wider goals with the client other than abstinence. Besides, as we shall see in relapse prevention later, a period of failed controlled use often prompts deeper reflection about one's use, leading to higher levels of goal setting. Motivational interviewing is useful in reducing and controlling use as well as with wholesale change. The decision must be made by the client. As we saw in the dissonance research, high choice invokes greater degrees of commitment. And the deep, public commitment to change is one of Prochaska et al.'s (1991) key mechanisms as we begin to shift out of contemplation and into preparation. They stress that the more public this commitment the greater the outcomes. Because if the client's stated ideal is change they will feel increasing dissonance should they recant and act in contradiction to this.

Tasks

After asking what the client wants to do about their problem (goal) we need to agree how they will achieve it (tasks). There are a greater diversity of services available now and also wider options in detoxification. As we saw in Chapter 4, methadone, buprenorphine and lofexidene are now widely available for opiate users. Inpatient, community and home detoxifications are also available offering varying degrees of support. Exploring the best option for the individual client is important. Understandably, they will usually want the option which elicits the least discomfort, but this may be a fallacy in that all options are strenuous in one way or another. For example, the grind of daily supervised consumption of methadone can be taxing in the extreme.

Whilst care pathways and models of care formalise the links between services of increasing intensity they may be double edged. We do not want to merely process the client through the conveyor belt of services. We must help the client identify what they feel is important in their journey to change. Furthermore, research shows that one treatment style does not work for all. Harris and Miller's (1990) research has unearthed an interesting finding. When attempting to measure treatment outcomes for those receiving support against a control group on a waiting list for help, they decided to send the control group some self-help material. What they found was that outcomes were the same for both the treatment group and the 'bibliotherapy' group. Indeed, what they concluded was that doing anything was helpful, as long as the client believed it to be beneficial. What is important is the client does things, and these things make sense to them.

The client may not know the full range of choices available to them. The worker has a much broader understanding of the support available to the client and so should present these options without prejudice. Under-selling these choices to the client is more effective than over-selling, which breeds resistance. The more choice the client has the more in control they feel, enhancing compliance. If we push the client into options we prefer they will only resist. Presenting options and inviting the client's opinion on different possibilities allows for the negotiation of the treatment plan with the client in control and making their own choices. What we will see in this is a natural difference between our late onset drinkers and our earlier onset drug users that we explored in Chapter 2. The tasks of treatment present very differently. Compare these two case studies.

Case Study: Comparison of tasks for an alcohol and a drug user in brief intervention

Case One: *A client began drinking at the age of 32, after the break up of his first marriage. He was the sole parent of a 12 year old son and his drinking had been out of control for the last 10 years. Arriving at the project in crisis, the counsellor used* *motivational interviewing skills to resolve ambivalence and develop the client's awareness of the consequences of use. In summary they asked the client what he was going to do. The client wanted to stop his drinking. Exploring how he could do that, he said he felt that he needed to get back to work, heal the rift with his family so his mother could look after his son in the day again, have a period of separation from his girlfriend to get this straight and use his spare time to get back on top of cleaning and repairing the house in the quiet time.*

Case Two: *An early onset heroin user began his drug taking career at 15. He grew up in London, but lived in an area where he only knew other users. He was very stuck, depressed and felt hopeless. He wanted to change but felt isolated and alone in his flat and that he would end up using again. After a motivational interviewing session the counsellor summed up the client's situation, asked what he would do? The client said he needed to change.*

The client said he needed to go home to London. He wanted to build on the progress he and his alcoholic mother had begun to make in rebuilding their relationship. And that he was going to sign up at a college course to get a qualification in carpentry, which he had a great passion for. The counsellor said 'Being at home can be hard, all the old family dynamics can come flooding back. Sometimes people find half-way houses helpful, to get more support and also meet a new group of people in the area. What do you make of that?'

The client considered it and thought it was a good idea. They began to look for a place in the right area that would appeal to the client.

You can see in both these case studies, that the clients did not want to follow standard care pathways, but both developed very clear and personal plans to achieve their goal. For the late onset drinker, he had the skills and experience to leave the session and go off and do these things. Indeed, he could not make his second session because he secured employment very quickly and continued to make significant gains. This may be why the preparation stage is not always apparent in an individual's change process as people turn these intentions into action immediately without the recourse for a great deal of planning. For the heroin user, this journey is more difficult. His lack of preparedness after protracted periods of exclusion since adolescence means he still needs to put a treatment and educational framework in place to support him. His treatment path is longer and deeper, and the preparation to enter into these support services is extended as the treatment path relies not on the client's own immediate efficacy but on identifying, negotiating and waiting on entry into services.

In this way we can see why motivational interviewing as a brief intervention enjoys good outcomes with late onset drinkers. For them, one brief session can equal the outcomes of 24 week psychodynamic programmes (Miller, 1992). Project MATCH, the multi-million dollar clinical trial of twelve step, cognitive behavioural therapy and motivational enhancement (a motivation interviewing based programme) demonstrated the same outcomes. The twelve step clients attended 24 counselling and group work sessions; the cognitive behavioural therapy clients attended 12 sessions; whilst the motivational enhancement clients were only offered four sessions. The non-attendance rates were approximately 25 per cent across all modalities meaning these clients made significant change in just three sessions. For the early onset drug users, the principle advantage of motivational interviewing is increasing compliance in subsequent services. Drug users who go through motivational interviewing do far better in a treatment journey which they have devised, chosen and owned for themselves (Miller and Rollnick, 2002).

Conclusion

Change is precipitated in the conflict between the positive and negative reinforcement of desired mood versus the aversive negative consequences. Paralysed between these forces the contemplative client waits for their situation to improve or deteriorate to shift the status quo of current behaviour. Crises points or opportunities often present, increasing motivation. However, it is how we as helpers respond in these moments that can determine whether these opportunities are taken or snuffed out. Recognising that motivation is incentive-led and that compliance is enhanced in the relationship can allow us to maximise our interventions at this stage. Ambivalence is the central problem here and raising the client's awareness of the pros and cons can begin to shift this balance towards change. This can be augmented by the use of reflective listening that allows the client to state their own concerns regarding the need for change. This can diminish the cons of stopping and strengthen the pros by operating on a deeper level, where values, beliefs and hopes for oneself will out trump rational argument. Such issues lie at the heart of our identity, and remaining consistent to this deeper sense of self is a basic drive in all of us. Chemical interactions, biology, social exclusion and poor self-belief may collude to create dependency and addiction, but it appears the desire to become who we really are can set people free of it. As such, increasing motivation will depend on how well we can increase the differential between the pros and the cons. Motivational interviewing has proved effective at reconciling these tensions and directing the client's concerns towards changing their consumption. In order to overcome addiction it has co-opted other strategies to develop the client's awareness of a more desirable life, which also increases the pros of change.

Chapter 6

On Preparation

There is wishful thinking in Hell as well as on Earth.
C.S. Lewis

Many problematic users are sparked into change by the crisis moment. However, the impetus for change can emerge in the opposite direction too. There appears to be a population for whom opportunity plays a more significant role than stress. For example, in the first ever self-help tract for those addicted to gin, Eliza Haywood (1750) observed that one woman managed to quit her habit through 'romances' (Dillon, 2002). If the decision to change is a balance between competing benefits and cost, then this balance may also be shifted by increasing positives of change. Whether configured as having too much to lose or so much to gain, both forces working in concert have a powerful influence on motivation. In contrast to motivational interviewing's emphasis on concern, this chapter will examine how we can strengthen motivation by cultivating the client's awareness of desirable alternatives to use. These alternatives need to feel achievable. This demands that we have the skills to fortify the client's self-belief that goals can be attained. Once again we will focus on natural remission studies and wider research to identify the underlying mechanics of change at this point in the process. We will then explore how we can best address these dynamics through the use of solution focused approaches with its emphasis on goal setting and mastery.

Preparation: a disputed stage

The preparation stage of change has the most chequered history. In the early work of Prochaska and DiClemente (1986) it appears as determination. This was a high state of resolve to put change into place. Even then, it was noted that people did not move uniformly from contemplation to determination, but could leapfrog straight into the action. A smoker who receives a diagnosis of heart disease might immediately quit without pause. Determination has now been succeeded by preparation. It is not defined by mechanisms of change but by the assumption that the client will change in 30 days. This seems prophetic and does not marry well with the other stages which are defined by distinct clusters of behaviours. This has been a source of criticism of the stage model (Sutton 2001). But equally, this uncertainty, as to whether preparation exists, is also reflected in the natural remission research and illustrates mitigating factors surrounding this stage of change.

One of the most famous natural remission studies conducted on heroin users was based on Vietnam War veterans returning to the US (Robins et al., 1980; Robins, 1993). This research highlighted that although 50 per cent of GIs were addicted to heroin in Vietnam, on returning home to their normal lives they simply quit their use without any recourse to formal treatment. The drastic environmental change made continued use redundant for these servicemen. When these GIs were flooded with the opportunities to get on with life the majority just stopped using. What is striking is that these veterans appeared in no way different to other users. Labouvie's (1996) aging out studies found that as individual users became more embedded in pro-social relationships across the life course their use faded. Stall and Biernaki (1986) found a different kind of opportunity prompted change in problem users. In their studies it was often a miraculous event that precipitated change, such as avoiding a prison sentence or a lucky near-miss in use which was interpreted as a significant sign to change. For Klingemann's (1991) cohort, 37 per cent of alcohol users and 50 per cent of the heroin users gradually ceased use and were not particularly conscious of the process of change at all. They too became immersed in other pursuits that simply become more of a priority in their lives.

Klingemann (1991) did recognise that conscious self-changers were characterised by one specific issue. Once the decision to change is made the user experiences a profound shift in stress. Rather than the external pressures they have had to outmanoeuvre when they were actively using, they now face a more difficult problem: confronting themselves. This increased the internal stress in the individual. This shift in stress levels is interesting and occurs when the change process reaches a critical juncture. The first half of the stages of change is dominated by *thought* processes such as raising awareness of pros and cons, self-re-evaluation, decision-making and commitment. Inviting clients to do anything in these earlier stages will yield little return. Once we cross the threshold from intention into action, thinking is no longer useful. It is what the client *does* that is important. The behavioural tasks of remaining drug free and rebuilding one's life in light of an uncertain future is far more demanding than merely thinking about it. Having made a commitment to change, clients now face the uncertainty of whether they can actually do it. Self-doubt is the product of the shift in demand.

Preparation and exclusion

The ease of this shift from intention into action may be determined by the degree of exclusion experienced by the user. For example, Biernaki (1983) found that those problem users who preserved connections to the non-using social groups could simply extend these existing relationships as part of their natural recovery. Conversely, those who were completely immersed in the shadow society of use had to reconstruct relationships from scratch. As a result, a new personality emerged in these recovering individuals that did not appear to exist prior to their addiction. This is a far more formidable task. So, for those with lower usage, high self-belief and preserved attachment to social structures of life the implementation of change is straightforward. Their partial connection to pro-social groups means that they remain in a position where enriching opportunities may still be available to them. And they may not even be cognizant that their priorities are shifting as they take up these opportunities.

In contrast, those who are high using, have low-self belief, and are wholly immersed in the shadow society of their use have a low probability of spontaneous opportunities challenging their consumption. For example, the individual who is using crack, heroin and is street homeless is unlikely to be offered meaningful employment or find love. If they want change they will have to identify opportunities and engineer the attainment for themselves. And even then, this may only be fully accomplished after more strenuous effort to detoxify. The necessity of preparation for change may be determined by the relative social exclusion of the particular client.

Certainly, clients who are committed to change become more future oriented. This takes both pragmatic and personal dimensions. Exploring detoxification options and strategies that we saw in the previous chapter becomes a central preoccupation. Besides this run deeper existential questions. Drug or alcohol use has become a dominant force in shaping their identity, relationships and purpose in life. The negative stress that compels change does not automatically drive the client into a more creative direction. The void that will be left through cessation needs to be filled with more desirable alternatives to use. As such, when working with change we need to establish two goals for the client (Gossop, 2003). What they want to do about their use in the short term, but also, what life they want for themselves in the long term. This is often over-looked but important. Diminishing the negative consequences of use alone tends to reduce motivation. To simply stop using without reconstructing one's life will end in failure because the factors that sustain use continue unabated. We have seen how motivational interviewing has addressed the decision to change substance use. We need to build on this by considering the life that will replace it. Therefore we must increase the benefits of change by helping the client map out their preferred future without drug and alcohol use. This new life needs to be culpably more attractive than what they have had. No one will put effort into change to be worse off than they are.

The creation of a more desirable alternative to use is more difficult for clients who have experienced high exclusion. Low self-belief in their capacity to change; the lack of preparedness for the every day demands of life; and their low self-expectancy can conspire to create self-defeating expectations even before the change process begins. The challenge for the helper working in the preparation stage is to help clients identify these more desirable alternatives to use and maximise their self-belief in attaining them. This will serve as an antidote to doubts that can derail change. The clearest articulation of these helping tasks is set out by solution focused therapy. This is a forward looking, pragmatic intervention whose central concern is what the client wants, instead of their problems, and how they can achieve this.

Solution focused therapy

The solution focused approach has emerged as a model in its own right and as an adjunct to motivational interviewing in the treatment of addiction. This chapter will explore the solution focused approach as a distinct approach. This will offer a deeper theoretical understanding of the intervention. So, whilst motivational interviewing aligns itself closely with the stages of change model, solution focused therapy acknowledges this framework but has developed its own terminology to describe the readiness of clients. This nomenclature broadly correlates with Prochaska and DiClemente. They separate clients into three distinct sub-groups (Berg, 1989). *Visitors* are people who are sent to see us by others or those who have to be seen to be doing something. As such they may be considered pre-contemplative. *Complainers* are those who want to ventilate feelings about their situation but do not necessarily want to change it. (This is seen as a legitimate human activity, but it is to be shared with friends and family rather than the counselling room.) These individuals equate to the contemplation stage. For solution focussed therapy, the *customer* is someone who has a goal and wants to do something about this. This supposes that the decision to change has been made but the means to achieve has not. Whilst solution focused therapy has produced strategies for pre-contemplative customers and contemplative complainants, it is the goal seeking client whose is preparing for change who is best suited to the approach.

Problem free talk

Solution focused therapy marks a radical departure from the assumptions of traditional counselling approaches. To understand this we must consider the basic assumptions which underpin it and compare them to traditional models. This is not to say that other approaches are wrong, but serves to highlight a profound revision of practice suggested by solution therapy. In Exercise 6.1, consider the list of questions in each column. What is different in the questioning styles of column A compared to column B? Answer the following questions to identify what is different.

Exercise 6.1: Comparison of questioning styles	
Column A	**Column B**
How long has this been a problem? How does it feel? When did you start using? When do you use the most? What happened when you were young? How old were you when you started using? Why do you think that you use? Tell me about the difficult times. Is this pain still with you? When does it hurt the most?	What is your goal in coming here? When is the problem not happening? What do you want to be different? If you could have anything what would it be? How did you overcome that? What did you learn from that which could be useful now?
What is different about these questions?	
What does the counsellor want to find out by these questions?	
What does the client end up talking about?	
How does the client end up feeling?	

Comparing these two columns we see that there is no such thing as a neutral inquiry in helping relationships. Questions are always loaded with suppositions which lead the client in a direction. Questions in column A are primarily about feelings and the past. Traditional therapy styles are often deeply concerned with historically difficult, painful or traumatic times. The assumption is that feelings are linked to behaviour. Thus, if we wish to help the client to address problematic behaviours, we must find the cause. And the cause may be locked in specific traumas that shape the client's current behaviour. The role of the helper is to fish for the 'real issue' behind the client's maladaptive behaviour in the hope of isolating the impulsive fears that remain active in the client's present life.

This demands that the client must discuss the most painful and difficult moments of their lives once again. They end up talking about their hurt, failures, helplessness and powerlessness. As a result, we may induce the very same feelings that we are attempting to lift. Talk to someone about their depression and they start to feel depressed; talk about their anxiety and they feel anxious; and talk about their use and they get cravings. This is because the human brain stores memories of like together (Lewis et al., 2000). Therefore, when we talk about painful times it lights up other memory circuits of pain. Not only that, but this signal will switch off positive memories. So when we are down we tend to remember other depressing times and when we are up-beat we tend to remember other up-lifting times.

Steve de Shazer was working at the Milwaukee family therapy centre and set a homework task for families to notice when the problem they sought to address was not happening. He noticed that when clients returned they could describe these other times and as a result they felt more positive, confident and clear. Dr Shazer then began to formulate other questions which assumed the client had the skills and ability to find solutions. We notice that questions in column B are concerned with the future. They are goal orientated and elicit the client's resources to solve problems. As a result the client does not discuss how they are overcome by more powerful external forces, but instead how they themselves overcome external forces. The biggest shift here is that De Shazer (1985, 1994) suggested that understanding the *cause* of the problem simply does not abate the problem. Instead, he looked to engage the client's own resources in implementing the solution they wanted, regardless of the cause. He reiterated the therapeutic curve effect in Chapter 3, where early gains were essential to client retention. As a result he suggested that the sooner we create these solutions the better the outcomes.

By talking about solutions and strengths the client describes their skills and resources. We draw upon the client's abilities, leaving them hopeful, optimistic and engendering self-belief in their ability to manage the demands of change. Dwelling on positive mood states invokes other positive memories. Selectively attending to one's success at performing a task appears important in developing self-belief, especially in the early phase of skills acquisition. This was demonstrated in a number of unrelated experimental conditions by Dowrick (1983) and Schunk and Hanson (1989). These researchers used video footage in teaching. They showed that editing film footage of people performing new tasks influenced subsequent performance. Footage that showed them getting the tasks right increased their performance whilst showing them getting it wrong decreased performance. Filming participants is not the only way to influence performance. In an experiment by Weinberg et al. (1979) bogus negative and positive feedback was given to competitors in stamina trials. Those who were told they had demonstrated superior ability outperformed those who had been informed they had less ability. When the physical demands were increased, our bogus positive group tried harder whilst the negative feedback group simply gave up. What we can see in these experiments is that success is dependent on maximising resources rather than dwelling on failures.

To put this to the test consider a problem that you have had recently that is solved. Answer the following questions in Exercise 6.2 as deeply as you can, recalling how it was when the problem was happening and then when it was resolved.

Exercise 6.2: Comparison of problem and solution questions		
	During the problem	**When it was resolved**
What were you feeling?		
What were you thinking?		
How were you acting?		
If I was to see you at this time, what would I notice that was different about you?		

Can you feel a different emotional tempo when describing these answers? Did you re-experience the problem mood against the levity of the solution mood? Solution focused therapy is often thought to be a shallow model because it is not concerned with the past. This is a mistake. Instead it invests in securing the detailed dimensions of the solution. Within this solution focused approach theorists vary in their willingness to engage in problems. Whilst De Shazer (1985) allowed his clients to talk about their problems, he would never ask about them directly. Whilst at the other end of the spectrum, Lipchick (2002) works more directly with the underlying emotional life of the client. She suggests that clients need to tell their stories and ventilate feeling. But we get alongside them to bridge them out into what needs to be done.

Solution focused assumptions

It can be very difficult to move the client out of their problems and towards solutions. I once set a depressed client with low self-worth a homework task. Before he went to sleep each night he was to identify one thing he had done that he was proud of that particular day. He looked at me blithely and said, 'Oh, I do that. I keep a diary.' I asked what he wrote about and he said that every night he wrote down all the bad things he did in CAPITAL LETTERS AND UNDERLINED THEM ALL. Recording his vicissitudes in such meticulous detail only served to educate him in his problems. Whilst not every client goes to such extremes, it is common for people to be drawn towards 'problem talk' at the expense of all else. As a result, they are so painfully aware of their troubles that they find it difficult to comprehend any solutions. Clients may also readily engage in discussing their problems in order to cultivate a deservedness that exonerates rather than changes them. Within this there is much that they are already doing towards change which they do not recognise.

'Problem talk' is often compounded by the helper trained in listening out for problems. We miss resourcefulness when drawn to troubles. Solution focused therapy demands a profound shift in the helper's thinking. Instead of seeing the client as the victim of external forces that cannot be controlled, we see our clients as resilient at all times. After all, every story the client tells about themselves is double sided. They cannot tell us stories of adversity, pain and suffering without also telling us of overcoming, perseverance or endurance. Our clients' stories are rich with the resources that they do not recognise, as problems bully their way into their attention. The role of the helper is to bring these resources into the client's awareness.

In order to do this, solution focused practitioners resists stock systems or rigid frameworks in which to help clients. This is because the solution focused approach is primarily a frame of mind where the helper abandons a preoccupation with problems in order to focus on solutions. Developing an ear for the client's resources demands that we work from a position of *not knowing* (Anderson and Goolishan, 1992). This means that we must be perennially curious about how the client does things. Our *not knowing* and desire to learn from the client keeps the focus on drawing out their expertness. When they educate us about their resources they also educate themselves. Even when the client makes their first appointment, the solution focused worker will set a different tone by asking the skeleton key question – 'Between now and when we meet I would like you to think of one of things you definitely want to keep happening . . .'

This curiosity is specific to each client's own experience. Solution focused therapy is not treating addiction, but each client's own experience of addiction (Berg and Miller, 1992). The effectiveness of counselling has never been determined by its solemnity. Rather strengths, warmth and humour are all important ingredients in the helping process. Not only does it take on a different tone but it has also evolved its own core assumptions of practice, and these are integral to the delivery of solution focused therapy. These assumptions provide the guiding principles of practice which are flexible, creative and responsive rather than prescriptive. Solution focused therapy can be described as a broad church, with variations on these themes amongst solution theorists. In order to deepen our grasp of each assumption, we will follow Walter and Peller's overview (1992). For each assumption there is question which invites you to relate the concept to your own life (see Table 6.1).

Joining the client

The first meeting with the client in solution focused work is to get the opening story and the background to the client's life. This involves getting to know the client, how they think and what they are wanting from their sessions. We may differ in the degree to which we allow the client to speak about their problems. If we have used motivational interviewing approaches with them we need not review them so deeply, but at a first meeting greater ventilation of feelings should be allowed for. But the solution work can still begin immediately. The helper can listen for the heroic story; the strengths of the client; any activities the client enjoys and even pre-session change. It has been well documented that making an appointment to see a professional is one symptom of change amongst many (Talmon, 1990). Exploring any changes the client has made in concert with seeking help can begin to highlight their resources and what works for them. Good opening exploratory questions are outlined in Figure 6.1.

- What brings you here today?
- How can I help you?
- What have you noticed about the problem since you made the appointment to come?
- How would you know coming today was really worthwhile?

Figure 6.1   Opening questions in solution focused therapy

Table 6.1 Assumptions of solution focused therapy

Assumptions of solution focused therapy	Consideration
1. Advantages of a positive focus Focusing on the positives, on the solution, and on the future facilitates change in the desired direction. Therefore focus on solution oriented talk rather than on the problem.	How does it feel when you recall a previous success or achievement in your life?
2. Exceptions suggests solutions Exceptions to every problem can be created by the therapist and the client, which can be used to build solutions. With drug and alcohol problems, whenever the client is not using, suggests that they have skills to make that happen.	Think of a problem in your life that is happening right now, when does it not happen?
3. Nothing is always the same Change is occurring all the time. Sometimes the problem is that there is too much change in our lives.	How much has your life changed in the last two years?
4. Small change is generative Small change leads to larger changes. In this way we need to get the client on track, which will lead to other opportunities, which taken, lead to others.	How did you end up in your current job?
5. Co-operation is inevitable Clients are always co-operating. They are showing us how they think change takes place. As we understand their thinking and act accordingly, co-operation is inevitable.	How do your clients tell you when you are getting it right or wrong?
6. People are resourceful People have all they need to solve their problems. People may appear as though they are barely coping, but they are always coping.	Think of a client who has surprised you by making great changes. What did they do?
7. Meaning and experience are inter-actionaly constructed We have experience, and we must interpret that experience for ourselves. There is no outside reality beyond our own interpretations.	Think of something that you once valued or believed in but have since changed?
8. Recursiveness Actions and descriptions are circular. Drugs and alcohol are a solution that is no longer helping but people are doing more of it, causing more problems, leading them to more use.	When you are under pressure, what do you do more of to manage it?
9. Meaning is in the response The meaning of a message lies in the person receiving it. We need to be clear what we are broadcasting to our clients.	Have you followed an instruction from someone else that was mis-communicated?
10. The client is the expert Therapy is a goal orientated or solution focused endeavour, with the client as the expert. Our clients know what they need and how they can achieve it. Our skill is not in providing the answers, but finding their resources.	How many workers have come up with great ideas to change your clients? How many have ever worked?
11. Unity Any change in how the client describes a goal and their future direction will influence others. Locked in a web or relationships of use or non use, if one person changes it forces a change in others.	How has a change that you have made in your life affected others in your family?
12. Treatment group membership The members of a treatment group are those who share a goal and state their desire to do something about making it happen.	What do your clients all have in common?

We can further build on this by asking the client what they want from us. If they have sought help before we might explore what the previous helper missed. Asking what the client was worried about in coming to the session might highlight concern and indicate what kind of relationship they need from us. Certainly asking outright, 'What could I do that would really screw this up for you?' will often bring a smile and an answer about what this client wants.

Treatment goals

As we saw earlier, increasing positive motivation is essential for the problematic drug and alcohol user to maintain change despite decreasing negative consequences. Negotiating the goal of the treatment at the outset is an important part of the solution focused process. It sets the tone of the rest of the session by keeping the client focused on what they are working towards. This goal needs to be very concrete so that they will know when they have reached this point. Framing the goal within the context of the length of the support you are offering can help shape this further, 'Well, we have six sessions to work together, what would you like to be different by that time?' Typically most clients seek counselling to reduce those negative forces in their lives, such as the consequences of their use; the impact it has had on their mental health; or have to work to keep legal or social services at bay. However, in solution focused therapy goals are more specific than this. It has its own clear criteria for what constitutes a workable goal. Whilst these can vary amongst different solution focused approaches they share core features. The criteria for goal setting outlined in Table 6.2 is based on Berg and Miller's criteria (1992).

This goal criteria appears complex at first glance. But each one is defined by simple questions which can firm up vague notions. Consider a problem that you have at the present. Work through the following questions to see if you meet the criteria for a well defined goal. In practice we would not do this in such a robotic way but tease out the facts and the details. Goal setting is a process of negotiation moving from these questions. Answer as many questions as you can in Exercise 6.3. If you cannot meet the full criteria it is not a problem. There are no such things as inflexible clients, only inflexible workers (De Shazer, 1995).

If you worked through this goal criteria and could answer every question fully, you will see that solution focused therapy makes the client work hard to create an alternative vision of what they want. As a result, this approach can be disorientating for the worker. Solutions working often take us so far away from the comfort zone of the perennial problems we are so well versed in, towards the idiosyncratic aspirations of the client. We are no longer discussing drugs, mental health, loss or distress. Instead we may be discussing qualifications in film studies, the desire for more solitude, setting up a motorcycle business or even love. We may not feel hardened substance use workers but traders in (im)possibility. This process must be guided by the natural curiosity of the helper as one can never legislate for what form the client's goals will take.

Wishes or complaints

If a client cannot fulfil the criteria for a well formed goal it is up to the helper to adjust their approach. This means we must not only be good at the central task of solution work, but also have subsidiary skills to support those that struggle with these questions. Clients may find it difficult to formulate the treatment goal for many reasons. Inviting some clients to consider the alternatives to the problem before they have vented feelings around it is often met with retreats

	Exercise 6.3: Shaping well formed goals	
Criteria	**Questions**	**Answers**
Problem:		
The presence of something	What would you be doing instead?	
Small	What will be the first sign that you are achieving this?	
Concrete, specific and behavioural	What will you be doing specifically to make this happen?	
Salient	What will be important to you about achieving this?	
A beginning rather than an end	When you leave here, and start this, how will you get on track?	
Realistic and achievable	Is this goal in your control? What is down to you?	
Involves hard work	Achieving anything takes hard work and perseverance, how will you know it is working for you? How would you know you were off track, and what would you do?	

into their struggles. Visitors or complainants may not have any clear goals at all. However, they may be 'hidden customers'. They may recognise a need for change but are unable to identify what form this change should take (Berg and Miller, 1992). Alternatively, some clients' goals are simply so vague that we need to firm their unspecified wishes for themselves. These are the clients who want to be 'happy', 'better', more 'able to deal with' the stressed they are under.

One way of helping clients formulate concrete goals is to use scaling questions. Here we ask the client to rate themselves on a scale of one-to-ten with regard to their situation, with one being at its worst and ten being at its best. We can then use the scales to calibrate what specifically contributes to the desired wish. For example, some clients want to be 'happier' but do not know what will make this concrete. We can ask the client to rate their current happiness on a scale of one-ten, with ten being at their most happy. Let us say a particular client gives a rating of four. We can ask them what makes it a four? What is life like when it is less than a four? What is life like when it is better than a four? By raising the bar on their happiness we are asking them to fill in the concrete detail of an abstract concept. Try this on yourself on the scaling map in Exercise 6.4.

Table 6.2   Criteria for a well formed goal (Berg and Miller, 1992)

Goals must be in the positive
A goal must be something that the client is doing as opposed to something that they are not doing. Typically, clients are apt to tell us what they want to stop being a problem. They do not want to be using; they do not want to be arguing with their partner; they do not want to be depressed. It is impossible to envisage yourself not doing something. But if the client is no longer drinking, arguing or being depressed some behaviour must replace it. Therefore it becomes important to identify what the client wants to be doing instead. And in identifying what it is that they will be doing instead, we begin to formulate concrete goals.

Goals must always be salient to the client
The goal should be what the client wants rather than ought to have. As such it must be meaningful to the client first and foremost, and not the helper or the programme. If the benefits of achieving the goal mean little to the client there will be no incentive to work towards it.

Goals should be small and manageable
Clients are more likely to engage in tasks that they are confident in completing. Large scale macro-goals – 'I will never drink again' can feel too out of reach to most clients.

A beginning rather than an end
Delaying the first joint until household chores are done; going to the gym in the week instead of smoking crack; walking a route that takes in a park rather than a bar on the way home from work; or seeing family instead of going out on Saturday night are all more manageable forms of self-control. These small changes can build to significant change over time. The client may have a larger macro-goal of abstinence, reuniting with family and regaining employment, but the solution approach wants the client to get on track with smaller steps.

Goals are well formed
Clients should not define their goals in broad terms such as to be 'happier', 'getting on better' or feeling 'less stressed'. When clients offer vague goals, there can be no way of telling when these goals have been achieved. As a result, the counselling process can become needlessly protracted as the helper and client deliberate over whether ethereal concerns have been addressed. Goals are defined, concrete activities. Vague wishes need to be unpacked to get the specific detail. How would you know you were happy? What would you be doing when you were getting on better? How would you know you were less stressed?

Goals must also be realistic
The client must be able to achieve the goal in the normal course of their life. This is a difficult area for the practitioner to judge. There may be significant disagreement between the client and the helper on issues such as controlled use. For example, the helper may feel controlled use seems unrealistic for some clients. The arbitrator of this is whether the goal is determined by the client. For example, a client may want to be re-united with an ex-spouse who has left them. This is not necessarily going to happen despite their best efforts to get clean. Empathising and reflecting on this difficulty can be helpful, before acknowledging that this is not going happen and moving on to more manageable goals.

Change is hard work
It is very important to stress this for several reasons. Firstly any past failures can be re-attributed to having not applied enough effort, which can change this time. Secondly, should the client suffer setbacks, it normalises the failure and can help foster greater perseverance necessary to continue by demanding greater effort. Thirdly, it negates other people who criticise or claim that simply saying no or staying with the programme will resolve all their problems. It can also serve to emphasise that change is driven by the client.

Exercise 6.4: Scaling goals

Consider your general happiness at the moment, on a scale of 1–10, with one being at your worst and 10 being at your very happiest.

- What makes it . . .?
- What is it like when it is lower?
- What is it like when it is higher?
- What else?
- What else?
- What would raise it 1 point?

This scaling approach can also be usefully employed in the life audit sheet from Chapter 4, if the client struggles to identify areas of improvement. Scaling questions offer a more systematic approach to assessing the client's life. But we must remember that in solution focused therapy we still need a central treatment goal that the client is working towards.

Hypothetical questions

For clients that still find it hard to formulate a treatment goal we can use the hypothetical frame. This is a technique which invites the clients to describe a hypothetical world where the problem is resolved. It aims to open up the possibility of the solutions actually happening. The most famous aspect of this is the miracle question that invites the client to consider that a miracle unfolds whilst they sleep and all their problems are resolved (Berg and Ruess, 1998). It then asks the client to describe what their waking and subsequent day would be like instead of having problems. This imagined day represents the outline of their goal. The pace and phrasing of the question is important. The first word, 'suppose', the slow pace and low tone of the question are aimed at inviting the client to suspend disbelief and consider their problems gone. Furthermore, no specific problem is referred to. The effect is to open up the limits of the clients thinking and not narrow them down to just a facet of their life (see Figure 6.2).

The question is powerful and usually catches clients by surprise. Leaving a long pause for them to answer is important. You can anticipate a deep response if the client pauses too and their eyes look to the horizon. Here the client is envisaging a response and should not be interrupted, no matter how long it takes. The follow up questions elicit what this world would be like in detail. They aim to establish what the client will be doing once the problems are gone. As such it must contain their thoughts, feelings and behaviours. We can reframe the event from an external perspective by asking what their loved ones or work colleagues would notice that was different too (Walter and Peller, 1992). 'What else?' will once again make the client work in fleshing out the detail of this other life. This is vital when working with addictions. The answer will be the germ of who they will be instead of the drug user they were. As such, the answer needs to be clear, concrete and more importantly, attractive to them.

We have to be careful because even as people describe their miracle they may describe what is not happening. It is easy for clients to slip back into telling us their problems. Gently asking 'But, what would it be like instead?' can keep the client on track with the task. At other times the client

> *Suppose when you slept tonight (pause), a miracle happens and the problems that brought you here today are solved (pause). But since you are asleep you do not know that the miracle has happened until you wake up tomorrow. What will be different tomorrow that will let you know this miracle has happened and the problem is solved?*
>
> - *What were you feeling?*
> - *What were you thinking?*
> - *How were you acting?*
> - *What would your partner/parents/children/goldfish notice about you that was different?*
> - *If I was to see you at this time, what would I notice about you?*

Figure 6.2   The miracle question (Berg and Ruess, 1998)

will pre-empt an answer with the observation that nothing can ever be perfect in life. Here we can compliment their realism and still encourage their 'flawed' miracle. What is striking in practice is that very often the client will give very humble answers to the miracle question. But even those that seem fantastic can be earthed to more everyday wants.

Case Study: The miracle question

Shelia was a single mother who was drinking heavily and suffering from depression. She felt very powerless in her life and reported just wanting to give up. 'So, suppose a miracle were to happen when you went to sleep to night, and all these problems were solved. How would you know when you woke up the next day?'

'I would have won the lottery!' she exclaimed.

'How much would you win?'

'Not much, about £17 million.'

'That is a lot to me! What would you spend the money on?'

'A big rambling house, walled with a huge garden and lots of rickety rooms.'

'Detached or semi-detached?'

'Detached, out in the country.'

'And what would be so great about all this for you?'

'I would have solitude.'

'Is solitude something that you need in your life right now?' She nodded, and spoke about how the demands of her family meant she had no time to herself, to do what she felt was important, and felt life was slipping through her fingers. 'So, if you had more time to focus on the things that are important to you, do you think this would be a helpful goal?' She agreed that this is what she needed. 'So, has there been a time when you have felt a little closer to this . . .?

The miracle question will give the client clues as to what needs to happen for change to occur as it focuses on the solution to a problem rather than a problem that needs solving (Berg, 1994). But sometimes we work with clients who want what they cannot have. Asking for their miracle may elicit a goal that is beyond their power to control or influence. In this situation we can ask a different hypothetical question. The deathbed scenario asks the client to project themselves forward to a future point in time and reflect back on this problem. How will it appear to them in twenty years time? This perspective often reveals dramatic shifts in thinking and comprehending the problem simply by changing the temporal perspective.

Case Study: The death bed scenario

A heavy amphetamine using client could not come to terms with his divorce. Two years later he was using more heavily than ever and would still cry at the sound of his ex-wife's name. He had even been discharged from a rehab for failing to make any progress on this issue. Now, he felt in complete despair. Not even the professionals could help him. In session, his keyworker was wary of asking the miracle question, knowing the client's miracle would be that his wife would be beside him. So, after listening empathetically, he asked. 'So when you're 73, and you're shuffling down to the post office to collect your pension, will you still be crying at the sound of her name then?' The client paused, laughed and said no. 'What will be different then?'

'Well, I hope that I will have moved on. Met someone else. Maybe even have raised a family of my own by then.'

'So you feel there is time when you will have over come this loss?'

'Yes, I guess. At some point. I have to start getting my life back together some time.'

'So, looking back, when you're 73, how might you see this time then?'

' [Long pause] I guess, as a time when everything came apart. When I came apart.'

'And what did you do?'

'I started again. Right from scratch. Rebuilt everything. I would be proud of that.'

'Are there any times now when you feel a little like you are rebuilding everything, from scratch?'

'Yes. Dog walking. I always used to have dogs, but I can't in my flat at the moment. But I have been thinking about become a volunteer dog walker for the local animal trust.'

Berg and Reuss (1998) have developed a fall back position for clients who cannot find goals, miracles or exceptions. They stress it is only to be used in these circumstances. They report that these clients are often waiting for things to get worse before they will initiate change. In response to this they have developed the nightmare scenario which is reverse of the miracle question (see Figure 6.3). It asks the client to envisage the worst case scenario if things continue as they are.

Just like the miracle question, the detail is unpicked. What would this be like? How does it feel? Who else does it affect? Then it can be converted into nightmare exceptions. Is some of this nightmare happening now? What is that like? All the same parameters are explored but in context to this worse case scenario. We can then ask, 'What would you need to do to stop the nightmare from happening?' And we are back into solution mode. What we can see here is that the nightmare scenario is more akin to the motivational interviewing skill of raising concerns. So for the very stuck client, stepping back into the negative intensity of the problem may elicit motivation

Suppose that when you went to bed tonight (pause), sometime in the middle of the night a nightmare occurs. In this nightmare all the problems that brought you here today suddenly get as bad as they can possibly get. This would be a nightmare. But this nightmare comes true. What would you notice tomorrow that would let you know you were living a nightmare life?

Figure 6.3   The nightmare scenario

to escape the undesirable before linking this back to the positive alternative of what they would want their life to be like instead.

Whilst the stock questions of miracles and nightmares are useful, there is also a danger in deploying them. As we saw in reactance, being forewarned is to be forearmed. The first time the client hears these questions they can be powerful. But on hearing a second or third time they become repetitive. They lose their novelty and with it their power. Clients will have arguments to counteract the technique. It is important to remember the function of the question is to open up possibility. These questions aim to knock the client out of an orbit of thinking that that is not working for them. Understanding this is important because it means we can devise our own 'hand grenade' questions to interrupt the client's stuck thinking. Making these questions relevant to the client's own story can increase their power and means the technique slips under their conscious awareness (see Figure 6.4).

To a woman feeling that nothing good ever happened in her life:
If that phone was to ring right now and it was really good news, what would it be?

To a young woman suffering from obesity, going to the gym, feeling self-conscious and hating it:
Well, if that gym got burnt to the ground tonight and there was no more of it, what would you do then?

To young heroin users thinking about change:
Well, if all this conflict in the Middle East got so bad that the heroin supply routes were cut, and there was no more gear, what would you do then?

Figure 6.4   Adapting the miracle question

The importance of the treatment goal lies in not only creating a clear target for the client to work towards, but also in creating the treatment goal in as much detail as possible so that the client will be able to recognise when they no longer need professional help. Whilst this may be a longer term process for many, it nonetheless ensures that the client is moving towards their own autonomy rather than more treatment. It implicitly and explicitly recognises that the client can and will achieve this independence in the world where their own relationships and aspirations will sustain them. It must always be remembered that the helping relationship is a poor substitute for loved ones and personal fulfilment.

Session goals

The first session in solution focused therapy is usually dedicated to the establishment of the treatment goal. This is what the client will want to have achieved by the end of their sessions with us. But as sessions unfold we need to identify the sub-goals that will lead us towards the ultimate outcome. The *session goal* is established at the start of each meeting to ascertain what part of the solution the client wishes to work on next. The session goal is always what the client feels is the next step they must take. One obvious session goal that demands attention is to consider what the client will do in order to manage or reduce their current consumption. If you have used motivational interviewing to achieve a clear goal around changing consumption, then the session goals can be used to monitor and evaluate progress. Session goals can be implemented immediately by those with substance misuse problems that do not require medically supervised detoxification. Clients who have alcohol problems as opposed to clinical dependence; crack and cocaine users; cannabis users; nicotine smokers; and those using amphetamine can begin to put this plan into direct action. For those with higher support needs the detoxification experience can also be included but any reductions will have to consider medical support. So for those clients who are dependent on alcohol, benzodiazepines and heroin any session goals regarding reductions need to be conducted in tandem with medical advice and an agreed timetable.

The scaling technique can again be used to help clients firm up session goals when they are unsure of their next step. Often used at the start of subsequent sessions, it asks the client to rate their own sense of progress since the last meeting (see Figure 6.5). On a scale of one-to-ten, where would they rate themselves last week, and then this week, this will give an idea of the client's progress. Then they are invited to consider what would raise this bar another point? The step up can be determined by the client's confidence. With a client with low self-belief we might ask what would raise it by half a point. For more confident clients we might set a higher step. The achievement of this step will be the session goal. Once again we ensure that the session goals are always as concrete as possible.

Again, solution focused therapy corroborates with motivational interviewing in allowing the clients to set their own goals with regard to abstinence or controlled use. Its deployment of session goals to break the treatment journey into smaller, more manageable units and constant reviewing of current progress against agreed targets lends itself well to the detoxification management. Gains can be trumpeted whilst setbacks addressed quickly and in line with the clients own want. This can be augmented further by solution focused facilitation of the client's own resources as a means to achieve their goals. Of course, this is not limited to the management of withdrawal but to the attainment of other positive gains in achieving their ultimate goal.

Direct questions to establish session goal:

- You have done a lot since we last met, how can we build on this?
- What do you want to be different after this session?
- How would you know that it was worthwhile coming here today?
- If I got run over by a bus tomorrow and we could not meet again, what would you have wanted to achieve by then?
- What is the next step?
- These changes you have put in place are great, where do we need to go next?

Scaling session goals:

- Where, on a scale of one to ten, were you last week?
- Where are you this week?
- What would raise this by one point?

Figure 6.5 Establishing the session goal

The Erickson code

Once we have established goals and made them as concrete and desirable as possible we must then identify the tasks in how the client is going to achieve them. To achieve this solution focused work draws heavily on Milton Erickson, who is often recognised as the first solution focused therapist (Berg and Ruess, 1988). Erickson broke the mould of traditional therapeutic practice by introducing brief and often dramatic interventions for clients. He believed that 'schools' of psychotherapy were misguided because every client was different. As such, he claimed to have no system of therapy but instead he claimed to invent a new therapy for every client he worked with (Lankton and Lankton, 1983). Furthermore, every client had the resources within them to resolve their problems and saw the principle aim of therapy to attend to the 'present and future adjustment' of the client. When reviewing his case studies one can indeed marvel at the sheer range and creativity of his approaches.

De Shazer (cf. Duncan et al., 2004) has been one amongst many to attempt to crack the Erickson code and glean the secret of his approach. His method was to sift through all of Erickson case studies and compile them into groups where similar approaches were deployed. The last of these piles was reserved for the miscellaneous studies where Erickson did a one off intervention which he never repeated. By organising them in this way he hoped to deduce the common pattern and trends in the techniques. Unfortunately nearly all the case studies simply fell into the miscellaneous pile. He failed to crack the Erickson code and gave up. However, we will attempt this very same task. Read the case studies in Exercise 6.5 and see what they have in common (Zeig and Munion, 1999). How does Erickson know how to apply each technique?

Exercise 6.5: The Erickson code

Case Example One

An old woman was both isolated and depressed. She lived alone and saw very few people. Erickson, who was visiting her home town, was asked to visit her in her home. They talked about her life, her loneliness and desire to break this cycle. She would go to church but slip out without speaking to anyone. On a guided tour of her house he noted a splendid African Violet flowering. Knowing this was a difficult plant to cultivate he gave her instructions. He told her he wanted her to buy starter pots and gift pots. And whenever there was any reason, such as a death, marriage or birth in her church, she was to send them an African Violet. By the time of her death she was known as the 'African Violet Queen' and her funeral was attended by hundreds of people.

Case Example Two

A 10 year old boy was sent to see Erickson about his bed wetting. The boy was embarrassed about the problem and reluctant to talk. Erickson asked him about the sports he enjoyed. They discussed the various games and what were needed to compete in them. Strong muscles, co-ordination and timing. This moved on to discussing different muscle types, flat ones, long ones and circular ones, like the iris in the eye, and how it needed exercising to work. From this the young boy stopped wetting the bed there after and it was never spoken of again.

Case Example Three

A married couple, both college professors, visited Erickson as they were having trouble conceiving a baby. They spoke in long and complex words that Erickson paraphrased. The trouble, as they saw it, was with philoprogenitive desires [the want to have children], despite marital union twice daily, and four times at weekends, nothing had happened. It was evident that the physiological concomitants [sex] did not result in pregnancy. Erickson recommended in these circumstances that psychological shock therapy could be helpful. But that they must agree to it and not speak until they got home. They deliberated amongst themselves and agreed to the shock therapy. Erickson asked them to grip the sides of their chairs to prepare for the shock. Then he said 'You have been engaged in marital union with full physiological concomitants to fulfil your philoprogenitive desires. Now, why in the hell don't you fuck for fun, and pray to the Devil she isn't knocked up for at least three months. Now please leave.' Three months later she was expecting.

What we see in case example one is that Erickson hears the client's goal and marries it to a skill that she already possesses. In the second example, the awkward and embarrassed child signals to Erickson that he cannot confront the problem of bed wetting and so Erickson finds a coded metaphor to engage the child and deliver advice that had not been received before. In the third case study Erickson recognises that the clients' solutions are their problem. As a result he wants to disrupt the way they are trying to solve it and open them up to other possibilities. He does this by getting close to their meaning in order to usurp it with a powerful punch line, but only after warning and seeking their permission. But how did Erickson 'know' what to do?

Erickson was once interviewed by a researcher, who was trying to elicit his secret (Haley, 1993). Erickson's reiteration that he had no theoretical approach was met with persistent challenge from the researcher. In the end Erickson invited the researcher outside and asked him what he saw. The puzzled researcher said he saw the street. Erickson asked what else he saw, to which the research replied he also saw the trees. Erickson asked what he noticed about the trees. After a short time the researcher said that they all faced east except one. Erickson smiled and said 'That's right . . . the second one from the end is leaning in a westerly direction. There is always an exception.'

A year after the initial attempt, De Shazer had an 'eureka' moment. He went back through the case studies and, instead of looking at Erickson, he looked at what the clients were doing. Erickson's approach became clear. He simply drew on the existing resources, meanings and skills that the client already had at their disposal but did not recognise themselves. He referred to this as 'utilisation' (Erickson, 1959). This demands the helper cannot have a model which they impose on their clients. Instead they have to enter into the client's frame of reference understanding how they make sense of the world and what skills they have which are both particular and important to them. The extraordinary techniques were derived from the observations of the client's extraordinary resources. It then becomes the marriage of the client's resources with their stated wants.

Exceptions and solutions

Solution focused therapy draws heavily on this approach. Without the observational guile of Erickson it has cultivated a more direct way to achieve the same aim. The idea of the *exception* is important in solution focused work and is comparable to the concept of utilisation. Wherever there is an exception, a time when the problem is not happening, it supposes that the client must be doing something to make this happen. If there is an exception there is a solution and for every problem there are exceptions. Whilst the problem may feel relentless there will always be times when this has been better or worse. Whilst clients report high and constant use in assessments in order to elicit deservedness, weekly use may fluctuate dramatically. Equally clients will have

---

Clients with high self-belief:

- Tell me about a time when you avoided this?
- When was the last time this was not a problem?
- Has there ever been a time when this was not a problem?
- Has there been a time that you have overcome this before?
- Has there been a day when you did not use?
- When is the problem not happening?

Scaling down the exception can help for clients with low confidence:

- When is it a little less worse?
- How is it when it is a little better?
- How have you stopped this from turning into an even bigger problem?

And for the client who has no self-belief:

- What is stopping this getting even worse?'

Figure 6.6 Eliciting exceptions

experienced periods of greater contentment in doing other things. These other times, close to the client's treatment goal, can be an equally useful area to explore in clarifying what the client did to make this happen. Furthermore, addiction is a relapse condition where people attempt change several times. Each change attempt can be understood as a partial success which offers clues as to the client's resources. Understanding what was helpful and eliminating what was not can help refine the next treatment event. In this way recovery evolves from previous change attempts.

In order to establish these exceptional times we can ask the client to describe what it is like when the problem is not happening. We can ask these questions directly to clients with high self-belief. Asking for exceptions from clients with lower self-belief will prompt retreat into talking about the problems. In this instance we can scale down the demand for the exceptions by asking when are things a 'little' better or a 'little less' worse? Where clients cannot suggest any times when the situation is better, we ask them what is stopping it getting even worse? After all, they may be barely coping but they are still coping nonetheless.

Again, we want the detail of these exceptional times. What happened? When did it happen? What were they doing, thinking or feeling that was different then? We can shift the focus to an external perspective on the exception. Who else noticed this and what would they say was different? This can be especially important when thinking about how significant others and loved ones appreciate them more at these times. This might be especially important to clients sensitive to the effect of their use on important relationships. Recognising what they did to achieve those times of greater intimacy can be a powerful reinforcer of this exceptional behaviour. If we recall any other aspect of the client's life that they enjoy or have stated as being important to them we can also draw upon this material too. For example if they enjoyed a close relationship with their father or respected his opinions we might ask how they would describe these times.

Case Study: Using exceptions

Alex had been a long standing service user at the needle exchange. Remote and aloof, he had a slightly menacing manner that kept others at bay. Clients and workers would avoid engaging with him when he came to the project. He would silently make his exchange and leave. This went on for 12 months. One day a practitioner, who had noticed the way in which no one spoke to Alex, began to engage him in conversation. He asked about his life in general and how he found the service. The client gave a long using history for himself and his wife who worked in the sex industry, whilst he looked after his daughter. The worker then asked whether there was a time when he was not using. 'Yeah', said Alex, when he had run his own garage. Suddenly this sombre man became animated with enthusiasm. The worker, knowing a little about mechanics, asked him about his time, business and his passions for bikes in particular. After a long discussion, Alex then told of how his wife losing a child meant they had gone back to using, but he missed those times. The following week he returned to see the worker with his daughter, then the following week with the whole family. They arranged for prescriptions and the client was suddenly on track, getting his family out of poverty and looking for work in the motor repair business. It all began with the one exception.

We always want the client to recognise what made these times happen and in doing so draw out their resourcefulness. As Anderson (Holmes, 1994) observed, the skills of the helper lie in how they elicit the skills of the client. We need to help clients identify the strengths which lie unobserved in themselves in order to achieve their treatment goals and session goals. This is important because the major source of our self-belief is in the mastery of experience. Eliciting the exceptions means that we draw upon skills, resources and abilities that the client already possesses and have successfully implemented on previous occasions or in other situations. As we saw in Chapter 3, only people with high self-belief persevere. Exceptions draw directly on their mastery which is the most potent antidote to self-doubt. Consider this for yourself – identify a problem that is occurring for you and answer the questions in Exercise 6.6.

Exercise 6.6: Finding exceptions

- What is the problem?
- When is the problem not happening?
- What is different about these times?
- What are you doing/thinking/feeling at these times?
- What would a loved one say was different about you at these times?

Scaling exceptions

Just as clients may not be fully aware of what they want to be doing instead of using drugs and alcohol in goal-setting, likewise they may not be able to articulate what they do at these times when the problem is not happening. When the client cannot identify exceptions we adjust. We can use the scaling technique on exceptions, just as we did before with goal setting. Here we ask the client to scale themselves from one-to-ten, with one being at their least confident they can manage this task, and ten being at their most confident. We then scale their score as before. For example, a client responds by scaling their confidence at three. We can explore what makes it a three and then develop this by asking what might need to happen to make it a four. Then a five. In this way we may pull out additional ideas of possible solutions too. We can also use this technique to scale historic goals (Seleckman, 1993). People do not always make the connection that skills acquired in one domain are transferable to other areas. If the client has low confidence in accomplishing a particular task we can use the scale to evaluate this first. If it is very low we use another scale to evaluate a task they do feel confident about accomplishing. We can then ask what skills they could transfer from the second scale to the first.

Case Study: Scaling historic exceptions

Young people on a relapse prevention programme were given workers' numbers to call if they were in danger of lapsing. Early one evening, James felt desperate and called his key worker, convinced he was going to lapse. After listening to James' concern the key worker asked him on a scale of one to ten how confident he felt in getting past this urge to use? '0' replied James.

'What was stopping it being minus 1 right now?'

'I don't want to wreck all the hard work I have put in.'

'OK, bear with me here. I know that you really like working out at the gym. At the gym you must have to go through the pain barrier right?'

'Well, yes.'

'On a scale of one to ten, how confident are you that you can get through that pain barrier without stopping?'

'Well. About 8.'

'An 8 is high. What makes it an 8?'

'Well, I keep my focus on what I am doing, and just keep going. I know that I will be finished after a few more reps.'

'What else?'

'Well, if you are going to get anywhere with it you've got to accept that is part of it I suppose. No pain no gain. It shows that it's working.'

'Anything else that makes it an 8?'

'I suppose it's about how bad you want something. Being prepared to make the effort or sacrifice.'

'Would any of these things be helpful to you in overcoming this urge to use right now?'

'No pain no gain. It is about how much I want it. I just got to keep on it I guess.'

Cheerleading

If we get an exception to the problem we gain considerable insight into the resources of the client. Exceptions can be of two types. Deliberate exceptions are when the client does something purposeful to make the exception happen. As we will see in Chapter 7, clients develop a host of techniques, strategies and self-help interventions to overcome their use. It is as almost as if the client develops their own programme, based on their own theory of change. These can include exercise, vitamin supplements, comfort foods, amongst others. As a result, the client may already have wide experience of developing their own idiosyncratic methods of dealing with withdrawal, cravings and recovery. Identifying which of these strategies would be helpful can increase the

- How did you do that?
- So, despite the fact that this has been a big problem for you, there were times when you have managed this well – how did you do that?
- What was that like?
- How did you decide to do that?
- How did you know that would be such a good idea?

Figure 6.7   Cheerleading questions

client's confidence and coping repertoire. Alternatively exceptions can be spontaneous. We have seen that not all changers are conscious strategists. The client might feel that they reduced or stopped because it just happened. We can try to firm up these exceptional times by making them feel as deliberate as possible (see Figure 6.7). This is sometimes referred to as cheerleading whilst other solution focused writers describe these as coping questions.

These questions are aimed at identifying the specific mechanisms that the client deploys in order to create the exception. Again, this makes the client work hard to discover their latent resources. They also get to hear themselves articulate their own strengths for themselves. Whilst they can be used as a tool to augment exceptions, many solution focused practitioners will make extensive use of these questions whenever the client highlights strengths or changes that they have put into place.

Case Study: Cheerleading exceptions

Two workers were running a group for young offenders with histories of violence and aggression. In the group programme the young people were asked to consider times when they did not get involved in fights with other people. Every young person could identify moments when they were not fighting or angry. Sitting back, one of the workers said. 'So, even though things are tough at home, on the out it feels like everyone wants to have a go at you and now you are banged up in here 24 hours a day. Yet there are these times when you deal with this without fighting. How do you do that? What stops you getting angry all the time?'

The group was quiet, until one said. 'Lose my privileges.' At this point the other worker tried to interject, as if this reason was not ethically valid enough. The worker politely restrained this line, and returned to the young offender. 'Privileges? Can you tell me more about that?' Cautiously the young offender began to speak. 'Well, it's all I got. The only thing to look forward to. If I think that someone is in my face I think is it worth it? I know I will regret it come Friday. I will have nothing and they will still be a dick.' Others in the group offered different explanations, wanting to get out, not wanting the hassle, tired of doing it for others. Some just did not know. None of these explanations were compatible with the second group worker's view of their world, but they were all useful to the young people in their world.

Bridging

Once we have identified the client's goal, through negotiation or the hypothetical frame, and then identified their resources though the exceptions, we can bring these two elements together. We

- So, if you could do more of this – these things which you find helpful – would you be on track to achieving your goal?
- How will you keep this going?
- How do you predict that you will keep this going?
- How will you know that you are keeping this going?
- What else would help you achieve this?
- How would you know if you were off track?
- What would you do to correct this?

Figure 6.8   Bridging statements

call this bridging. Here we formulate the client's solution by asking the client whether they can apply the resources, strengths and coping strategies we have identified to achieving their goal (see Figure 6.8). Having a contingency plan can also be helpful. Assisting the client to recognise what being 'off track' would entail can then trigger a second plan of action to address this quickly.

Feedback and suggestions

Coupling the goal and exceptions thus closes the loop on the approach and provides a clear treatment plan based on the client's own wants and resources. Asking the client what else they feel would help them creates scope to develop any concurrent support or after care plans that they feel might be helpful. This may be more important for clients with early onset addictions and protracted periods of social exclusion.

The client's stated aspirations or the nature of their exceptions might give clues as to what support may be beneficial. For example, clients with very low confidence might find skills based programmes more helpful; whereas those who use prayer might find a more spiritual based programme such as Christian houses more useful. Prior treatment episodes can also be evaluated in terms of exceptions. Here the client can consider what helped them and what did not in order to refine the support they feel would be useful. If previous treatment did not work, it is worth exploring whether their previous programme missed something or whether they themselves did not make the most of the opportunity. Again we should always remind clients that when treatment works it does so sooner rather than later.

Within this it is also important that we anticipate setbacks in the implementation of these session goals. The client is standing on the cusp of having to turn their intentions into actions. In many ways this is the biggest shift in the stages of change. Preparing and normalising setbacks in this are very important. Helping to develop the client's awareness of where they may drift off course will alert them into taking clear action more quickly when needed.

Feedback and tasks

In its pure form solution focused therapy is conducted in counselling rooms where a second practitioner, or even team, observes the session through a two way mirror (Walter and Peller, 1992). Towards the end of a session the helper leaves the client for short while to discuss the session with the team. They then return to the client and give them feedback on the session and a task to complete between now and the next appointment. Whilst this is a luxury most of us cannot afford in daily practice, the concept of positive feedback is important. Although we may not have colleagues to consult with, never the less taking time to sum up can augment the progress of the session. There are three elements to this feedback.

The first function of feedback is to compliment the client. Clients do not know what we think of them and this can create a blank canvas to project fears or inadequacies on. Complimenting the client by acknowledging the resilience, skills and progression they have shown in the session supports change and builds on the relationship. I recall talking with an extraordinary bright young woman who was depressed. Listening to her speak I said to her that she seemed really good at grasping the essence of things. A beaming smile of pride stayed with her throughout the rest of the session. We do not want to flatter the client. Our observations must be accurate. But normalising the client's situation, their response and valuing their achievement is important in bolstering their gains.

The second function of the feedback is the message. The message is anything that you have heard in reading, training, supervision, that you think will be useful for the client to hear. It is your chance to have your say. Feeding back this information, which seldom percolates to clients, can help endorse and sustain the changes over time. Again, it must support the client's direction of change. The message can also set the scene or provide the rationale for the task.

The task is important in shifting the client's gains out of the consulting room and into the real world. At the beginning of this chapter we saw that the client was poised on the threshold of turning intentions into action. Now it is what you begin to do that is important. Crossing this threshold is difficult. Setting tasks begins this process by having the client going away and doing something. In the following session, the client can review the progress of the task. The type of task can vary, but some standard tasks are included in Table 6.3.

We can also draw upon wider resources which are relevant to the client. Rosenthal's (2000) excellent compendium of homework assignments is a great resource for this. This book outlines a vast number of varied and interesting homework tasks that can be usefully applied to specific problems. Wherever the client's tasks are drawn from, it is important that the client knows that the task does not have to be a success. We want them to simply try it. The primary function of tasks is to up-grade the client's mastery of experience. For example, asking the goal-less client to think about what they want from the session is helping to establish the goal. Then asking this client to pretending the miracle has happened gives us a spontaneous exception. Asking them to do more of it provides a deliberate exception and so on.

Tasks are always learning experiences regardless of whether the client achieves the targeted behaviour or not. If the client comes back reporting the task was a complete disaster, we simply use exactly the same skills that we have reviewed. For example the disastrous task can be met with – 'If it had gone really, really well, what would have been different?' Alternatively the partial success can be met with exceptions. 'When it was going well, what were you doing then?' Whether clients perform and succeed at the task; ignore it; or struggle with it reveals something. It may reveal their motivation, whether they need to revise goals or whether their confidence is very low. Clients are always collaborating with us even when it appears as though they are not (see Figure 6.9).

Table 6.3 Tasks in solution focused therapy

Task	Function
Go away and think about what you want from these sessions	For clients who have trouble forming goals, reflection may help them clarify what they want to be different in their life.
Notice when the problem is not happening	For clients who find it hard to identify any exceptions, or have low confidence which may prevent them doing more proactive tasks.
Pretend the miracle has happened	For clients who do not have any exceptions but have a goal.
Pretend you are doing it on purpose	For clients who have identified spontaneous exceptions.
Before you go to bed each night, using the scale that we showed you, make a prediction on how the next day will go. The following day consider whether you prediction was accurate, if so, what made it accurate or out.	Good for clients that can only identify spontaneous exceptions but do not know what is making them happen.
Do more of it	For clients that have identified deliberate exceptions.
Slow down	For clients who are making good progress but as a result may be putting themselves under a lot of pressure to succeed.
Flip a coin each day if it comes up heads then do X, if it comes up tails then do the opposite.	Good for ambivalent clients who do not know whether they want to use or control it, use or stop. Also, for partners and carers who might want to end the relationship with user, to act as if they do on the heads day, and as if they don't on the tails.
Do the opposite	Good for people who are stuck in their solutions that are not working anymore. For example, a partner who forces the user to promise to stop. Doing the opposite can open other possibilities.

Subsequent sessions

In the first session of solution focused work we spent a great deal of the time formulating the treatment goal. In subsequent sessions we focus on developing exceptions. Berg and Reuss (1998) have developed a simple structure for the follow up sessions to which I have added a slight amendment. I have included session goals to initiate the next step in the session (see Figure 6.10). They describe subsequent sessions in terms of the acronym EARS. This stand for Elicit, Amplify, Reinforce and Start again. You will see that these are simply a re-application of the skills which we have already identified. By *elicit* they refer to asking questions about what has changed since the last session – not is anything better. If the client complains we ask what it was like when it was going well. If they have had profound setbacks we can explore what they learned. Investigating what keeps them trying can shore up doubts. So, even if the client is struggling with difficulties, we can explore how they manage to cope with that.

Amplify refers to deepening the client's awareness of the changes they have made. When the exceptions are stated we want to know the what, where, when and how this was managed. Who

---

The Compliment

What can I say positively about the client that can promote a positive atmosphere?

What is the client already doing that is working, positive or exceptional that I can highlight as encouraging?

Are there fears about being judged that I might want to alleviate?

Are there any apparent fears or expectations about change that I might want to alleviate?

Is there anything about the client's situation that I might want to normalise?

How can I give credit to the client for changing?

Even if there is more than one person present, how can I support each individual's perspective?

The Message

What message would I like to give the client about people in this situation?

The Task

Figure 6.9   Template for informative feedback

else noticed this change and how they responded to it can strength positive reinforcement for change. *Reinforcement* can also come from our response to the client's exceptions. Our reaction of amazement, pride, surprise and enthusiasm can reinforce the progress that the client is making and underline their gains. It provides an opportunity for us to enjoy the gains with the client and compliment them on their success. Even clients who have not implemented gains can be complimented, 'Yes, I think you're right to do this more slowly.' This will make it sound a deliberate choice that is still contributing to change. And finally, *starting again* involves all the above on the next exceptions. 'What else has changed? Once we have worked through every exception we can set the next session goal. 'So where do we go from here to build on this?'

Reporting positions

Taking an overview of solution focused therapy we can see there is something simple and something complex in the approach. De Jong and Miller (1995) have suggested that solution focused work can be reduced to five basic questions. These questions are those which take advantage of pre-session gains, find exceptions, elicit the miracle, scale solutions and questions of coping. These skills are established in the first session and in the subsequent ones that follow, though the ratio of goal setting to exceptions finding shifts. Once we have these basic skills we need to be flexible in how we apply them. Especially when the client cannot respond to the helper's questions and demands that we change our approach. You may have noticed that the suggested questions and case studies in this chapter are posed from different perspectives.

Elicit information about positive change

1. Open the session by asking | What has been better?
   What have you been doing to make life better?
   What would (significant other) say was better?

2. If the client complains, ask them about the best day, identify exceptions and cheerlead | How did you do that?

3. If the client reports setbacks | What have they learned?
   What makes them continue to try?

4. If the client has had difficulty | How have you managed?

Amplify by asking for the details of positive change and exceptions

1. When | When did this happen?
   Then what happened?
   Then what happened?

2. Who | Who else noticed?
   How did they respond?
   How did their response change things?

3. Where | What was going on that helped?
   Could you do the same thing everywhere?

4. How | How did you do that?
   How did you know that was the right thing to do?
   How do you know that you can do more of this?

Reinforce by making the client aware of and value of positive change

1. Non-verbal: Show signs that you are impressed by the client's gain.
2. Verbal: Interrupt the client by saying 'Tell me that again' or 'You did what?' in the face of gains.
3. Compliment the client for the progress. Compliment clients who have not made change by telling them they are wise to take it slow.

Start again by focusing on client generated change

1. Review as many exceptions from the previous week.
2. Invite the other perspectives on gains.

   Next session goal . . .
   How can we build on this?
   What is the next step?
   You have done a lot since we last met, how can we build on this?
   What do you want to be different after this session?
   How would you know that it was worthwhile coming here today?
   If I got run over by a bus tomorrow and we could not meet again, what would you have wanted to achieve by then?

Figure 6.10 EARS for follow up session (Berg and Reuss, 1998)

Sometimes questions are asked directly to the client (What do you do?). At other times, different perspectives are brought in (What would your partner say?/What would I say was different?). This refers to the reporting position. In solution focus therapy we can change the way we ask questions in order to get different perspectives and angles on the same solution. The conversation matrix (See Walter and Peller, 1992) in Table 6.4 describes these different reporting positions and where they are most effective.

Table 6.4   Conversation matrix (Walter and Peller 1992)

Reporting position	Goal	Hypothetical	Exceptions	Guidance
Self	What is **your** goal in coming here?	What will **you** be doing differently if the miracle occurred?	What are **you** doing differently?	Useful when: (1) The client presents the solution as their own responsibility.
Other	What would your **teacher** say was your goal in coming here?	What would **your partner** notice that was different?	What would your **parents** say that you are doing differently?	Useful when: (1) Client believes that the solutions are in someone else's control. (2) For helping realign differing goals between two people. (3) For the involuntary client, who can be asked from the referrer's perspective.
Detached	What would **I** say was your goal in coming here?	As a fly on the wall, what will **I** see you all doing differently?	If I were a fly on the wall, what would **I** see you all doing differently?	Useful when: (1) Clients believe that they will just be feeling different rather than acting differently.

Changing the reporting position can be useful for a number of reasons in solution work. We usually work from the self position, asking the client what their miracle would be like or what they are doing when the problem is not happening. When a client fails or finds it difficult to answer a question from this self reporting position, we can simply ask it again from a different reporting position. For example, when working with a client who struggled to find any exceptions themselves you might ask 'What would your partner say was different at these times?' Usually you will suddenly get a full answer and one that contains the intimate understanding that only a concerned other would know about them. Likewise, asking questions from the detached position – 'What would I see that was different?' often opens up an objective, outsider's view. These simple shifts can help the client a great deal.

The *other* reporting position is used extensively with couples where it may increase empathy and mutual understanding of the wants, hopes and behaviour of the other. But it is also deployed when working with involuntary clients (Lipchick, 1998). When involuntary clients are referred, the conversation begins by focusing on the referrer's position, not the clients. We establish what the referrer identifies as the problem, what they believe the client must do and what they want to be different before we ask the client if they share this view. This allows rapport to open without making any assumptions about the client or their need to change. Once this is established we can ask the client whether this is what they want. If the client does not believe they have a problem we once again take a more motivational interviewing angle and ask what are the consequences of not doing anything about the problem. If they cannot live with the consequences of not seeking support then the goal setting begins. As such, once again we do not sell the benefits of change

- Whose idea was it for you to come here today?
- What makes X think you should be here?
- What does X want you to be doing differently?
- Is this something that you want?

If the client says yes proceed to goal setting, if they say no then –

- What are the consequences of not coming?

If the client cannot live with these consequences, proceed to goal setting. If they can live with these consequences, then terminate warmly.

Figure 6.11 Template for involuntary clients (Lipchick, 2002)

to them. If the client can live with the consequences of continuing their behaviour we thank them for their honesty, offer an open door policy and wish them well.

Conclusion

The client in the foothills of change faces three key issues. They need positively reinforced motivation to work towards what is desirable; must overcome the internalisation of stress; and finally they must start to turn best intentions to effortful actions. These mechanisms are not clearly enunciated in Prochaska and DiClemente's work because of the difference between their subject group of dependent smokers as opposed to those who experience the more profound social exclusion of addiction. The high degree of cultural separation demands greater planning that encompasses wholesale life revision. And the means of achieving this requires more than resolve, it requires careful construction. Solution therapy addresses these issues through its development of concrete goals to create a preferred future that is more desirable than use. It then encourages the client to step into behaviour change by reaffirming the tasks that they have already mastered, minimising performance anxiety. Harnessing the motivational impetus to avoid the increasing consequences of use with the desire for more fulfilling alternatives is essential to maximise motivation in the pre-change user. We must remember that change does not occur until a clear differential is achieved between the two forces. Motivational interviewing and the solution focused approach offer the helper practical tools to augment this separation by reducing the cons and increasing the pros of change respectively. This is essential when working with pre-change substance users. But once the client initiates the change process new challenges appear on the horizon. The question then becomes how to weather becoming drug free and sustain these changes in the long term.

Chapter 7

On Implementing Change

You may send Hell packing, but it can return at a gallop.
Roger Caillois

Stepping over the behavioural threshold of change is difficult. The discomfort of withdrawal and urges to return to use run alongside convincing sceptical others to support the user through these changes. This must be done without the principle coping mechanism that insulated the client from the collateral damage inflicted by use. When confronting these realities, it is understandable that the decisional balance of change can swing back in favour of the comfort of self-sedation. In this chapter we will explore the key mechanisms of implementing change, based on both the stages of change and remission research. This will examine the key mechanisms and skills people deploy to maintain the direction of change. We will then augment this with consideration of the lapse process and how it unfolds. This will assist us to help maintain the client in the early stages of change and minimise the risk of relapse.

For Prochaska and DiClemente (1994) action is a mechanism-rich stage of change which places the highest demands on the individual. It spans the early period of recovery, from the immediate cessation of problem consumption through the following six months (Conners et al., 2001). They highlight key behaviours which are important in self changers during this phase. Firstly, environmental control is essential in abandoning the old world of use and incumbent triggers, and placing oneself in an environment where new affirming opportunities are available. The substitution of old behaviours for more healthy coping strategies has to be negotiated. Learning counter-conditioning mechanisms such as eating comfort foods instead of smoking or using relaxation techniques when stressed are equally as important as the new environment the individual needs to create. These new behaviours need to be reinforced if they are to be built upon. Rewards for gains not only lift mood but also provide recognition of gains made. As we saw before, rewards need not be material but can include social relationships: recognition as well as value based. Rewards are used heavily by successful changers in order to provide additional reinforcement to gains made. As such, the 'instead' behaviours that we saw in the last chapter that replace the problem activities are very important. And finally, helping relationships are essential to the recovery process. This does not just refer to the therapeutic relationship with a worker but instead to wider social support which can include self-help, family, new non-using peers and employment that increase pro-social support.

Natural remission in action

In studies of those who change without formal treatment we see that they all invent their own techniques to deal with cravings and urges to use once they put their commitment to change into place. This broadly parallels Prochaska and DiClemente's findings. Stall and Biernaki (1986) found a common strategy was separation from environments that supported the old behaviour and to co-opt support from others. Their group showed that the public pronouncement of change was the principle means of securing this support from others. The negative experiences which initiated change featured heavily in their attempts to convince others of their sincerity. They also developed other strategies to counter cravings such as fooling themselves that they were still using. Amongst problem drinkers this included adding lemon to drinks to give it more bite for a short period after cessation.

Burman's (1997) problem drinking cohort made more extensive use of environmental control measures such as throwing away alcohol and seeking out more rewarding activities. Her study demonstrated the necessity of absolute separation from old drinking relationships. People even changed their careers to avoid work-social patterns dominated by high consumption. Again, gaining the support of others featured heavily. 'Stress buddies' – people who would remind them of their gains and cheerlead their successes in moments of doubt – proved a powerful antidote to resist cravings. Some made use of substitute drugs, such as cannabis, but soon abandoned the strategy, whilst others made more extensive use of this drug as a means to recovery. The use of 'bargaining' with time to limit commitment to abstinence for shorter more manageable periods of time was common through this group. Positive self talk, reminding others of their decision to reinforce their commitment and extensive journaling were also widely used coping strategies. What also seemed useful to this drinking group was holding on to painful memories and mementos of their drinking. These two terms served as painful reminders of the old life.

Klingemann (1992) has conducted extensive research on the specific coping strategies of problematic heroin and alcohol users in the early stages of recovery. His research identified a spread of experiences. As we saw in the last chapter, some simply matured out and made no conscious attempt to change. Others reported a quantum experience which was so powerful and encompassing that no 'tricks' were necessary to support this transformative change. However, the majority were intentional changes and drew on three core strategies. These were the management of the withdrawal and craving for the drug; separation from the relationships which supported use; and building up resilience to risk.

In terms of stopping, many remitters tended to stretch the intervals in-between use. This was also done through staging their own reduction programme by diluting alcohol with increasing amounts of water. Replacing drugs and alcohol with comfort food, coffee, water, vitamins and (for some heroin users) alcohol was important across all users. Cultivating negative expectations about the effects of even using a small amount also helped. This was again augmented by removing oneself from the social and environmental conditions which supported use. In contrast to the previous American research, Klingemann's Swiss cohort kept their change attempt secret in order to lower performance anxiety. Many isolated themselves in remote areas. Clearing the home of drugs and alcohol were symbolic moments of separation in the early drying out period.

These aids were all perceived as temporary measures though, and the next challenge became 'hardening' oneself to temptations through overcoming exposure to the drug and successfully resisting. For some this was done even in the face of other life adversities such as the loss of a loved one. These events, common in the natural remission studies, were always perceived as consolidating the individual's conviction to change as opposed to reasons to resume use. Some even made a sport of knocking back offers to drink, hanging out in bars deliberately to refuse offers of alcohol. Non-using relationships were also important in sustaining change. Even strangers were seen as supporting the process and the interaction as an endorsement of gains made.

In summing up these findings it is clear that during this phase of treatment these are the critical elements that we must address to support people though the early recovery process. These research studies converge on the same themes. Individuals need to separate from environments and social networks which promote use, develop a range of behaviour based skills to manage cravings and break old habits, develop new relationships that will support them in the crisis moments of doubt and finally the individual must learn to master risk situations. They are never going to be free of risk or temptations. They must foster the self-belief that they can resist these situations rather than perpetually avoid them. We shall see how the skills and techniques of structured relapse prevention match these components of recovery in order to assist the recovery process.

Control use controversies

What recovery may not be dependent upon is substance use itself. As we have seen, many people use heroin, crack or even consume high amounts of alcohol without necessarily becoming addicted. Similarly, people recover without recourse to total abstinence but go into controlled use. This is the most controversial area of substance misuse research and the publication of research findings that identifies problematic users who regain control over their consumption has cost many researchers their reputations and have opened them up to both professional and personal vilification (Haskell, 1994). It is not the quality of their research which is attacked, but the nature of their findings which is considered heretical. However, despite these moral objections numerous research studies have demonstrated that alcohol users can switch from problematic consumption to controlled use (Sobbell and Sobell, 1978; Marlatt, 1983; Amour et al., 1978). Heroin users can achieve prolonged controlled use (van Bilsen, 1994). Even heavy users of cocaine could move towards controlled use (Erickson and Hadaway, 1989). Whilst research suggests that up to 20 per cent of nicotine smokers are recreational users (Schiffman et al., 1994) there is no research available on how many heavy smokers go on to become occasional users.

This research demonstrates that some people can shift from problem to controlled use, and indeed it may be a legitimate option treatment goal (Marlatt and Gordon, 1985), but it does not suggest that this is viable for all treatment seekers. For example, it might be doubtful that those who have experienced clinical alcoholism may be able to return to normal consumption. After small doses of alcohol the newly restored tolerance to alcohol appears to collapse very quickly in this small group, with chronic withdrawals emerging after 72 hours (Edwards et al., 2003). The reasons for this are not fully understood but the phenomena appears limited to the toxicity of alcohol. But just as those attempting to maintain total abstinence can relapse, so too can those seeking control. As we have seen in previous chapters, arguing with clients over the viability of controlled use may be counter-productive. Instead it can be better to work with the client's stated goal non-defensively and review progress. Repeated failure may indicate abstinence is a better option in light of their experience, rather than the beliefs of the helper. Indeed, enforced abstinence may be unhelpful in dissuading people from entering into treatment. This is especially true of young people. If we consider that the heaviest users of alcohol are people in their twenties – but they rarely present for any treatment.

When working with individuals who wish to resume consumption after abstinence the following areas can be important to consider. Firstly, why does the person wish to resume use? Any indications that this is a coping strategy for sedating stresses and pressures runs the severe risk of leading back into problem use. It is important to explore the expectations of use. For those feeling confident and desiring to return to 'normal' social interaction, it is important to analyses their peers' drinking and using patterns closely. What do they expect drinking to be like? What do they see when their peers are drinking? Is what they want actually contingent on alcohol consumption, for example feeling accepted, having fun or feeling at ease?

Setting concrete milestones is important. Those who use subjective measures to calibrate when enough is enough tend to mis-judge their consumption levels. Combined with this is the fact that taking alcohol may influence judgement. Therefore setting concrete limits to drinking at the outset is vital. Education about the bi-phasic nature of alcohol can be important too, recognising that whilst it lifts mood initially it depresses it soon after. And for those who lapse when drinking has exceeded set limits, dealing with the consequences and learning from the experience are important aspects of the journey. In other words, we must investigate the client's considerations and take them seriously. Having explored these areas with clients prior to resumption in drinking some have successfully go on to become controlled social drinkers, others have decided to not even bother and remain abstinent, whilst others have tried, and returned to abstinence. People may move back into dependency, and there may be health risks to themselves which they are willing to take in light of the benefits of use. But this is not the same as addiction if their use no longer interferes with their functioning or takes precedence over their choices and relationships. A classic mistake is where, after a period of abstinence, people may simply assume that they can now use recreationally, *even though they have acquired no skills in the interim whatsoever*. A period of abstinence does not teach intoxication management skills and as such, these attempts are doomed from the outset. Clients must understand that managing controlled use is more difficult than managing abstinence.

Blocking medications

There has been increasing availability of medications to support those that cease problematic drug and alcohol use. Naltrexone has become widely prescribed for heroin abuse. Naltrexone is an opioid antagonist. This means that it binds to the same receptors in the brain as heroin but it does not activate them. This effectively caps them and prevents the action of heroin. Because of this people should be heroin free for seven days before commencing the prescription otherwise the drug will trigger withdrawal. This offers the newly drug free individual an insurance policy. If they take the Naltrexone that day then heroin use will have no effect. But this relies on the person being motivated enough to take the drug; if they are it buys them time and will eliminate spontaneous use.

Naltrexone can be administered orally (50 mg a day), three times a week and does not appear to cause tolerance. It can cause side effects of abdominal pain, nausea, joint pains and dysphoria. The main problem with Naltrexone is that whilst it appears a useful relapse prevention drug, very few clients ever maintain their prescriptions on it. For example, in one study of 386 drug users (Greenstein et al., 1981) only one per cent continued to take the drug after one year. Such poor outcomes have been found in other studies (Azatian et al., 1994; Kosten and Kleber, 1984). Outcomes for Naltrexone can also appear poor in comparison to other drugs. Clinical trials often compare it with high dose methadone maintenance and buprenorphine. These drugs tend to be more useful for clients in the lower stages of readiness. Certainly, the problem with Naltrexone is that if there is a lapse people cannot resume the drug for a period of seven days (Sullivan et al., 2006). Highly motivated clients and those with good social relationships appear to be the best responders to the drug (O'Brien, 1994; Tennant et al., 1984). Rounsavile (1995) has suggested the drug should only be prescribed in tandem with relapse prevention support work in order to maximise its effectiveness.

Naltrexone is increasingly being used as a rapid detoxification method. Its high affinity for opiate receptors in the brain means it will readily displace opiates causing abrupt withdrawal. This has been used as a very rapid flushing detoxification for patients under high sedation which may be conducted in less than 24 hours. Here, the drug is administered until withdrawal symptoms abate and the client is opiate free. However, the outcomes of such detoxification are poor and most experts in the field advise against them (see Gossop, 2003; Strain and Stritzer, 2006).

Naltrexone has also been used in the treatment of alcohol abuse. It would appear that alcohol's global action on the brain includes opiate receptors, though to a far lesser extent than heroin. Administered in doses of 50 mg per day, the drug appears to reduce the euphoria associated with drinking and may reduce cravings (Volpicelli et al., 1995). It is less effective in reducing abstinence though and, once again, needs to be administered within the context of psychosocial support (O'Malley et al., 1992; Volpicelli et al., 1995).

A second drug used extensively for alcohol clients is disulfiram (Antabuse). It is administered in doses of 100–200 mg per day and its slow absorption rate means it can take several days before it reaches a therapeutic threshold. Disulfiram does not block the effects of alcohol. Instead it inhibits one of the enzymes that metabolises alcohol. This leads to an accumulation of acetaldehyde in the body if alcohol is consumed; causing a reaction that includes vomiting, sickness, headaches and increased heart rate. This makes it unsuitable for those with a history of coronary problems and the action of the drug on the liver makes it unsuitable for those with hepatitis. Again, like Naltrexone, if the drug is administered that day, it can prevent spontaneous relapse though it may also reduce cravings. The severity of symptoms induced from drinking with disulfiram can vary from individual to individual. Some individuals can drink their way through it regardless. Disulfiram pellets can be surgically implanted but the outcomes are poor. They do not always deliver an effective dose and patients have been known to scratch the pellets out from under their skin. Even though disulfiram has been available as a treatment since the 1940s its outcomes remain limited. Once again, the drug only appears useful for highly motivated clients when administered as part of a psychosocial support package (Edwards et al., 2003).

It appears the medication that can block or create aversive reactions on resumption of use have little efficacy as a stand alone treatment. The central aim of recovery is to address the environmental pressures that make use meaningful and the client's ability to address them. Whilst prescribed drugs may interfere with the action of drugs, we cannot prescribe for the results of long term addictions. This demands wilful effort on behalf of the client as we have no practical means to short cut this process.

Relapse prevention: an overview

To understand the underlying mechanics of relapse we will use the social learning model utilised by Marlatt and Gordon (1985). Within this programme, use is seen as a habit rather than a biological compulsion. Whilst there are physical consequences of excessive use, this is not to imply high consumption is a physiological process. Rather consumption is a pattern of behaviour which is learned, and it can be changed and modified like any other repetitive habit. As such it assumes that high consumption is driven by over-learned behaviours which are augmented by the anticipated reinforcing effect of the drug. This can be the desirable high induced by the drug or the way in which the client perceives use as a means of controlling undesirable stresses. Thus it is the expectation that is critical in driving use, with the individual's mind set and environmental setting exerting greater influence than the pharmacology of the drug itself (Marlatt and Rohsenow, 1980). This demands that new patterns of behaviour need to be established. As the problematic user has always used when confronted with a substance, their awareness of other choices is narrow. Furthermore, even if they are aware of alternatives to using they have very low self-efficacy belief that they can resist. As such the underlying strategy of cognitive behavioural therapies is to increase client awareness of alternative choices other than use and nurture their self-belief that they can employ these alternative strategies effectively.

So, regardless of the amount people are consuming, the action phase can be considered as a chance to unlearn old habits by developing new skills to conquer old challenges. By using cognitive and social psychology principles, Marlatt's relapse prevention model aims to provide key skills to assist the individual in remaining drug and alcohol free, or indeed, even switch to controlled use. This has been done on research studies of the lapse process to indicate the specific challenges that the newly drug free individual needs to master and the pitfalls they need to avoid. Consider the following questions in Exercise 7.1 that lead us through the lapse process. Think of behaviour that you tried to change but slipped back into. What happened in the build up to the lapse?

Marlatt's lapse model begins with the lifestyle balance of the individual. An imbalance between the demands that you 'should' do, as opposed to the things that you 'want' to do impact on the feelings of the individual. 'Shoulds' are those negatively reinforced behaviours where we strive to reduce undesirable mood states such as stress, such as working to avert debt, going to treatment to avert lapse, meeting the needs of others to avert conflict etc. 'Wants' on the other hand are those tasks we engage in to increase desirable things in our lives. These positive rewarding activities include activities such as going to the cinema, socialising with friends, or just relaxing in front of the TV. The individual who is constantly locked into performing tasks they 'should' do soon begins to feel deprived, tired and resentful. This can be further fuelled by reactance, if an individual feels bonded or forced into meeting these incessant demands. This fosters a sense of self-mutiny against these regulations. The desire for indulgence becomes greater as an attempt to re-balance the disequilibrium between 'wants' and 'shoulds'. How many times have we heard ourselves say – it's been a tough week I deserve it? The expectation is that engaging in these low skill/high reward behaviours will act as an antidote to the stresses we are experiencing. As a result, impoverished environments tend to drive up our emotional needs and with it our substance use.

These desires for release can trigger or modify physical and thought processes which begin to shift the cost benefit analysis back towards increasing the pros of use and decreasing the cons of change. Physical urges can appear as a sudden impulsive desire to engage in the old behaviour, whilst cravings are the desire for the effects or consequences of use. These can be amplified by the forbidden fruit effect. Inflated expectations lure us to believe if we could just have one drink, one hit or one cigarette it will make all these life stresses dissolve. The expectation of release that this old behaviour will offer, no matter how unrealistic, is a powerful motivator to resume use.

Similarly the want for the old behaviour can affect our thought processes. We may start rationalising how using was really not that bad. As we saw in Chapter 5, reactance occurs when we feel we have lost our personal freedom, we want to take it back, no matter what the cost. This can manifest itself in our thinking as a desire to test personal control, to demonstrate to ourselves that we can manage it now. We see that very few people go out and use overtly: to do so would invoke too much guilt and dissonance. Instead of making a direct choice to use, people take small steps towards it, and let the opportunity present itself. This is called Apparently Irrelevant Decisions or AIDs (elsewhere these are referred to as Seemingly Irrelevant Decisions or

Exercise 7.1: Antecedents to lapse (Marlatt and Gordon, 1985)

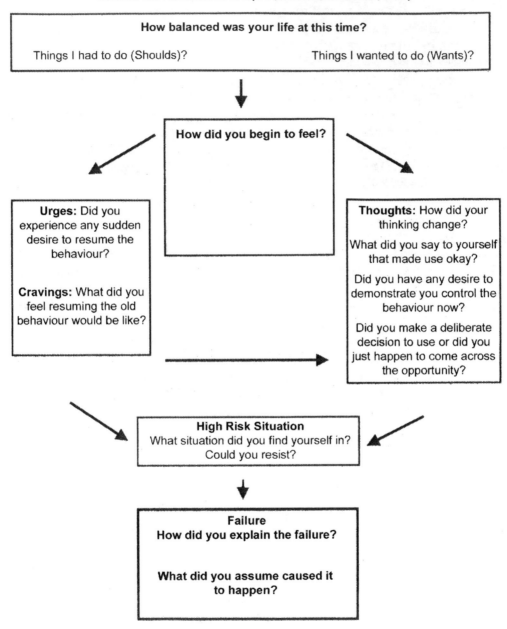

SIDs). This is a set of mini-decisions which are innocuous in their own right but slowly lead us, step by step towards temptation to use. We can lapse back into the old behaviour feeling that in these circumstances of high availability we had little choice but to use; even though we put ourselves in that very position.

Lapse and relapse

Once we are exposed to high risk, with powerful expectations of the positive effects of use and little confidence in resisting, lapse becomes inevitable. The difference between lapse and relapse is critical, and research studies often use very different criteria to define the two. Typically a lapse is considered as a single using event, whilst a relapse is defined as five days continuous use (Connors et al., 2001). However these are not universally accepted criteria. This leads to some confusion in research where 'any use' may be quantified by some research as relapse whilst a short time limited episode of use is deemed a lapse by others. Thus one research study (Armor et al., 1978) that defined relapse as the return to pre-treatment levels of drinking found 50 per cent of their subjects relapsed; whilst Orford and Edwards' (1977) study using 'any consumption' as indicative of relapse found that 90 per cent of subjects relapsed. In Hunt et al.'s (1971) comparative research of relapse rates amongst smokers, drinkers and heroin users post treatment indicated strongly that the majority of people relapsed in the first three months, but their relapse rates include anyone who used, even once, as equal to those who used at pre-treatment levels. This research was also criticised as producing a mean average score that was not reflective of any individual's actual experience (Marlatt and Gordon, 1985).

Problems in understanding relapses is further compounded by the fact that relapsed clients defy statistical analysis. Prochaska et al.'s (1994) initial statistical analysis of the stages of change made no sense, until they took the relapse group out. Only then did the process of change achieve statistical significance. This has lead Prochaska and DiClemente to define lapse and relapse not as stages of change, but as events in the change process. Relapsed clients may also revert to either pre-contemplation or contemplation stage. As such, the lapse event is not necessarily uniform or predictable. Some clients rapidly lapse and turn it around quickly; some relapse after long periods of abstinence; whilst 'chippers' appear to the world as drug free but continue to use in private. The idea that lapse leads to relapse in either abstinent or control users is spurious (Heather et al., 1983). It must also be remembered that what we tend to see in treatment is that change is accumulative. Every change attempt or treatment episode tends to reduce consumption. And according to Prochaska and DiClemente's change model, we see that individuals make between 5–7 change attempts before they achieve their goals.

One of the reasons why the response to lapse appears variable may lie in the explanations that are offered by those that have slipped. They have to explain this failure to themselves or to others. Marlatt (1978) describes this as the abstinence violation affect. If we consider the lapsed individual, their actual behaviour is now in contradiction to their ideal of themselves. This recreates the dissonance we saw in Chapter 5. The strength of this dissonance depends upon the degree of personal commitment and effort the individual has made towards abstinence, the length of sustained abstinence and the value that the change behaviour held for the individual. The stress generated from the dissonance effect impels the client to reduce this psychological discomfort. They may do so with the same rationalisations and minimisation that we saw in Chapter 5 to protect themselves from failure. Lapsed individuals tend to attribute the cause of their failure to their own internal weakness. Wortman and Brehm (1975) refer to these conditions as 'helplessness training', where an individual's previous experience leads them to believe that a desired outcome is uncontrollable. Hence in the light of failure, self blame confirms to the under-confident client that they are innately unable to manage change so succumb to a relapse that is perceived as inevitable.

Whilst much is made of relapse as being physiologically driven by the priming dose of the drug, we actually see expectations play a critical role in determining relapse rates (Curry et al., 1987). For example, the twelve step treatment programmes teaches the belief that one lapse will inevitably lead to relapse and the progressive destruction of the individual. Whilst learning models suggest that lapse should be interpreted as a learning experience that can assist the process of change. Both approaches can be double edged. The twelve step view is useful in warning people away from use but then fosters the expectation of complete loss of control in light of a lapse. Whilst the learning model removes the threat of lapse by making it manageable but then offers the means to overcome it. In comparisons of treatment outcomes for these two approaches we can see how these expectations are enacted in the recovery process. We see more days of continuous abstinence in twelve step treatment, followed by longer and deeper lapses. Whilst conversely we see less days of continuous abstinence in learning models but shorter lapse episodes (See Miller et al., 2001).

This overview provides insight into the nature of treatment responses to individuals in the early stages of recovery. Learning to manage lifestyle balance, feelings, urges/cravings and negative thoughts are critical. This is referred to as *phase one* relapse prevention work in targeting the immediate and practical skills in early recovery. When clients are newly drug or alcohol free their confidence in managing risk situations will be very low. These skills need to be mastered in the first month of being substance free. These are taught as skills in group or one-to-one sessions. As such, little is provided in terms of self-reflective counselling at this juncture. It should be remembered that if individuals' use is driven by negative mood states, the deep exploration of past trauma may be counter productive until the client has developed more self-management skills.

Relapse prevention: phase one

The first area we need to consider in relapse prevention work is the lifestyle balance of the client. After protracted periods of use and social exclusions, the person in recovery needs to begin to impose routine on their day. As we saw in the last chapter, lifestyle balance underpins the lapse process. Keeping busy is a great asset in the early stage of recovery and figured highly in many of the natural remitter's stories. It is therefore important to help clients structure the early clean time purposefully. This can be done by drawing up a timetable of their typical day, from waking to going to sleep. Marlatt and Gordon's (1985) Should-Want Tally is a very useful tool in this but a simpler timetable can done (see Figure 7.1). Basing this on the last few days previous to meeting, this timetable should account for every activity that they have undertaken. The client then lists their activities and evaluates whether each one was a 'should' or a 'want' by ticking the relevant column. Remember, that 'shoulds' are the things the client has to do whilst 'wants' are the things that they enjoy. They then rate their level of satisfaction from 1–100 for each section of the day, morning, afternoon and evening. From this it is important to identify the lifestyle balance. For example, do they get up and do all the things they like, neglecting the demands of household chores, finances and food shopping, leaving them under pressure? Or do they throw themselves into demands without respite, leaving them drained, tired and resentful? Are they aware of any recreational or social activities that are available or are they living in isolation?

Client's with long using histories will have tended to organise their time around the things they desire rather than the mundane tasks of life. Procrastination can have a powerful impact on us though. Not attending to tasks does not make them go away but increases stress. Knowing that

Time	Activity	Want should rating						
		Should			Mixed		Wanted	
		1	2	3	4	5	6	7
Morning (rising–noon)								
Overall satisfaction at the end of the morning? (1–100)								
Afternoon (noon–5.00 p.m.)								
Overall satisfaction at the end of the afternoon? (1–100)								
Evening (5.00 pm–retire)								
Overall satisfaction at the end of the evening? (1–100)								
Total overall satisfaction with the entire day?								

Figure 7.1 Based on Shoulds–Wants Tally (Marlatt and Gordon 1985)

important but uncompleted tasks await us saps our energy and dampens mood. A useful way of helping the client organise their time in these early days is the Premack principle, named after the psychologist who derived it (Premack, 1965). Premack's principle states that when low frequency behaviours are linked to high frequency behaviour, it increases the rate of the low frequency behaviour. This is to say that if we take a task that we find onerous and link it to a rewarding task, we are more likely to complete the onerous task. For example, a child may not tidy their bedroom very often (low frequency task) but if this is dependent on going to the cinema (high frequency task) they suddenly do more of it to gain the reward. As a result, Premack's Principle is sometimes referred to as Grandma's law.

Making rewarding tasks contingent on completing onerous ones helps overcome procrastination but we must structure this carefully. For example, if you are studying a college course and your homework is mounting up, you might pledge that you will do two hours of your essay and then watch your favourite DVD as a reward. But you are now bonded to the onerous task of homework for two hours no matter what you do. Time drags slowly, you clock watch and the investment of your efforts makes little difference to the duration of time you must spend on the task. And to compensate you watch hours of DVDs. Instead, with Premack's principle, the onerous task is not divided into time units but work units. Reward behaviour is stated in time units. So it is better to state that you will write 800 words of your essay, and then watch half an hour of the DVD. This means that as soon as the 800 words are written you can engage in something that you enjoy. This can be a very useful strategy in helping clients plan a more balanced day. Onerous activities need to be augmented with rewarding ones. This ensures the client has a balance between what they must do and what they like to do. Being proactive in managing the demands of life increases our sense of competence and allows a better quality of life. Keeping busy in these early days of recovery is important as a general distraction from thinking about use as well as increasing the sense of progress in the client.

Sleep hygiene

Linked to lifestyle, an area of difficulty reported by most clients in early recovery is poor sleeping patterns. Sleep is integral to human functioning in allowing the body to shut down, replenish energy reserves and dream. Whilst the vast majority of clients often complain about not being able to sleep, further investigation is important. They may not have a sleep disorder but have simply poor sleep hygiene. People with insomnia tend to over-estimate the time it takes them to get to sleep (Healy, 2002). Addiction for the most part operates on a nocturnal time schedule and clients must adjust from late night using to early morning rising. For the individual who is newly clean there is nothing worse than the isolation of being sat up all night alone, pondering one's life or the frustration of missing important appointments the following day. It is lonely, depressing and exposes the user to old cues for use. As a result, the evening can be a prime time for lapse (Marlatt and Gordon, 1980). Educating clients about good sleep hygiene is therefore very important. Before going to bed they should avoid stimulants such as tea, coffee, nicotine and alcohol except if it is part of well established routine. Routines and ceremonies are important cues to the body to prepare for sleep and so clients should try to identify and rehearse their going to bed routine regularly to signal to the body to begin to shut down. For clients who are finding it difficult to sleep, the techniques in Figure 7.2 have proven effective in alleviating anxiety about not sleeping once in bed.

Establishing a new sleeping pattern is essential. The human body operates on regular rhythm called the basic rest-activity cycle (Waterhouse et al., 1990). This operates on peaks and troughs of energy and arousal on a three-four hour cycle. The same cycle also underpins sleep, as we pass through deeper phases of sleep. Some individuals go to bed and report feeling awake once they are there. This may be because they have waited until they feel utterly exhausted before retiring. They are now turning a corner with their rest-activity cycle, which having dipped to its lowest point it is now reviving. In this situation the individual should rise and do something else relaxing rather

Sleep Techniques
Ice Station Zero (Rosenthal, 2001): Whilst in bed the client imagines they are going to live in an arctic ice station for 6 months. They can only take 10 items with them. What items would they take?
Paradoxical Intentions (Frankl, 1985): This paradoxical intention is for the individual to get into bed and instead of dwell on the fact that they cannot sleep, which promotes anxiety, they must instead concentrate on staying awake for as long as they can.
Muscle Relaxation (Healy, 2002): Starting with the toes, the client focuses on tensing these muscles as hard as they can before relaxing them. They then focus on tensing the tendons in the feet, and feeling them relax. Then the calf muscles, thighs and all the way up the body, working up and relaxing all the muscle groups.

Figure 7.2 Sleep techniques

than remain in bed. They also need to learn to read their body dip sooner and go to bed before it troughs.

It appears that our body clock is set by the time we rise rather than when we sleep. Getting up at a regular hour will soon adjust the body clock over a matter of days into a new sleep pattern. But people should avoid napping in this cross-over period. On the whole, sleeping tablets should be avoided. Benzodiazepines are often used but have a great deal of abuse potential and may only lead to broken sleep which interrupts the bodies own rhythms. Furthermore, these may make acute anxiety and post-traumatic stress disorders worse (Elkin, 1999). There are a number of sleep disorders which may influence sleep patterns. These can include anxiety and stress disorders, post-traumatic stress, depression and insomnia related sleep problems such as sleeping too early or late. Clients experiencing these repetitive and protracted problems should seek medical assistance.

Relapse prevention techniques

Besides creating a new pattern of life the client must also dissociate from the old world of use. This means that the most effective techniques to deploy immediately are distancing themselves from old using connections. The primary methods for both natural remitters and treatment seekers are escape and avoidance. It is easier for illicit drug users to escape temptation. Once drug users escape from the shadow society of use, temptations are reduced as they are no longer exposed to the public consumption of others. Problem drinkers face far higher social pressure to drink as alcohol has a common currency within mainstream structures. For example, where does one socialise which is alcohol free? Smoking tobacco is considered the hardest drug to quit not simply because of its pharmacological properties but because of the higher degree of social acceptance in a wide variety of social structures. With increasing social and legal restriction on smoking it will be interesting to see if the perceived difficulties of quitting begin to wane. Avoidance and escape are considered the most basic coping strategy people must master (Myers and Smith, 1995; Annis et al., 1996; Marlatt and Gordon, 1985). In any future exercises that the client seeks to undertake, if they are not confident in their ability to manage this challenge, they should always revert to these basic strategies.

For escape to work well, the client needs to anticipate situations where they may encounter other users who may offer them drugs or alcohol. Getting the client to describe the likely scenarios where this might happen can help alert them to the potential danger times and places. Thinking through and rehearsing strategies in advance can prepare them for these situations. Having a prepared script to say in the event of being offered a substance is useful but it is not simply the words that are important. It is the way they deliver the message that signals their confidence and assertiveness. Any hesitancy or pause in how these messages are delivered will signal to the interloper whether this person can be persuaded to yield. Figure 7.3 describes the key elements of escape.

In general, set techniques do not always translate well from the counselling room to the real world where the rehearsal is often too shallow and conducted without the pressure of competing sub-goals. As a result, when rehearsing skills it is good to practice them in role play situations where the helper takes on the role of the persuader. In groups, having individuals stand very close and face to face with each other and talk can replicate the changes in body language and pitch that can occur when we are under pressure. Teaching the client to relax, lowering the pitch of

Risk situation: I am likely to come across drugs/alcohol in:	
Strategy	**Response**
Make an excuse to escape quickly	What excuse could you use if you bumped into someone on the street?
Say no	How would you phrase the response that felt natural and comfortable?
Watch body language	How could you do this in a way that made you look confident?
Change the subject	How can you steer the conversation away?
Confront those offering	What questions might you ask the person who insists on you using?

Figure 7.3   Escape strategies (Myers and Smith 1995)

their voice and speaking fluidly whilst under duress can offer better preparedness for real situations. It can also be useful when discussing escape and refusal skills to get the client to consider why, as they invariably will, current users constantly offer drugs and alcohol to those that are trying to quit. At a pragmatic level this is because they will suspect that the recovering user has access to money to enable their own use. At a deeper level, the ex-user's attempt at change may raise dissonant self-judgements about their own continued use which they can assuage by changing the other person. Understanding that the other person's motives are purely self-directed can alter expectations and loyalties.

Avoidance is the next significant skill clients will have to learn to master. Natural remitters may leave their homes or districts in order to escape old ties, even if this for a short period of time. Avoidance is not simply of people and places but also of objects. When developing an avoidance plan with a client it is important to identify the key triggers to using. Furthermore, the easier it is to do something the more we will do of it, whilst the harder it is to do something, the less we do. Avoidance strategies must always be designed to make use as difficult as possible by reducing all the means to accomplish it (see Figure 7.4).

The client needs to be wary of any individuals who will have a negative impact on their recovery for whatever reason. This may extend well beyond active users and dealers. Friends, family or neighbours who sap their conviction and confidence in staying clean are equally as dangerous. Remember the sources of self-belief we explored in Chapter 3: it is far easier to undermine people's self-belief than it is to fortify it. Ironically, the client will also have to avoid many support agencies that were once the source of help as they are often open to a wider range of clients who are still actively using. Having out of hour services or specific venues for clients who are drug and alcohol free can be a great asset to those in recovery.

Equally, removing the means to use is also important; objects that make access to using easy should be avoided. There is an argument that individual's who used IV drugs should have an 'emergency' pack of needles handy so that they are not in the position of having to share in case of lapses. This argument has some merit to it. For some it may be an important safety net in the worse case scenario but for others is may be a means to an end. This should be discussed with the client before enforcing options here. We should also be careful to look at other objects that facilitate use. The classic is the mobile telephone and address book. Destroying telephone numbers and changing personal numbers to sever connection with using others is a major step forward in

---

Avoidance Plan

List all the high risk people that you need to avoid at this time:

- Other users: Bill, Pete, Sam and Tracey as I will be tempted to share.
- Dealers: Max and Jim who give me heroin and coke on tick.
- Family: Step father – find him negative about recovery.
  Sister is very draining and loads me with her problems.

List high risk places that I need to avoid at this time:

- The old neighbourhood where I used to score.
- The Drugs Project as a lot of people are using still. Easy access to needles.

List high risks things (such as drug paraphernalia) that I need to avoid at this time:

- Needles, bins and clippers.
- Too much cash. Have housing benefit paid straight to landlord.
- Get rid of cash point card.
- Dealers numbers and address book.
- Change mobile phone number.

What are some safe activities that I can get involved in now?

- Swimming and the gym to get fit.
- NA meetings – not the one at the community centre as people are very aggressive but will attend Tuesday at the hospital and Saturday nights at the church as it is a high risk time for me to use.

Where can I seek out support or who can give me support?

- Father Joseph at the mission centre.
- Dave my sponsor.
- My mum.
- My step brother Andy who has been through it and is clean.

Figure 7.4 Avoidance plans

separating from using others. Likewise, having easy access to cash, credit cards or cash point cards is equally dangerous in enabling easy use. A client I once worked with would freeze his cash point card in a bowl of water and defrost it when he needed it. It would never prevent him from accessing it to get funds for use, but the thawing processes would buy him just a little time to question what he was doing.

Activities available to the client should be rewarding and non-compatible with use. Swimming may be incompatible with drug use in a way DJ-ing in a night club may not be. Finally, people need to draw upon support in difficult times. They should never be over reliant on one person, but instead have a diverse support base that offers them something different and unique. This prevents one person feeling overloaded, and in the event of conflicts, it mans that other sources of support will be available. In drawing up an avoidance plan it is important that you help the client see them through. This hemisphere of the stages of change is about doing. Developing awareness is not sufficient. It is what the client does that will count, and we should always be looking at setting plans into action with clear dates and concrete outcomes.

Cravings and urges

Cravings and urges to use are common in the early stages of use. Again, educating the client to the nature of cravings is important. Marlatt and Gordon (1985) have stressed that there are common misunderstandings about the nature of cravings. Many clients believe that craving, a strong desire for an expected experience, are continued symptoms of withdrawal. Whilst this may be true in the initial throes of detoxification, most cravings are the product of external or internal cues. These trigger positive expectations through classical conditioning. As we saw in the first chapter, tolerance may be driven by psychological expectations. In situations where the individual has habituated themselves into using, their metabolism may adjust in anticipation of the drug. Cravings may be the result of this increase or decrease in their metabolism that is not countered by the drug. Cravings can be considered as the re-education of the body. We need to help the client re-attribute the craving not as an innate physical want but the desire for relief. The second mistake is that the craving forebodes imminent relapse. Instead, the client needs to understand that cravings are a natural response to cues and expectancies, which if overcome, will fade in time.

Clients need to recognise the onset of cravings. They may vary a great deal, from the taste of the drug in the mouth; a searing sense of anxiety; or a hyper-irritable state. At present, we can see that the craving is akin to a rush of anxiety (see Figure 7.5). Whilst their stress levels will fluctuate throughout the day, the onset of the craving feels like a deep and searing desire that increases dramatically over a short span of time. As this desire increases in intensity the client can become superstitious, believing that the craving will continue to intensify until it becomes so overpowering that they die or go insane. It is at this point the client may use to abate it. But this is a false economy. Using will only strengthen future cravings. Only resisting the craving and working through it does the client break the craving pattern and weaken its power.

We must develop the client's awareness of the external situational cues as well as the internal emotional prompts for cravings. It is important to include both these elements as expectancies

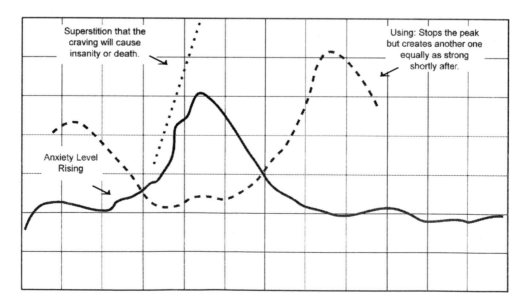

Figure 7.5 Diagram of craving

differ according to these two mediating factors. For example, using crack when angry is different when using with like-minded others in peer groups. Drinking alcohol at a funeral is different to drinking at a party. Expectancies are therefore specific to both emotional states and situations. Learning what these triggers are, the external and the internal ones, becomes essential in anticipating or avoiding cravings. Furthermore, exploration of craving events provide clues to what other strategy might fulfil the client's wants at this time. Most textbooks recommend that clients keep craving diaries, but in clinical practice I do not know of any clients that actually maintain them. Therefore, direct explorations of the kind of situations and moods the client is in when they have had recent experience of cravings may be more useful in assessing the expectations that trigger them and alternative fulfilments. People may also use activities to ease cravings. Going into environments where there is no association with use will also abate cravings.

Case Study: Managing cravings

On a relapse prevention programme for young people, each client was given a worker's mobile phone number for emergencies. One young person rang a worker and said he feared relapsing. He bought and hid a six pack of beer and had enough money to buy heroin with. The worker asked what he hoped the alcohol and heroin would do for him right now. The young man said he just wanted to be out of it for a bit, escape daily life for a short while. Well, the worker concluded, that is a lot like going to the cinema, to sit and be in a fantasy world for a while and forget everyday hassles. The young person had not been to the cinema in years and would not have thought of it. He realised if he went to the cinema he would not be able to afford the heroin either. As a result, he went to the cinema and the lapse was avoided.

Getting the client to recognise the times, situations and mood states associated with the cravings is an important part in avoiding them. However, as stated earlier, cravings and urges are a natural and unavoidable part of learning to manage a drug and alcohol free life. As such there are a number of behavioural strategies which can be useful in learning to manage the craving. These are listed in Figure 7.6. Consider each one and think through which would be best as the craving sets in, as it happens and finally what the client might do after the craving has passed.

In practice the client would not use all of these techniques. Instead they would develop their own routine, using skills from each section. The craving may make it hard to focus. Therefore a clear, simple and well-rehearsed repertoire or coping is better in the pressured reality of the experience. The importance of the management of craving and urges may not be locked into the specific technique itself but the belief in the technique. In parallel research, in the 1980s biofeedback become a popular treatment strategy for ailments such as tension headaches. Clients would be connected by electrodes to feedback machines and given information about degrees of relaxation, teaching them how to stop tension headaches. Holroyd et al. (1984) took a group of tension headaches sufferers and divided them into two groups. One group was given the feedback to teach them to relax, whilst the second group were actually taught to tense but were told they were relaxed. The outcome for both groups was exactly the same. What appeared to be important in the treatment of tension headaches was the belief that they could be controlled. This may be the same for cravings, where the greater the individual's belief that they have the ability to control them the greater the effect.

Behavioural techniques to manage cravings
Before the craving
Recognise the craving Cravings can vary from tasting the drug, thinking about the drug, people you used with, places associated with using. It is important to recognise the symptoms so you can respond to it. Say to yourself something like 'I am having a craving but I do not have to use. Nothing bad will happen, it will pass.' *Be positive* It is really important that when you feel anxious that you see yourself in a positive light. Think of something positive about yourself such as being a good parent, worker or student. Or a quality that you have, that you are a caring person, you make others laugh or that you are a good friend to someone. *Relax* Cravings may make you anxious, speed up your heartbeat, make you breathe rapidly or perspire. It is important to relax. Breathe in through your nose very slowly. Hold your breath for three seconds and then breath out through your mouth. Count to three and repeat. This will bring your heart beat down and help you feel calmer and more able to manage the craving.
During the craving
Delay Tell yourself that you will wait ten minutes and see how you feel then before making a choice. *Rise above the feeling* Separate the feeling from you. Rather than saying to yourself 'I am craving for a drug' see it as 'I am having a craving which will pass.' Try to use visualisation techniques, imagining the craving as something separate from yourself. *Distraction* What could you do to distract yourself from the craving? Phone a friend? Go for a walk? Eat a favourite snack?
After the craving
Reward yourself Reward yourself by buying yourself or allowing yourself a treat, like a new CD to just congratulating yourself for succeeding in beating the craving. Talking to others about how they might reward you for beating a craving in advance means that you could get positive praise from others when you do it. *Think about the craving* Work out what the triggers were that set off the craving. Keeping a craving diary can help you to see patterns and help you anticipate triggers. You may also notice that the cravings die down, happen less and become less powerful. What helped you overcome it?

Figure 7.6 Strategies to manage cravings (Annis et al., 1996)

Visualisation techniques

Visualisation techniques allow the client to externalise urges to use. Rather than being submerged in the feeling that they are craving, they reframe the craving as a passing phase. One way of doing this is through *urge surfing*. The client imagines that they are a surfer and a large wave (the craving) comes sweeping through them. Just like a surfer they must ride the wave out until it breaks, staying balanced and feeling the wave rush beneath them until it subsides. In the *samurai technique*, craving, urges and triggers are viewed as a mortal enemy. They lie in wait for you anywhere and attack when you least expect it, a little like Cato in the Pink Panther movies. The client must visualise their enemy, be alert to sudden attacks and be prepared to out-battle them. This is a strategy preferred by males on the whole.

One of the most common tricks used by people, and reiterated by Burman (1997) is *thought substitution*. This is when an overtly positive expectation is replaced with an overtly negative one. This only works when the negative expectation is truly noxious and repellent to the client. For example, a female quit smoking after a cervical scan revealed treatment was needed. When she looked at cigarette packets she would think of that image from the scan being in the pack. A client trying to lose weight visualised plates of take away food as warm congealed fat. A heroin user who had bad abscesses imagined that poison in the barrel of the needle. These need not be health related but could also be about important values that are contradictory to the experience of use. Peele (1995) re-tells how his Uncle Oscar stopped smoking after being teased by co-workers about giving away his money to the corporations. As a staunch union man smoking was incompatible with his world view and so he stopped. Miller (1998) likewise tells of a smoker who left his child waiting in the rain whilst he nipped around the shop to buy cigarettes. Finding her wet and bedraggled after it took invariably longer than he had previously cared to admit, shocked him into change. Finding the most reprehensible image to that individual is thus vital to its success. Research (Connors et al., 1998) showed that the strategy of recollection of previous problems associated with use figured in 61 per cent of abstinence periods of women and 80 in per cent of men. Many natural remitters held on to painful mementos of their use like old photographs or arrest cards to augment these negative memories.

Besides the thought substitute, reward substitution is also a highly prevalent strategy employed in these early days of recovery. Here cravings and urges are countered by the client deploying other rewards to dupe themselves into achieving some form of satiation. Identifying and deploying these countering techniques is important, and often intrinsic, to successful change. Comfort and sugary food appear particularly popular but anything that the client believes will help usually does. For example, in Klingemman's (1992) research some found taking vitamins helpful, on the premise that they were restoring what was lost, whilst 51 per cent of the heroin users found cannabis useful. Many might consider this simply trading one addiction for another, when it actually served as a useful bridge out of heroin consumption and into normal life.

Cognitive processes

The second problem area in the early strategies of recovery is the effect on thought processes. The self-mutiny that reactance can inspire may drive people to test personal control in order to regain the personal freedom they have lost, or becomes rationalised as denied to them. Self-tempting thoughts such as 'I will quit tomorrow' or 'I can control it now', or 'I will do it just the once' can haunt the client and undermine their resolve. This has to be combated with self-affirmation statements or attributions which minimise the situation as not being that bad, or that these urges will pass. Certainly the biggest trap individuals may succumb to is Apparently Irrelevant Decisions, which seduce the individual to orbit ever closer to temptation. The client may happen to find themselves in a situation where the drug or alcohol is so immediately available that they would have to be superhuman to resist, and as this was not a covert choice of their own, it alleviates guilt by making lapse appear understandable. Educating clients to the nature of these decisions is important to halt the seduction process.

One way of doing this is through behaviour chains. The lapsed client often feels they had no choice in the lapse processes. The behaviour change diagram can help them unpack the experience and help identify where they were active agents in the process. Here we explore the details in the build up to the lapse and record it on the chain. Each 'spike' on the chain represents a point of choice leading to the event. Once the story is told, you then explore what other options were available to them at each point of choice, what they could have done differently along every step of the way. This behaviour chain is useful in that it provides clients with a visual overview of the process and seeing themselves in the process of self-deception is often met with laughter as it is with realisation. Shortening the spikes as the chain progresses gives a sense of narrowing down of options. See Figure 7.7 for an example of a completed chain for a smoker, who initially reported that they felt that there was no build up to the lapse. What were her other options?

Acting sooner, when at home and restless, is far easier than taking action when sat with the means of indulgence at one's disposal and those who might encourage resistance are removed from the picture. Secondly, if a different choice is made along the way, the whole outcome can change. This means we not only educate the client to the process and the consideration of choices, but may strengthen the belief that they have greater control than they are consciously aware of. Behaviour chains can also be useful in identifying the factors that initiated the behavioural response in the first place. Whether it was an external cue of seeing others drink alcohol or an internal one such as feeling depressed. This can teach the client what their risk factors are and help us to target our interventions at teaching them other ways to deal with these typical moments of lapse. This is important as lapse and relapse appear to be initiated by a limited number of factors.

Phase 2: stress inoculation

At some stage in the client's recovery, the individual is going to have to confront and overcome risk situations if they are to maintain drug and alcohol free lifestyles. Klingemann's (1992) heroin and alcohol using cohort began to make extensive use of this strategy once they had moved through the early period of recovery. Phase 2 of relapse prevention work aims to address this directly through the development of a comprehensive coping skills programme, targeted directly at managing risk situations. This has been termed the stress inoculation training (Meichenbaum, 1992). Marlatt and Gordon (1985) describe the three core components of the model as the conceptualisation of the risk situation by the client in relation to their coping skills; the development of new coping skills; followed by the rehearsal and implementation where the client both practices and then applies the new skills to real situations.

The first component demands a deep analysis of the client's risk hierarchy. Research into relapsed users has highlighted that there are eight key determinants of relapse (Marlatt and Gordon, 1980; Cummings et al., 1980). Five of these determinants were categorised as intrapersonal, as they were primarily the result of interactions within the person. Whilst three others were defined as interpersonal as they were primarily driven by interaction with others (see Figure 7.8). In their initial findings, Gordon and Marlatt (1985) identified that 82 per cent of

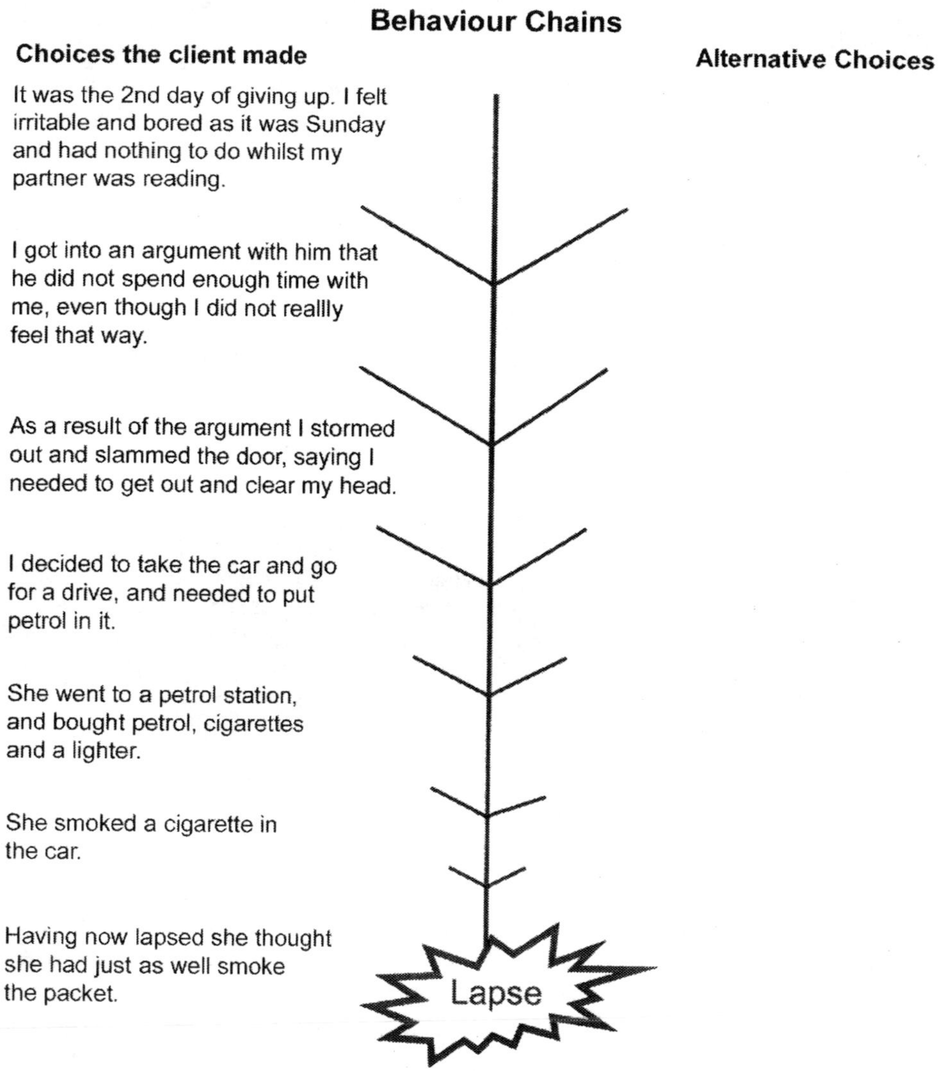

Behaviour Chains

Choices the client made   **Alternative Choices**

It was the 2nd day of giving up. I felt
irritable and bored as it was Sunday
and had nothing to do whilst my
partner was reading.

I got into an argument with him that
he did not spend enough time with
me, even though I did not reallly
feel that way.

As a result of the argument I stormed
out and slammed the door, saying I
needed to get out and clear my head.

I decided to take the car and go
for a drive, and needed to put
petrol in it.

She went to a petrol station,
and bought petrol, cigarettes
and a lighter.

She smoked a cigarette in
the car.

Having now lapsed she thought
she had just as well smoke
the packet.

Lapse

Figure 7.7 Example of behaviour chain for smoking

intrapersonal relapse occurred due to frustration and anger. In the interpersonal categories other emotions accounted for 85 per cent of the relapses. These findings have been broadly supported by other researchers, but Wallace (1989) and Heather et al. (1991) also identified that relapse was driven not by a single discrete determining factor but by several in operation at the same time.

In stress inoculation, the individual's susceptibility to each determinant is assessed. This can be done in several ways. Autobiographical explorations may highlight consistent patterns of causes of previous lapse. Alternatively exploring the client's fantasies about what conditions would most likely make the relapse can also identify vulnerabilities. If the relapses were caused by several determinants the client should choose the most potent. There is a problem in these scenarios in that they rely on recall or forecasting based on memory which often contains bias. We tend to

Intrapersonal
(1) **Unpleasant emotional states:** People may use to deal with difficult emotional states. These include negative feelings such as frustration or anger due to hassles of daily life or incorporate wider feelings of loneliness, boredom, worry or depression.
(2) **Physical discomfort:** Drugs are used to ease physical pain. This includes physical states which relate to prior drug use such as physical withdrawal or cravings. It also relates to non drug-using physical discomfort such as illness, fatigue or injury.
(3) **Pleasant emotions:** Here drugs are used to enhance positive emotions such as feeling joy, in control or happiness
(4) **Testing personal control:** This is the ex-user's desire to test their will power by using drugs in moderation or 'Just the once' to see if they can manage it now.
(5) **Urges:** This is where use is resumed through an inner temptation or deep urge to use. This may be accompanied by cravings. It can be triggered by finding oneself exposed to a situation where the substance is there to be taken. Alternatively it can come as an urge to seek it out where no substance is immediately at hand.

Interpersonal
(1) **Conflict:** This is where drug use is resumed after arguments or disagreements with other people. Often these encounters leave people in a negative emotional state such as frustrated, angry or guilty. At other times people might feel anxious, apprehensive or worry about the implications of the conflict.
(2) **Social pressure:** Drug use can start as a result of other people's drug use tempting people back into usage. This can be direct as in being offered the drug or it can be indirect through the ex-user just observing others, such as an ex-drinker walking past a pub and seeing others through the window.
(3) **Pleasant times:** Drugs can be taken to enhance a pleasant occasion such as a wedding, sex or other celebrations. Although this enhances a positive mood the drug is taken as part of more social interactions.

Figure 7.8   Determinants of relapse (Marlatt and Gordon, 1985)

remember emotionally powerful events which may generate misleading data. An excellent assessment tool has been developed by Annis et al. (1996) called the Inventory of Drug Situations which systematically asks the client about a variety of setting for previous use. The measures can then be extrapolated in graph form, highlighting the individual risk hierarchy.

Certainly we tend to see a general divide between long term users and young people. Older, long term user's consumption tends to be negatively reinforced in that they use to stave off or control negative emotions or stresses. Young people's use appears positively reinforced. They are more likely to use in positive situations and in positive moods. Very few relapse prevention programmes teach the management of these times as a risk factor and therefore may not be as efficient in dealing with young people's needs. In general terms then, relapse is not necessary limited to stereotypical negative emotions, but may be linked to the intensity of the emotion. In high emotional states we are more likely to see the world in the black and white contrast of our wants. Hence the person that has quit smoking is just at risk after a bad day at work as they are at a party having a good time.

Coping responses

The client's risk hierarchy can then be compared to an assessment of their coping strategies. A coping strategy is any response that allows the individual to manage any risk situation without relapse. Coping strategies can be drawn from four key domains. These are included in Table 7.1:

Table 7.1 Coping strategies

Coping domain	Examples
Cognitive (Thought based strategies)	Problem solving skills Reframing: Finding good in a bad situation Anticipating consequences Thought substitution and visualisation Self-praise and validation Planning
Affective (Emotional based strategies)	Ventilating feeling in the gym Expressing feelings through creative arts Communication skills Assertiveness training Anger management Refusal skills Dealing with negative mood states
Behavioural (Action based strategies)	Social skills training Avoiding risk situations Stress management techniques Recreational activities
Interpersonal support (Help from others)	Stress buddies Emergency contacts Social groups that do not support using behaviour

This is not an exhaustive list, but a typical range of skills that are taught in relapse prevention programmes to augment the coping repertoire of clients. Rather than carpet bombing clients with skills, a detailed individual assessment is important. Careful assessment of coping can highlight strengths and deficits and indicate to both the helper and the client areas they need to work on in order to develop resilience to risk. There may be some clues gained from the assessment of determinants. For example, someone who scores highly in succumbing to social pressure may find refusal skills and assertiveness important. Alternatively an individual who scores highly on negative mood states and low on positive social occasions probably isolates themselves when depressed. This might mean that they need to find ways to call on support from others when low and learn how to self-sooth in crises moments. In group situations it is more difficult to tailor skills training to the individual, yet at the same time the group can provide a bank of experience and resources for individuals to call upon. Allowing the clients to choose which groups and subjects they would like to do, as well as having free air time to discuss each client's weekly progress before commencing in the skills based work can be important in ensuring the programme feels relevant to all the members (Kadden et al., 1992).

Assessing coping is difficult as a client that lacks particular coping skills in any given domain cannot tell you what they do not know. This is important because we do not want to know what the client could do in a risk situation, but what they actually do. A good method of assessing coping skills is the situational competency test developed by Chaney et al. (1978). In the situational competency test the client is given ten brief scenarios that are typical stressors for relapse. These can be further divided between negative emotional stresses, positive occasions and neutral events.

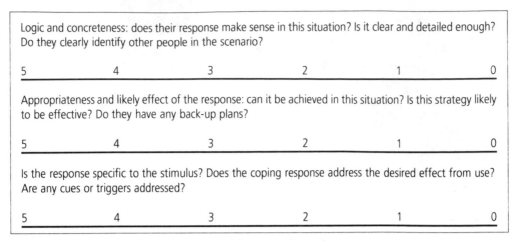

Figure 7.9 Situational competency evaluation (Chaney et al., 1978)

This might be an argument at work; attending a wedding where everyone is drinking and having fun; or just being sat at home alone feeling bored. Basing them on the eight determinants of relapse may test how specific their responses are to different vulnerabilities. The client is asked to imagine entering into these situations and describe what they would do or say to avoid lapsing. A short time limit of 30 seconds can be enforced in order to replicate the real-life pressure that they would be under to respond if the given situation where real. Their answers are then scored up to five points on the following dimensions (see Figure 7.9). The situational competency test should be done at intake into the treatment programme and can be repeated as the client works through the programme.

The client's final score will give a baseline measure of their coping, as well as indications of their coping style. If the client has a narrow range of skills it will give clear indications of what other skills they may need to augment their recovery. The situational competency test can also be used as an outcome measurement tool. Repeating the test monthly or at treatment completion can reveal which skills the client has acquired. Again, giving this feedback directly to the clients can shore up their gains by allowing them to evaluate their own progress in a concrete and impartial manner. Comparing clients scores across a programme may also show patterns or common weaknesses which will indicate which of the skills you are teaching are translating well to the group. This can be useful in evolving programmes and stopping them becoming stale.

I also use an amended situational competency test in measuring the outcome of longer training programmes for substance misuse workers. Taken prior to training and at completion, they are more sensitive to change and progression than evaluation sheets and they are hard to fool, as students will have acquired the new skills, or not, as a result of training (Harris, 2002). These measures appear sensitive to change, even at one year follow up. For example, when these test are conducted on workers who have gone on to use the training materials as supervision aids to other students, they preserve their scores. In comparison a slight decay happens in those who just practice.

Skills training

The skills training aspect of relapse prevention is then tailored to the individual client's weakness in relapse risks and the deficits in coping strategies. Again, the more these tasks feel relevant to the client, the greater the engagement will be. A common error in delivering relapse groups is that very often they are delivered as lectures and lack an experiential element. In order to acquire any skills from any programme clients must rehearse, practice and evaluate if they are to truly assimilate new skills. The strong theory base behind relapse prevention work, combined with its more educative approach makes informing groups tempting. But it is the doing that remains important if these skills are to not only embed but also be automatically available to people in the high pressure environment of a risk situation. Research has demonstrated that specific skills based treatment can show superior outcomes than generalised counselling (see Jones and Lanyon, 1981; Roth and Fonagy, 1996).

In order to further enhance self-belief, relapse prevention will set homework tasks where the client must take these newly acquired skills into challenging 'dry run' situations. Marlatt and Gordon (1985) recommend these tasks only be attempted once the client has acquired the basic coping skills. These can be programmed homework tasks. Annis et al. (1995) recommend choosing a determinant where the client feels most confident first, and build up to increasingly challenging situations. An objective is then set for the client. For example, if the client felt confident in resisting social pressures to drink, his task could be to walk down a drinks aisle of a supermarket; enter a bar without drinking; or walk through an old neighbourhood where the client once scored. For those with low self belief they may be accompanied or go as a group to discuss their reactions and feelings.

The preparation for the event is important. Before entering the risk situation, the client must 'live it' mentally so to speak. Working with the helper they describe the sensations, reactions, cues and doubts and weaknesses they may feel going into this situation. Together, the helper and client identify what coping skills and strategies can be used when and how. Role play, rehearsal and more skills training may be needed. Once the client has acquired these skills they repeat what they will do and how they will do it with as much detail as possible, like a story. This is rather akin to the mental rehearsal we may do in preparing for an interview. We might imagine waking up in the morning, getting to the venue, waiting, entering the room and responding to each specific question we presume we will be asked. It can raise the heart beat in anticipation, creating a real time level of stress that we must master. But having rehearsed it, we have a script and we know what cues we must look for in managing these pressures in real life (see Figure 7.10).

There are limits to stress inoculation in that you can only invite the client to enter into environments which may elicit urges to use. One cannot set a homework task based on the emotional distress. For example, you cannot set tasks to feel depressed or have an argument with someone. Instead I tend to explore the risks that the client faces in the coming week. If the risk feels too challenging then we go for avoidance as the primary strategy. If the client feels able to deal with it then the situation is explored, risk and vulnerabilities identified and stratagems rehearsed. But the caveats of self-efficacy need to be remembered in the application of these skills. The tasks must be challenging but do-able. Early failure can have a devastating effect on self-belief. Alternatively task that are not challenging enough will fail to develop self-belief and increase resilience.

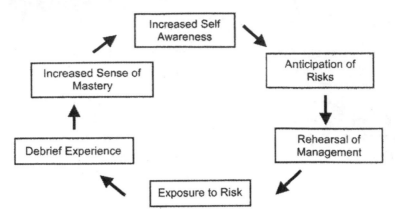

Figure 7.10   Stress inoculation approach

Case Study: Stress inoculation

A stimulant user had achieved his first month of sobriety when he visited the drug project in a state of anxiety. The previous day he found a lump on his testicles, and had made an emergency appointment to see a doctor who conducted tests. The results of these tests would not be available for four days. The client was distressed and fearful when he came to see his case worker. The case worker remained calm and confident as he listened to the client's fears. Whilst acknowledging the stress he was under he put the situation in perspective, deliberately modelling confident and clear behaviour. He reminded the client that there was no reason to fear the worst. On balance of probability it was more likely to be a cyst, and, even in the worse case scenario the prognosis was good. They had four days to manage before they could make any decisions. He reminded the client of the problem solving training the previous week, how it was important to break problems down into smaller parts. The client recognised this. Together they explored the difficulties over the next few days, what emotions the client felt might trigger use, when were going to be the most difficult times and how confident he felt in overcoming them. They then explored what coping strategies could be most effective. Once the four days were planned the client reiterated the plan. The night times when he was alone felt the most difficult. He had no confidence he could manage these times. Instead he would stay with his parents for the remaining nights. He rehearsed what he would tell them and how he would approach it. As they were elderly he did not want to worry them overly and so his rehearsed approach was confident and underplayed the situation, presenting it as if he was not feeling that well. The days were easier but he feared he would not sleep well at night, so he arranged to rise early, and do an early morning session in the gym. He would then attend the support group and one-to-one sessions each day to review progress. A late afternoon swim would ensure he felt physically tired. In the evening he would remain active, not engage in passive recreation that would allow him to dwell. Instead he would cook for his parents and read a particular book which he found inspirational. If he felt overwhelmed he would journal his thoughts to alleviate concerns, but these had to be strengths based rather than the worst scenario. His worker would attend for the results

with him and they would make another immediate plan the day they were out. The client
stayed clean and the test results came back negative for cancer.

Just as setting homework task for dry runs, it is important to set a plan for lapsing in advance, using a simple set of actions as well as debriefing to augment the learning and evaluate changes in self-efficacy. Working in community settings, with the client exposed to risk on a day-to-day basis means that those on relapse prevention programmes often face more lapse events in the initial stages of treatment. But the continued exposure, partial success or overcoming means that their self-efficacy begins to increase over time, with results snowballing over a two year period (Marlatt and Gordon, 1985). Conversely, those in residential rehabilitation units are often protected from risk, meaning they do better in the short term, but once outside the protective environment lapse increases.

Working with lapse and relapse

Whilst lapse is seen as set-back it need not be the case that it will inevitably lead to relapse. Fortunately, the idea of removing clients from treatment programmes who have lapsed is becoming outmoded. Lapse on programme can be a useful learning experience for the client. It is better that it occurs within a supportive framework that can provide guided mastery and assistance in helping the client make the connection between the skills they have been taught and their experience.

Case Study: Working with lapse

On a programme for young people, three clients relapsed and the workers were
disconsolate. They demanded that the clients have emergency methadone, as if the
whole process was ruined. One key worker reminded these colleagues that they had just
spent two months training these young people to overcome such set-backs; they wanted
to see two things happen. Firstly, what did the young people believe they should do.
Secondly, the workers themselves needed to show faith that they could turn it around.
Their negativity was the problem as it transmitted a complete lack of faith in the young
people. If these young people could overturn this event it would be an important learning
experience and increase their mastery. This was an important part of the treatment.
Discussing this with the young people they decided to set about a rapid home
detoxification, and were back on the programme within the week.

Lapse events can also be useful in addressing the forbidden fruit effect. The forbidden fruit effect was the amplification of positive expectancies we saw earlier. Exploring what expectancies prompted the lapse, whether it is urges or craving, in contrast to the actual experience, can be useful means of bursting the bubble of expectation. Research demonstrates that what is hoped for in use is rarely achieved (Cappell and Greeley, 1987; Wilson, 1982).

Case Study: Forbidden fruit effect and lapse

Rachael had given up drugs and alcohol after several residential treatment attempts.
However, back in the community she continued to lapse back into alcohol use. After a

very bad day at work she was feeling very depressed. A colleague sympathised and suggested they go for a drink after work, ending in a heavy drinking session. Exploring this with the Rachael the next day, the helper asked what did she think that the drink would do for her when her colleague invited her out? She thought it would lighten her mood and relieve the stress of the work problem. 'Then, when you started to drink, what actually happened?'

'I became more obsessed with the event, brooding on it and finding it impossible to discuss anything else.'

'So, what did you do next?' The client decided to drink more, thinking it would induce a more positive mood, that she would be up and dancing. 'What actually happened?' I asked the helper She reported that she began crying and felt even more depressed.

'So do you still feel alcohol is the best way to lift your mood?'

'No. It is just making it worse.' Lapses became infrequent from then on, even in the light of major life changes.

In dealing with lapse or relapse it is essential that the client responds quickly. The abstinence violation effect can generate intense dissonance in the client. Attributions that they are a failure may augment the belief that relapse was inevitable. Furthermore, if all the means of success are put at your disposal and you still fail, this can prove even harder. Our continued message of change being hard work is important at this juncture. The client may feel that they have let you down and isolate themselves from support. Annis et al. (1995) recommend a rapid assertive outreach response to clients who miss appointments. Telephoning, or handwritten but professional letters, reminding them of the next appointment and expressing an open door policy if their priorities have changed is extremely useful in clinical practice in returning people back into treatment. Research showed that sending letters to clients who missed appointments reduced drop out rates from 51 per cent to 28 per cent (Panepinto and Higgins, 1969). Personal calls have also been shown to have a big impact on retention (Intagliata, 1976). For dual diagnosis clients I would include a SAE, pen and paper. Whilst I feared that this might be seen as patronising to begin with, all the clients, especially those with episodic problems or agoraphobia were touched and responded by post, rejoining services when they felt able to continue.

When working with clients that have slipped it is important to recognise whether lapse or relapse has occurred. This may be evident in terms of the length of use, whether it has exceeded five days of continuous use, but also in the client's attitude. Resignation to the event may indicate deep dissonance and acceptance of the failure. Strengthening the belief that the failure was inevitable reduces internal stress. For the client who fears or has lapsed it is essential to reframe the slip as a learning experience. Learning this the hard way is difficult, but important none the less. The lapse needs to be seen as a specific event, not who the client is. Re-attributing cause can be vital here. Those who attribute failure to innate, uncontrollable circumstances are far more likely to relapse more deeply. Asking the client what was happening at the time of the lapse will automatically direct them to discussing the external factors around the lapse. Reminding the client that all change is hard work can diminishing failure, recasting it as a lack of application rather innate deficiency. Most importantly, the client must recognise all is not lost. The sooner they implement change again the greater their chance of success (Prochaska et al., 1994). For the relapsed client, they may re-enter pre-contemplation, but there will be an underlying dissonance having invested a great deal in the change attempt. As a result motivational interviewing skills can be used to kick start the process of change. And as such, the intentional change process loops around once again.

Conclusion

The early stages of recovery are dominated by the mastery of substance-free life. Here the client must overcome the wake of their dependence. Where self-belief is low all measures must be taken in order to augment the client's belief in their capacity to establish new patterns of behaviour. Avoidance, escape and distraction are important facets in this process. Whilst urges and cravings are a central obstacle, the neutralisation of overtly positive expectations with the painful realities of use remains a powerful and aversive strategy. The client can only barricade themselves against temptation for a short period of time. Learning to confront risk, deploy key strategies and demonstrate to oneself that temptation can be overcome becomes an integral part of this process. Mastery of this experience is the key to a different life. It demands persistence, clarity and faith. Whilst the number of reasons determining relapse are limited, the means to overcome them are not, and a sensitive optimism from supportive others is essential in bridging this transitory moment from one life to another. Laying down the foundations of a new life structure is integral to all of this. But this life must evolve into a more rewarding existence if the benefits of change are to establish themselves as a preferred norm.

Chapter 8

On Maintenance

At the Day of Judgment we shall not be asked what
we have read but what we have done.

Thomas A Kempis

Once the client has ceased problematic use and managed the early problems such as withdrawal, cravings and urges, they must now maintain these changes in light of obstacles and setbacks. Prochaska and DiClemente's research suggests that sustaining the momentum of helping relationships, countering and rewards are necessary for the continuance of non-smoking. But the dependence on nicotine does not demand the total abandonment of one's life, only elements of it. For those submersed in the exclusion of addictions it demands a more radical lifestyle change. Once they have broken their dependence they must overcome their addiction. They must replace the life they have lost with a more rewarding and enriching existence. A striking feature of addiction is the time and energy it consumes: are problem users lifestyle and identity structured entirely around acquiring the funds for drugs, taking the drugs and sitting through the effects before commencing the cycle once more. As we have seen, use is bound up in a shadow network of like-minded others that mutually sustain it. At the same time, the problematic user may not feel competent in initiating or dealing with mainstream demands of life after long periods of social exclusion. Therefore we shall review the findings of successful natural recovery and consider how we can replicate these lifestyle changes within treatment situations. This demands less in the way of formal treatment and more in assisting people to reintegrate with the social structures of mainstream life. This chapter will describe how this can be done systematically, building on the natural motivations of the client and sustained over time.

What is recovery?

Once again, reviewing the natural remission research we see wide agreement on the recovery processes. Burman's (1997) natural remission research highlighted that in the final stages of recovery a new identity emerged in her drinking cohort. This entailed finding new responsibilities, interests and placing greater value on social norms. This self-driven recovery was also inspired by others who had achieved sobriety. This vicarious learning was augmented by the rewards which came with improvements in family and social relationships. Many had previous failed attempts at controlled use, before identifying and maintaining sobriety as a goal. Greater access to environmental support played a very important role in sustaining recovery, particularly in the areas of employment, non-drinking social groups, broader social interests and long term relationships. These all provided increased stability in individuals' lives.

We see similar results in Stall and Beirnaki's (1986) review of natural remission studies. New identities and the immersion in non-using social groups were essential to their recovery. Alongside this was a new spirituality in individuals, as was strong feedback that affirmed their gains. We have already seen how Beirnaki's (1983) research observed that the degree of self-reinvention necessary to overcome addiction was dependent on the relative immersion in the shadow society. Those heavily embedded in their use constructed a new persona that did not exist prior to the addiction. Those who were less consumed in this using world were able to build upon or extend the remnants of an identity that was not catastrophically eroded.

Klingemann (1992) found the environment played a significant role. As these changers continued to progress, approval from others in their life augmented their gains. Family, bosses and even casual acquaintances were all cited as important in the recovery process. The initiation of stable drug-free relationships provided more rewards and a higher quality of life. For many, reinstating old hobbies, and a desire to make up for the time lost to their addiction offered a new appetite for life. Again, in parallel to this was the emergence of new identities. This was expressed as finding a new meaning in life that 'filled the hole' drugs and alcohol had left behind.

This new identity took three distinct but interrelated forms. Firstly was the emergence of what Klingemann called post-materialism. A new set of heightened values established themselves and were articulated in terms of either religious or spiritual beliefs. Others found more secular avenues to express these values such as politics, feminism, ecology or art. Secondly, people found a new compatibility within the social roles of being the father, mother or employee. In this normalisation process they were able to fulfil societal expectations and abandoned idealistic or anti-establishment notions. Thirdly, this new ethic became expressed through helping others. They offered their time and skills to assist others in settings such as drug and alcohol treatment centres, people with disabilities or those with mental health problems.

Becoming a professional in the welfare field is a very common experience after overcoming addictions. After long periods of social exclusion it could be suggested that their past using experience qualifies as a form of specialist knowledge. And as adults we must all operate in a labour market that buys and sells specialist knowledge. As such the past using experience becomes a marketable commodity. This often replaces the skills gap after long periods of social separation and offers an in-road back to the work force. At the same time it also allows the recovering user to find purpose and meaning in their past experience if it serves to help or alleviate others' pain. But this expression of helping is not only limited to the work place, but also manifests in helping others in the family and associates. Again this suggests the emergence of a deeper ethic that is expressed in a global shift in values.

These emergent values may be closely linked to the crisis in values in the contemplation stage, where we saw that a breakdown or perceived clash in values were so integral to the motivational process. It is not clear from the research whether this is the reassertion of deeply held beliefs, smothered by years of normalised anti-social behaviours; a re-formation of values in the light of the fragmentation of previous beliefs; or simply the natural expression of the maturing personality which has been impeded through years of social exclusion. But what is clear is that it emerges in all the remission and treatment research. This has led to renewed interest in the spiritual aspects of recovery. However, there is nothing in the research that suggests that there is a particular faith necessary to change. What is important about the emergent values is that they foster negative expectations of use. It is the function of the individual's belief rather than what they believe as such. This was one of the principle differences we saw between non-users and users in Chapter 2.

Comparing the process of change in both treated groups evaluated by De Leon (1996) with the natural remission studies of Stall and Biernaki and Klingemann, we see the reintegration of new social roles and values is prevalent in both groups to a far higher degree than identified by Prochaska and DiClemente's smoking group (see Table 8.1).

Table 8.1 Comparative models of recovery

Prochaska and DiClemente	De Leon (1996) Treated Remission	Klingemann (1992) Natural Remission	Stall and Biernaki Natural Remission
Contemplation to preparation	**Pre-treatment** **Denial:** No acceptance of problems **Ambivalence:** Inconsistent awareness of problems for self and others **Extrinsic motivation:** Problems recognised but attributed to external events **Intrinsic motivation:** Recognition of problems associated with use **Readiness of change:** Considering options without seeking treatment **Readiness of treatment:** Acceptance of the need for treatment	**Motivation stage** Negative motivation: *Hitting rock bottom* *Deterrence* Positive motivation: *Maturing out* *Positive life-turning points*	**Stage 1** Problems associated with substance use Possibility of significant accidents 'Psychic change' (sudden or gradual change in perspective towards substance) Decision to quit (or initial attempt) Continuing possibility of significant accidents
Preparation to action	**Treatment stages** **De-addiction:** Withdrawal and detoxification **Abstinence:** Stabilisation of drug free state **Continuance:** Sobriety and commitment to maintain drug-free lifestyle, behaviour and values.	**Action stage** Diversion: Problem related strategies: *Everyday concepts* *Substitutes and consequences* *Distancing*	**Stage 2** Public announcement of the decision to quit Claim to new non-stigmatised identity *(Recidivist 'Chipper' continues to use privately)*
Action to maintenance	**Integration and identity change:** The resulting treatment experiences culminate in self-perceived change in personal and social identity.	**Maintenance stage** *Tricks and renewed confidence* *Protecting the achievement* A new life: *Becoming a helper* *Post-materialism* *Peace of mind and reconciliation*	**Stage 3** Ability to successfully renegotiate identity Successful in eliciting significant other support Ability to manage cravings Initial integration into non-using social groups Lessening of craving (2 years) Resolution/stabilisation of a new identity

What we see as a common theme across these natural remission studies is the normalisation of life perspective, re-establishment of pro-social groups and the expression of new values which facilitate the establishment of intimate and meaningful relationships. These might be considered the core ingredients of individuals formulating a new and meaningful life. As such, recovery is concrete in the reintegration into structures such as housing, relationships, family, work, education, recreation and hobbies. And it is aesthetic in the expression of values, greater personal control, intimacy, spirituality and acceptance. Throughout this book our working definition of addiction has been the erosion of relationships in pursuit of one satisfaction. Recovery is the re-instigation of relationships and satisfaction derived from diverse sources of enrichment.

In the early chapters we identified that the central problem of addiction is the exclusion resulting from this breakdown in relationships. Exclusion from an increasingly complex life leaves the early onset addiction clients with little preparation for re-entry in adult life. This places immense pressure on individuals to catch up and acquire the life skills that they have missed. This can feel overwhelming as they struggle to master the tasks of self-care, relationships and employment alongside the demands of treatment and lapse vigilance. These multi-dimension pressures can generate a deep malaise in the individual. They may attribute this to their perceived innate inadequacy, depression or even imminent relapse. But the struggles they experience will indicate the very skills that they now need to acquire. And the exploration of these problems can re-attribute the cause of the problem as indicative of a need to learn rather than innate deficiently.

Case Study: Developmental delay and recovery

A probation office referred a 38 year old client to a drug counsellor for a one-off session. The client was a long term heroin user, who had successfully completed residential treatment and lived for six months in supported housing. Now with his own flat he felt chronically depressed but could not bear the thought of yet more treatment. He was buying cd's compulsively and those in his NA group continually warned him this was a sign of obsessing that would lead to relapse. He felt that this was true and that it was only a matter of time before he succumbed and went back to using. He was desolate. Listening to this story, the counsellor said, 'You are also buying a lot of junk food and have Hep C which is making you feel even worse.' The client was surprised at this, and said that he was doing just that, and asked the counsellor how he knew that. The counsellor said 'You are living like a student. Why do students live that way?'

'Well, they have just left home, and don't yet know how to manage I suppose.'
'And for you?' At this the client laughed.
'Yes, this is my first real place.'
'How do students learn to manage differently?'
'Well they fuck up and they learn from it.'
'And for you?'
'I am just fucking up!' The client continued to laugh. Suddenly he reframed his experience. He understood himself not as a pathologically inferior, but as entering into the catching-up process. The things he was finding difficult were helpful signals directing him to what he needed to learn. He shrugged and remarked how strange it was, that recently in the probation office he saw a poster for free cookery lessons. He wanted to attend but did not know why, as he had never considered it before.

We must recognise that the central obstacle in recovery is overcoming the social exclusion of use. For the most eruditely rehearsed refusal skills will mean very little for the hopeful user that remains locked in the shadow society of use and has no practical means to escape it. When we consider the question of rehabilitation, we might ask for whom? The individual user is implicated in this, but so is the wider society that may deny opportunity for reintegration due to stigma and prejudice. Addiction is about a relationship between the individual and environments they occupy. As stressed earlier, too often addiction treatment has remained overtly focused on the removal of the biological or psychological want for the substance without any regard to the environmental factors which play a substantial role in initiating and maintaining addictions. Greater focus is needed to create access to those environments which preclude use and provide competing incentives to help sustain these changes. We are now seeing the development of relapse prevention models which account for this relationship between the individual and environment. Pre-eminent in these developments is the Community Reinforcement Approach (CRA).

Community Reinforcement Approach

CRA is based on behavioural therapy principles (Bellack et al., 1990). As such, it seeks to understand how behaviour occurs in relationship to the environment. The intervention relies heavily on assessment of the target behaviour, the environments in which they occur, selecting appropriate interventions and evaluating their effectiveness in changing behaviour (Nelson and Hayes, 1986). This is then augmented with environmentally based supports. As such, Corrigan (1997) identified the key advantages to behavioural therapy over other approaches. It is precise and measurable; enables individuals to express greater control over their environments; and assists in formulating treatment planning. It has also been effective with a wide range of disorders and ability levels.

To fully grasp behavioural therapy we need to understand the basic principles. In order to change behaviour it is important to understand its function. Behaviour can be understood functionally when we consider the factors that precede it and the consequences that follow it. For example, a person in recovery feels bored, seeks out his old dealer, uses and then feels relieved but frustrated in that he has lapsed and let people down. We can see this behaviour has a function in alleviating negative moods. It also has antecedents that stimulate the desire to use (boredom, meeting dealer) and consequences (short term relief and longer term disappointment). This process may also be influenced by other factors, such as the individual may be suffering from depression at the time which makes them feel pessimistic that they can do anything but use. The positive or negative consequences of behaviour will increase or decrease the probability of that behaviour happening again in that situation.

As such, behavioural therapy relies heavily on the idea of consequences working as reinforcers of behaviour. We have already reviewed this process in Chapter 5, but we will summaries it again as these terms can be confusing on first exposure to them. Reinforcers are consequences that increase the frequency of the behaviour. Positive reinforcers are those that add something desirable to the individual environment such as the pleasurable feeling of the drug. Negative reinforcement occurs when it removes something negative from the user's environment – the feeling of boredom. Conversely punishments are consequences that decrease the frequency of the behaviour. Positive punishments occur when something undesirable is placed in someone's environment, such as the user's partner shouting at them for lapsing. Whilst negative punishment removes something desirable from the person's environment, such as the partner giving the lapsed client the cold shoulder because of use. Extinction occurs when the behaviour is no longer reinforced. For example, if the user was able to successfully pressure their partner into giving them money to buy drugs, it would have positively reinforced the behaviour by adding something desirable to their environment, money for use. However, when they stop giving them money the pestering behaviour will intensify as the user persists and this is called the extinguishment burst. This burst often undermines the establishment of new boundaries. Because the behaviour gets worse for a short period, people read this as a signal that the intervention is not working. They then give up before the extinguishment occurs.

The community reinforcement approach borrows heavily from these principles and applies them directly to the treatment of problematic drug and alcohol use. The approach was developed by Hunt and Azrin (Miller 2001) in the 1970s. They felt that an addiction was greatly influenced by the user's social environment. The positive and negative reinforcing effects of alcohol in inducing desired feelings of intoxication and alleviating negative mood states could be interrupted by adding competing sources of satisfaction. Likewise the punishment of use could also be increased by allowing the natural consequence of high consumptions to be felt unhindered. They predicted that drinking could be reduced if attractive non-drinking activities were more available and contingent on not drinking. As such, CRA can be understood as a systematic analysis and rearrangement of the individual's environmental reinforcers in order to increase non-using behaviour whilst decreasing using. It differs from other counselling approaches in that it relies upon concrete rewards in the user's environment rather than insight to address these issues. CRA may resemble other skills based approaches at a superficial level, but its relentless focus on providing reinforcement to augment change makes it markedly different in practice.

The early CRA studies showed very promising results and led to the evolution of the programme that aimed to increase the satisfaction with all the other aspects of the problematic user's life. This includes marriage, family, employment, social skills and recreation amongst others. This has seen new approaches to the treatment of alcohol (Meyers and Smith, 1995); cocaine (Budney and Higgins, 1998) and heroin/methadone use (Stitzer et al., 1977). Whilst each of these programmes has its own unique elements, especially in the provision of alternative reinforcing behaviour, they also share a great deal of commonality. We shall describe these common themes first before exploring the particulars of each approach.

Therapeutic relationship in CRA

The treatment process begins before setting goals and tasks, as the behaviour of the helper is seen as critical. The position adopted by the helper should be one of directive-ness without confrontation. This can be a difficult balance to achieve. Certainly, the helper themselves must model the behaviours that are expected in the client, and again can serve as a source of learning simply by example. Key qualities outlined by Budney and Higgins (1998) include optimism, forward thinking and positive attitude towards achieving goals. The worker must exude confidence that the client can achieve their goals. There is a proactive tone in their interactions with the client and involved others. This demands vitality in approach, where obstacles are to be expected and seen as challenges to be overcome. In a similar way to solution focused therapy, we can empathise with the frustrations of set backs, allow some ventilation of feeling but it is then what we do about the situation that matters. A worker beset with doubts or negativity will transmit this to the client. As such it is important that the helper always models behaviour in the light of set backs and obstacles.

Workers also need a great deal of flexibility, particularly in the early stages of treatment. This involves negotiating appointments with clients around hours that best suit them and offering additional sessions per week if they are necessary. Even if the client attends a session 40 minutes late, the worker will still accommodate the client, thank them for coming and use this time to review progress on goals and tasks. The worker must also be actively involved in the process. Adults find it hard to enter into pre-formed social groups. Getting the client over thresholds of support services, job clubs, day care, social and recreational activities is difficult. Escorting them to make the first steps is essential in overcoming the fear barrier and helping create new social networks. To evaluate your performance consider the Exercise 8.1 below, and rate yourself on the following scores. What could you do to improve your performance in each area?

Exercise 8.1: Therapeutic alliance in CRA		
Quality	**Rating**	**What would raise this score?**
Flexibility: How flexible are you in appointment setting in the early stages of treatment?	1 2 3 4 5 6 7 8 9 10	
Empathy: How non-confrontational and understanding are you when working with clients?	1 2 3 4 5 6 7 8 9 10	
Active involvement: What support do you offer clients in practical terms outside the counselling session?	1 2 3 4 5 6 7 8 9 10	
Optimism: How optimistic are you that clients can achieve their goals?	1 2 3 4 5 6 7 8 9 10	
Modelling: How effective do you feel you are in modelling behaviour for clients?	1 2 3 4 5 6 7 8 9 10	

Goal setting in CRA

CRA uses an extensive one-to-one case working model alongside skills based group work. This is because each individual's reinforcers are unique to them. Identifying the client's reinforcers must be done meticulously for the programme to work well. The primary source of reinforcement of non-using behaviour is derived from the community of the user themselves (hence the name). As such, CRA makes extensive use of treatment planning assessment tools like the life satisfaction audits that we have already seen in Chapter 4 (see also the Happiness Scale and the Relationship

Brief: Statements of goals are kept as brief as possible to minimise confusion.
Wrong: Well, I am going to get my life together. I just want to be normal again-do normal things and get on with it. I need to sort stuff out with my wife, make it up to her and the kids.
Right: Spend time with my family every Sunday.

Positive: The goal must be something that the client is going to do rather than not do.
Wrong: I am not going to the pub or drinking with that old crowd anymore.
Right: I am going to get involved in the drama society again.

Measurable: Only use measurable, specific goals. The must be concrete descriptions of behaviour which is clear has been achieved.
Wrong: I will start checking job ads soon.
Right: I will look in Thursday's newspapers and contact four job advertisers the next week.

Figure 8.1   Goals in CRA (Meyers and Smith, 1995)

Happiness Scales, Meyers and Smith, 1995). Using these tools, we ask the client to rate their current levels of satisfaction in each domain of their lives. Listening to the positive and negative aspects they identify in each domain can offer clues and insights into past sources of reinforcement that could be amended to the present situation. We can then ask what would improve their scores in each area. It is important that we support the client to be honest in this process. It is not what they feel they ought to do but instead what they want in each domain of their life. Although not part of CRA in a pure sense, the scaling techniques we saw in solution focused therapy can be usefully applied if the client finds it difficult to identify other sources of satisfaction.

Once the client has identified areas for improvement we then set treatment goals. Behavioural models place heavy emphasis on observable behaviours. As such, CRA has clear criteria for well formed goals, akin to those of solution-focused therapy that we looked at earlier. The criteria for a goal demands that they are stated in the briefest form in order to remove degrees of ambiguity. They are in a positive form, in that they must be something that the client does rather than refrains from. And they must be measurable in that the concrete achievements can be observed to have happened (see Figure 8.1).

Goals must be set in every domain, closely targeted at the client's particular concerns. Not all goals need to be done in session with the client. Once we have demonstrated the criteria for setting goals, and observed the client identifying goals for themselves, we then ask them to complete the rest as homework tasks. This has two principle functions. Firstly, it teaches the client skills in how to target their own wants. Secondly it sets the tone for the rest of the sessions. They are expected to be actively involved in the development of their own recovery.

The recommended number of goals varies in different subtreatments in CRA. Whilst Meyers and Smith (1995) set goals in every domain, Budney and Higgins (1998) suggest identifying four to five to begin with. It is best to negotiate the number of goals with the client. We do not wish to run the risk of over-taxing them, but at the same time we need to provide goals that will help to structure their day purposefully. Alongside this it is important that goals set are not all chores, but also encompass rewarding recreational behaviours as well. These can then be combined using Premack's principle.

Prioritising goals is a flexible process. Problematic users often have multiple and inter-related problems. Targeting behaviours needs to be negotiated between the helper and the client. This can be done by asking the client what they feel is the most severe problem at present. For example, the client may state anxiety attacks are causing them a great deal of distress and so this may be an important priority to tackle first. Alternatively, selecting a behaviour that will have an impact on other domains may be a useful strategy. If the client believes getting back to college will help them with employment, boost confidence and increase their social circle, this could be a useful priority. Sometimes the most manageable goal can be the best starting point to build the client's confidence and self-belief. Each case can be different, but agreement on the goals must always be sought and given a measurable outcome. This outcome needs to be as concrete as possible. Indicators of outcomes could be frequency of family visits a week, a deadline to prepare a c.v. by two weeks time, to attend two AA meetings week etc. Reviewing progress toward goals, and offering informative feedback on progress, can be a great reinforcer in itself to support the client's progress.

Interventions

The intervention is a clear statement of the tasks that the client will perform in order to achieve their goal. Once again, for every goal the client must be given the means to achieve it. These tasks must feel manageable to the client in the way we explored in Chapter 3. The performance of task often relies upon the development or deployment of skills. These are usually taught in group settings and then role-played. They are then developed further in one-to-one sessions. Corrigan and Jakus (1994) have developed a process model for supporting skills development in people with severe mental illness, but this structure can also be a useful checklist in working with problematic users when assessing their competence (see Table 8.2).

In order to perform a skill we need to acquire it. We can learn these skills or observe others perform them. For those clients with a history of prolonged exclusion, there may be large gaps in their skills in managing everyday tasks that we may take for granted. Problems with acquisition need to be addressed through training. The teaching of skills is very important in CRA to close this gap, alongside consistent and good modelling by the helper. One to one role play can be used extensively with clients to develop and illustrate new skills from communication, to refusal skills,

Table 8.2   Process model of skills development (Corrigan and Jakus, 1994)

Cognition	**Acquisition**
Are there any negative thoughts that undermine the skill deployment?	Does the client have the necessary skills?
	Do they learn better in groups or one-to-one?
	Do they have a learning style?
Are there any learning impairments that would interfere with deploying the skill?	Can they repeat the skills to demonstrate understanding?
	Performance
	Where can they practise this skill?
	What could reinforce practising this skill?
	Can you observe the individual deploying the skill?
	Generalisation
	Can the client recognise where these skills would be useful?
	Have they tried this skill in other situations?
	Does the deployment of the skills still need reinforcement?

initiating conversation and social skills. These needs to be rehearsed and practiced until they become embedded in the client's memory.

However, people only perform skills when there is a reason or incentive to do so, and no direct barrier preventing the deployment. Problems in performance can be overcome by adding incentives contingent on their deployment. Incentives can include improved social contact, praise, activities and privileges, tangible rewards, or generalised reinforcers such as money or vouchers.

Generalisation is the aim of the skills training and also the biggest weakness in skills based recovery programmes. A skill becomes generalised when it is deployed in different forms, in different situations and across time. We also want to encourage the client to see how skills can generalise to similar situations. For example, teaching someone assertiveness may encourage them to take a dress back but that very night they might receive a really poor meal in a restaurant and say nothing. Young people can be especially prone to this. We send young people on outward bound courses in order to prompt change in other behaviours. But they do not make the connection that the skills they deployed in climbing a mountain may be similar to those needed to overcome drug use. As such clients may be able to acquire skills, perform them but are not able to apply them to diverse situations. In order to encourage the generalisation of skills they are heavily reinforced to begin with, and then reinforcement schedules diminish allowing the behaviour to be repeated without inducements. As skills do not automatically generalise across settings, skills generalisation needs to be practiced in a variety of real life situations and settings where the client learns to transfer the skills. This can be done in a 'live' setting. For example, rehearsing a telephone conversation asking for a job application is then followed by the actual call which the worker can observe and offer feedback on. Again we see a strong focus on enabling the client to master the experience, refine performance through feedback and transfer these skills to other similar challenges.

Cognition refers to the mental process of problem solving, remembering, planning and decision making. We also need to consider if there is any impairment to the thinking which may interfere with the deployment of skills or the management of tasks. People who hear voices may not recall information discussed in session and so writing lists may help them. Likewise, people with depression may have negative expectations and anticipate failure in advance. This will need to be challenged before engaging in the skills deployment. Helping people overcome these obstacles, especially when working with dual diagnosis or young people is important in facilitating all skills.

Within this the specific skills in CRA are all aimed at facilitating greater social involvement with others. Interpersonal skills are particularly important in this as are communication skills. In CRA the client is taught how to interact with others assertively but in a non-confrontational way. This is achieved by teaching the client to use 'I' to statements to assert their needs; to state what they want from others as opposed to what they do not want; alongside showing understanding and willingness to co-operate. Problem solving skills invite the client to identify the specific problem. Then they brainstorm possibilities before eliminating what they feel are the weakest options. They then try the solution and track it to see if it is effective and refine it where necessary. These basic skills can then be incorporated into more strategic approaches. Employment skills look at how to identify work from informal networks. Relationships skills teach partnering and can include the significant other. Social and recreational counselling help identify cost-effective hobbies, activities and social groups that the client can access. Wherever possible the client is encouraged to step out of the ghetto of support services and back into the social structures that everyone in the community draws upon.

Case Study: Goals and interventions using CRA

Victoria was middle aged when her relationship broke down and her drinking accelerated out of control. She felt isolated and drank heavily every night by herself. She finally presented for treatment. In the first session she discussed her problems and conducted a life satisfaction audit. She scored herself low across every domain including health, mental health, relationships and worst of all, social and recreational life. She felt she had no confidence and nothing to look forward to in life. Evaluating which of the goals would be most helpful, Victoria made constant reference to her isolation as it seemed to compound many of her other problems. Therefore this was to be the first priority. In talking to her about her social group prior to drinking, she reported she was once involved in an amateur dramatics society. She had stopped attending at the breakdown of her marriage. Since her drinking had escalated she felt unconfident in making contact. Victoria and her worker explored various strategies about how she could renew contact. This included who she would need to call and rehearsing what she would say. Victoria reported low confidence in doing it and they explored the obstacles. The key worker reminding her that she had once enjoyed it and that the group had always needed people to get involved. She was resolved to the task and agreed that she would telephone the co-ordinator of the group on Saturday. She would inform them that she would really like to get back involved and could they meet to discuss it. She followed this through and soon began evening rehearsals for a new play they were about to perform. After rehearsals she would go to friends for coffee. Getting involved in the new production raised her confidence and gave her a sense of purpose and fun. Furthermore there was a positive consequence. The fact she had things going on her life that she could talk about positively improved her communication and engagement with others outside the amateur dramatics circle.

With clearly identified goals, negotiated and rehearsed interventions and clear deadlines, CRA provides each client with an intensive and specific care plan. As we have seen, the helper will then work closely with the client to provide the support and energy to help them act on these goals. But at all times we must remember that this is not simply about intensive case planning but looks to identify, engage and sustain environmental benefits at each step of the way.

Functional analysis

CRA makes use of another well established behavioural assessment tool called the functional analysis (see Figure 8.2). Functional analysis is conducted to establish the function of the target behaviour. In this case it will be drug use. It describes it function by identifying what preceded use (antecedents) and what followed it (consequences). In this way it hopes to establish the relationship between triggers, thoughts, feelings and behaviours. As such, the functional analysis antecedents identify triggers that need to be avoided or that serve as an early warning signal to the client of imminent temptation to use. The functional analysis accepts the positive reinforcing effects from use as well as the punishing aspects of use. Typically, drug and alcohol have short term immediate benefits, alongside long term damage. The assessment thus helps clients recognise the losses in their use, in terms of significant people, opportunities and old sources of

External triggers	Thoughts	Feelings	Behaviour	Short term consequences	Long term consequences
I am most likely to use cocaine with Ben and Sam	I am usually feeling like I deserve a treat after a long week at work	I am usually drunk, but feel like I want some fun	Alcohol, I drink about eight pints	Fun	Feel rough the next day
We use this on Friday nights	I know my girlfriend will just want to go to sleep at this time of night	Feel resentful that my girlfriend will be on my case when I get home	Cocaine, snorted, two grams	Laugh	Bad come down
This is usually at Sam's house after we have been drinking	I know my girlfriend will be angry and I think to hell with her, I can do what I want	Feel like I am being deprived of something I want		Relief	Miss the weekend recovering
After the pub closes		Have fun with Ben and Sam as nothing really matters to them and they do what they want		Real buzz	Headaches, I can't think clearly
				Do not care about anything else	Emotionally drained, irritable and depressed
				Confident	Lose my job if I got one
				Powerful	Spend over £200 at a time, struggling financially. I am in debt
					Big arguments with my girlfriend. Hard to see her so upset
					Feel like I have let everyone down.

Figure 8.2 Organismic aspects

satisfaction. The organismic section is designed to include any fixed aspects of the individual that may influence the process of use. For example, heavy drinking may impair thinking which might influence these outcomes. This could also include illness or a bipolar episode for a client with a dual diagnosis.

The assessment begins by getting the client to identify a typical situation in which they might use. In the first column they begin by identifying the external triggers that surround this typical using event. Who are they with? Where are they? When is the risk time? Are there specific events when use is more likely to occur? Once this is established the client is then asked to identify the internal triggers to use. What are they thinking and feeling at these times? As we saw in Marlatt's determinants, extreme emotional states and conflict can figure heavily in lapse events. In the behaviour column we explore the drugs used, the amount and the length of the using episode. This data can be important. When we repeat functional analysis as the client progress through treatment or lapses, it will give us a clear idea of whether the interventions are working and use is declining. In the consequences column we then explore the short term benefits and the long term consequences of use. In terms of long term consequences these are mapped out in each domain of social functioning so the client has a deep insight into the damage use has on other more rewarding aspects of their life. And once again it draws the client's attention to the cost-benefit analysis of use in the same way we saw in Chapter 5.

Further details of reinforcers can be taken from partners, parents or significant others who are encouraged to attend the sessions. These are referred to as 'network sessions' as they are open to the client's wider pro-social relationships. They can endorse or challenge the client's perspective and provide additional insight into their use. They may have a much deeper insight into the patterns of use than the user themselves. And, as close relationships are an integral source of reward (and punishment) the significant others can play a substantial role in the treatment, being present as it unfolds. These reinforcers are kept in mind and drawn upon as the treatment process unfolds.

Meyers and Smith (1995), in their treatment model for alcoholism, also conduct a functional analysis on non-using behaviour. They report that it is often a surprise to clients who have had a lot of treatment experience to be asked about these other aspects of their life. Here the client is asked to identify one pleasurable activity that they enjoy and explore the antecedents, behaviour and consequences in the exact same way. This might be a hobby such as a going to see a football match, the cinema or spending time with a loved one. This must be a behaviour that is in their control and is enjoyable, rather than unpredictable. Again we want to be precise in what is enjoyable about this activity. We need to listen to hints, clues and resolve any ambivalence about this behaviour. We explore the consequence in the reverse manner. Identifying any short term consequences of engaging in this behaviour highlights any obstacles that prevent or hinder engagement. We can apply problem solving skills to this area to facilitate greater ease of engagement. Think of a behaviour that you currently engage in and complete the functional analysis on yourself. Get as much detail as possible in each area. Then consider the questions in Exercise 8.2.

Exercise 8.2: Evaluating functional analysis

- What is the relationship between the trigger and the thoughts?
- What is the relationship between the thoughts and the feelings? What is the relationship between the feelings and the behaviour?
- What might this individual's early warning signs of lapse be?
- What could they substitute for using which might also meet their needs?
- Have they done something different before to break this chain? How did they do it?
- Do you have any suggestions to assist them to identify and act on a different behaviour?
- Does this demand the acquisition of new skills that they do not currently have?
- Does this demand the support of others that they can draw upon or need to develop?

We continue to conduct functional analysis assessments throughout the course of treatment. This is done whenever the client is tempted to use, lapses or in the light of triggers that have not been avoided. We can understand the function of using behaviour in specific circumstances and help identify alternative means to achieve the same function without recourse to use. We can also use it to focus on these alternative and more rewarding behaviours instead.

CRA and alcohol

Whilst CRA models have evolved on these core principles, they have also been adapted in the treatment of different substance misuse problems. The most expansive CRA programme that has been developed from the original work of Hunt and Azrin (1973) is for treating alcohol users. Goals are set in each domain of a life audit with measurable targets which the helper and client both work towards achieving. This, along with the detailed functional analysis of both using and non-using behaviour provides the central spine of the treatment programme. Additional medical support can be offered through the daily administration of the drug disulfiram (Antabuse), which makes the individual violently sick if they consume alcohol whilst taking it. Azrin et al. (1982) have emphasised that disulfiram is a core component of the treatment. In CRA alcohol programmes the partner of the client is taught how to administer it daily in order to reinforce compliance. The effect of drinking and making the client violently ill sits neatly within the ideological framework of providing a positive punishment for drinking behaviour. However, research by Miller et al. (2001) did not find that disulfiram improved the efficacy of CRA's outcomes. Reinforcement always works better than punishment.

Sobriety sampling

Alongside the life audits a second procedure has been introduced called sobriety sampling (Meyers and Smith, 1995). Sampling is used to introduce the reluctant client to the idea of abstinence without overwhelming them with what may feel a formidable or unappealing task. Regardless of whether the individual wants controlled use or total abstinence, sobriety sampling is introduced to all the clients entering into programme. The client can consider this as time out from use for an agreed time. The helper initially suggests a period of 90 days, as this is considered the optimal time of relapse (Marlatt and Gordon, 1985). If the client baulks at this period, it can be negotiated downwards in steps, even to a day.

This period of time allows clients to experience the sensation of being alcohol and drug free on a daily basis after many years of use. Although this may be difficult initially it will allow them to think about the positive benefits of being drug and/or alcohol free without long term commitment. They can then make a more informed decision regarding continued use. As we have seen in the natural remission studies, commitment will also be viewed positively by family, non-using peers and supportive others as the client appears more sincere in this change attempt. This gesture will therefore provide them with affirmation and understanding that helps reinforce change. Sobriety sampling can also inform the treatment process itself. It prevents the reliance on using as a coping strategy, and instead gives the client the opportunity to deploy new coping behaviour. It can also afford the client practice in setting and achieving manageable goals, which then works to enhance self-esteem and confidence. In the event that the client experiences difficulty in maintaining sobriety during this monitored period, it provides useful insight into the vulnerabilities that they need to learn to address.

CRA does not trust the existing resources of clients and instead aims to teach skills to assist in the attainment of positive goals in every domain. They have developed a wider behavioural training programme that incorporates relationships, communication skills, problem solving, social skills, employment training and relapse prevention skills amongst others. As stated, positive and negative reinforcement exists in the environment. When the client occupies impoverished environments or has limited access to a quality one, *synthetic* environments have been developed. CRA treatment programmes vary in their modular structure but have included elements such as job club, literacy and education, marriage therapy and weekend drug and alcohol-free social clubs. Saturday nights can be a prime time for relapse and so alternative social interaction can provide competing reinforcement to use. Where there are no significant others in the clients life, a buddy-ing system may help provide surrogate involvement. Whilst the recovery process demands that the client must rebuild their entire life, it also provides a blank canvas for them to shape the kind of life that they want for themselves. Work placements and college taster sessions can do much to introduce clients back into the work place slowly, alleviate fears and also gain up-to-date references. Whenever the client is reluctant to enter into these new activities the sampling method is used to encourage them to try it without any long term commitment.

Another core feature of CRA and alcohol developed by Azrin et al. (1973) has been the evolution of marital therapy with the purpose of making the relationship a positive reinforcing experience for both the user and non-using spouse. This reciprocal counselling model uses similar tools as the core assessment of the main programme. Both partners are asked to complete a Relationship Happiness Scale (Meyers and Smith, 1995) that charts the level of satisfaction with each individual aspect of the relationship. This is done on a scale of one to ten and includes household chores, affection/intimacy, social life, child rearing and independence amongst others. Each partner rates their own level of satisfaction. From these evaluations, goals are set based on what the other partner could do to improve each domain. Partners are then taught communication skills in how to make a request from the other. The other partner cannot say no, but can offer an alternative. This helps with learning negotiation skills. Once the goal is agreed, the other partner makes their request and the same procedure follows. In this way, both partners strive to improve concrete areas of their relationship for the other, and in return have their own wants reciprocated. This is then reinforced through reminders to be complimentary, supportive and affectionate to each other every day. This must be done regardless of whether it is reciprocated. This prevents the stand-off situation where both are waiting for the other to make the first gesture.

CRA alcohol outcomes

CRA for the treatment of alcohol problems has continually demonstrated superior outcomes compared to traditional approaches in clinical practice. In the very first randomised study (Azrin and Hunt, 1973), the six month follow-up demonstrated that the CRA treatment group drank for 14 per cent of the follow-up days. This compared to the standard twelve step group who had been drinking for 79 per cent of the days. Furthermore the CRA group were unemployed for only 5 per cent of this period and needed hospital treatment on 2 per cent of the follow-up days. This compared to unemployment of 62 per cent and 27 per cent hospitalisation for the twelve step group. In the second major study that introduced disulfiram (Azrin, 1976), similar patterns were found. CRA clients achieving drinking levels of two per cent of follow-up days, unemployment of 20 per cent and no hospitalisation periods at all. This compared to the standard treatment group, who drank on 55 per cent of follow-up days, achieved 20 per cent unemployment days and were hospitalised on an average of 45 per cent of the follow-up days. A large scale randomised control trial did not find such a significant difference between CRA and twelve step treatment programmes at two year follow-up. But it did find more rapid improvements in the CRA group and shallower lapse periods (see Miller et al., 2001).

CRA performances with the most excluded homeless alcohol users also showed impressive results compared to standard treatments (Smith et al., 1998). Both CRA and twelve step models substantially reduced average daily drinking consumption from 19 drinks a day to 0.9 and 3.8 daily drinks respectively. This difference in daily consumption could have been higher but many of the heavy drinkers in the standard treatment programme could not be found. Again, the use of disulfiram did not lead to improved clinical outcomes for the CRA group.

CRA and cocaine

Significant outcomes have also been achieved in CRA programmes focusing on primary cocaine users with equally impressive results (see Budney and Higgins, 1998; Silverman et al., 1996; Higgins et al., 1994). CRA has been adapted in order to overcome the high drop-out rates shown by cocaine users entering treatment. This can be as high as 50–75 per cent in the first few weeks of treatment (Higgins and Budney, 1997). Furthermore, reinforcement sourced in the individual's environment takes a longer time period to establish. To compete with the reinforcing effects of cocaine more rapidly, a voucher system was introduced that rewarded clean urine samples immediately. This is a form of token economy where desirable behaviours become rewarded in order to increase the frequency of their performance. Token economies demand that the target behaviours are clearly identified. It must state precisely the contingencies under which the reward will be provided. This means that all exchange rules are determined in advance (See Ayllon and Azrin, 1968; Ayllon, 1999). In cocaine treatment trials, urine testing was conducted three times a week and the value of the vouchers increased with each consecutive negative urine test (see Figure 8.3). Positive test results set the user back to the start. The clients were never given cash but vouchers which could be exchange for desired goods. The client would inform a staff member

Negative urine specimens earn points that are approximately $0.25 each during weeks 1–12 of treatment.

The first negative specimen is worth 10 points or $2.50 ($0.25 × 10 points).

For each subsequent, consecutive negative urine sample, the value of the voucher increases by 5 points (e.g. second = 15 points or $3.75, third = 20 or $5.00, etc.)

The equivalent of a $10 bonus is earned for three consecutive negative urines in a week.

Positive specimens or failure to submit a specimen on schedule resets the value of vouchers back to the initial $2.50.

Five consecutive negative specimens after submission of a positive specimen returns the value of the vouchers to their level prior to the reset.

During weeks 13–24, the magnitude of the reinforcer is reduced to one state lottery ticket for each cocaine-negative specimen.

Figure 8.3   Cocaine token economy (Budney and Higgins, 1998)

who would then buy it for them. The token economy ran alongside attendance in relapse prevention groups and one to one sessions.

Research has continually identified superior results for the CRA and voucher programmes. The first clinical trial (Higgins et al. 1994) compared CRA plus vouchers versus standard CRA approaches. Here, 75 per cent of the voucher groups completed the programme as opposed to 40 per cent of the standard treatment group. Continuous cocaine abstinence was approximately 11 weeks in the voucher group and 6 weeks in the standard CRA treatment group. These results were then compared with a standard non-CRA treatment group. In both the voucher and non-voucher CRA programmes, clients outperformed standard treatment on every measure. In another study (Higgins et al., 2000) cocaine users were randomly assigned to a CRA and vouchers programme dependent on negative urine tests, and a CRA and vouchers programme with vouchers and no testing. This allowed the identification of the contributing factor of the vouchers in the programme. Retention rates were the same in both groups, but cocaine abstinence varied considerably between programmes. In the vouchers contingent on negative urine tests, 36 per cent of clients sustained abstinence for twelve weeks. Whilst in the non-contingent voucher group, only 12 per cent remained abstinent for twelve weeks. The results endured over 12 months. The biggest predicator of abstinence at one year follow-up appears to be directly related to the number of weeks abstinence achieved on programme. As a result, the advantages of CRA and vouchers are carried over into the long term where CRA clients continue to outperform the standard treatment models (Higgins and Abbot 2001). This has also been replicated with wider ethnic groups (Rawson et al., 1999; Silverman et al. 1998) and in reducing adjunct cocaine use in methadone treated opiate patients (Silverman et al., 1996, 1998). Whilst the voucher system rewarded non-cocaine using behaviours it also had a significant impact on reducing continued illicit use of opiates on top of the methadone prescriptions. (*Note: A free complete CRA programme for cocaine users (Budney and Higgins 1998) can be downloaded from the NIDA website.*)

CRA and heroin

CRA has been found to be extremely effect in providing adjunct psychosocial support to those on substitute prescriptions. In the McLellen et al. (1993) study, clients were randomly assigned to methadone only, methadone and CRA and methadone and enhanced CRA treatment groups. Outcomes were predicted by the degree of psychosocial treatment provided on the programme and not methadone. Two thirds of the methadone only group had to be transferred to the standard CRA programme for their own protection where they made immediate and substantial gains. We see similar results favouring CRA over other interventions in methadone maintenance programmes (Onken et al., 1995; Silverman et al., 1996), even when these treatment programmes do not use additional voucher systems (Abbot et al., 1998). Conversely Bickel et al. (1997) studied the effects of detoxification that involved CRA and vouchers. Half the vouchers were awarded for negative urine testing and the other half for attendance in treatment activities. In this study 53 per cent of the CRA and vouchers group completed the 24 week buprenorphine detoxification programme compared to only 20 per cent of the standard drug counselling group.

A variation of the standard CRA programme has been developed for those on methadone maintenance programmes by Stitzer, referred to as contingency management (For review see Stitzer et al., 1979; Strain and Stitzer, 2006). What is significant about these programmes is that they have developed aspects of methadone prescribing itself as the reinforcement for abstinence. Methadone clinics can be an ideal forum for this type of behavioural change because of the relatively long term treatment course. These programmes make the assumption that those on methadone prescriptions could refrain from using opiates in addition to their prescribed drugs but simply lack the motivation to do so. Therefore making rewards and privileges contingent on abstinence can increase abstention. This is a form of behaviour contracting which has been found useful for a range of problematic behaviours (Kirschenbuam and Flanery, 1983; O'Banion and Whaley, 1981).

Behavioural contracting demands that the client enter into a formal agreement which spells out the exact nature of the rewards and the conditions of the procedure. This contract must state four key elements of the contract. Firstly, it must specify the target behaviour to be addressed through the contract. This could be either attending treatment sessions or remaining drug free. Secondly it should state how and where this behaviour is to be performed. For example, if the target behaviour is to attend a counselling appointment the contract should state exactly the time and place of the session. If the target behaviour is to remain drug free the contract would state the frequency of random urine tests. Thirdly the contract must state clearly the reward. This could be privileges such as take home doses, increased doses or vouchers. Exact amounts should be specified. Finally the contract should state the rules for earning the rewards. For example, whether the client will receive vouchers for every drug free week or for attending every third appointment. This is then formalised into a contract which the client signs. This contract must then be strictly adhered to by both parties. If the agency fails to maintain boundaries and provide frequent urine tests the strategy will soon break down and prove ineffective.

The rewards that could be applied are broad. In Chutuape et al.'s (1998) review of methadone services as treatment reinforcers, they identified 21 items which could be used as reinforcements for abstinence (see Table 8.3). These items were evaluated in numerous ways to identify the most desirable. Take home doses has been consistently ranked higher than increase doses and

Table 8.3   Comparison of reinforcers evaluated by clients (Chutuape et al., 1998)

Twenty-one items compared by per cent of clients that ranked them in their top 5	Twenty-one items compared by mean rank
• Receive three take home doses of methadone a week. • Receive payments for food, fuel or rent. • A permanent methadone increase. • Control your own methadone dose. • Receive medical care at the clinic. • Receive occasional take home doses of methadone • Get help finding a job. • Receive vocational training at the clinic. • Get help finding housing. • Select your own clinic attendance times. • Select your own counselling schedule. • Attend weekly counselling sessions. • Get financial advice from clinic. • Select your own counsellor. • Receive single day methadone dose increase. • See a psychiatrist at the clinic. • Get legal advice at the clinic. • Receive family counselling at the clinic. • Participate in monthly clinic outings or parties. • Act as a client representative for the programme.	• Receive three take home doses of methadone a week. • Receive medical care at the clinic. • Receive payments for food, fuel or rent. • A permanent methadone increase. • Receive occasional take home doses of methadone. • Control your own methadone dose. • Receive vocational training at the clinic. • Get help finding a job. • Select your own clinic attendance times. • Get financial advice from the clinic. • Receive retail items from the programme such as clothes, entertainment events etc. • Attend weekly counselling sessions. • Receive single day methadone dose increase. • Get help finding housing. • Select your own counsellor. • Receive family counselling at the clinic. • Get legal advice at the clinic. • See a psychiatrist at the clinic. • Act as a client representative for the programme. • Participate in monthly clinic outings or parties.

additional support in many other similar studies (see Stitzer and Bigelow, 1978; Kidorf et al., 1995).

Contingent prescribing has had a dramatic improvement on reducing the adjunct use of illicit opiates on top of prescriptions. For example Iguchi et al. (1998) were able to increase the number of drug free urine samples from 18 per cent at the start of the contingency programme to between 35–65 per cent by including take home dosage privileges. Contingency management has also been used effectively to increase rates of attendance into additional support services. For example, Kidorf et al. (1994) were able to improve attendance at additional therapy through increasing take home privileges based on the number of sessions attended. However, mere attendance alone did not produce reductions in use. Similar findings were replicated in the Iguchi et al. (1996) research where take home privileges were used to increase attendance on problem solving groups. It is necessary in any behavioural contracting to clearly state the target behaviour to be changed. Splitting the incentive between reductions in counselling on top use and increased attendance is necessary to maximise these treatment interventions.

Aversive consequences

Research has also been conducted into the effect of increasing punishments for use on top of prescribed drugs. Treatment regimes that punish drug-using behaviours show higher outcomes.

For example, Iguchi et al. (1988) designed a study where both positive and negative sanctions were applied to use of heroin on top of methadone. Using on top of the script triggered a 10 ml reduction in dose. Negative sanctions did increase drop-out rates in this study. But those who stayed with the programme did better than subjects who were on a positive reinforcement schedule. Furthermore, the study subjects also had the option to return to mainstream prescribing and those who experienced continuous reductions for use on top did just that. This really removed the aversive aspect.

Other studies have demonstrated stronger associations with adverse consequences to use on top use. McCarthey and Borders (1985) compared 69 clients on unstructured and structured methadone programmes. Those on the structured programmes would have rapid reduction prescribing and exit the programme for use on top. The structured group achieved greater periods of abstinence and higher general treatment outcomes than the unstructured group. It also retained 53 per cent of clients compared to only 30 per cent on the unstructured programme. Numerous research studies have demonstrated that the threat of withholding treatment can increase motivation (See Kidorf and Stitzer, 1993; Dolon et al., 1985). However, it remains unclear as to what happens to those who do not meet the demands of the programme and exit treatment. They may have made less, but important gains, on low threshold methadone. Less dramatic aversive consequences such as split dosing methadone between the morning and evening can generate increased compliance. The nuisance value of having to visit the project twice can be effective in reducing illicit use on prescription without terminating treatment. As can placing the client on a higher demand support scheme.

In their meta-analysis of contingency management (a means of amalgamating the results of over 30 different studies), Griffith et al. (2000) found several key advantages for this approach. Their analysis showed the largest reductions in illicit drug use were achieved by increased methadone doses and take home privileges. The efficacy of these outcomes were significantly improved if the reinforcing reward was delivered to the client quickly. Contingency management was most effective when there was a clear target drug selected for reduction rather than multiple drugs. Urine sampling must be intensive and consistent in order to increase the client's fidelity to the programme. This is the only way to eliminate the client gambling that they could get away with adjunct use and sustain privileges. Finally, and most importantly, was who the intervention had the biggest impact on. Research has consistently shown that between 17–25 per cent of heroin using clients show no improvements on any measures in methadone treatment (see Gossop et al., 2000; Belding et al., 1998). Griffiths et al., (2000) demonstrate that it is these very clients who show the highest response rates to contingency management. This has been substantiated by other research (see Belding et al., 1998).

Community reinforcement and family training

The shift in focus from targeting individual use towards understanding the impact of the environment on consumption has lead to the development of new treatment approaches. These do not in themselves even work with the identified client directly. Community Reinforcement and Family Training (CRAFT) has developed as an off-shoot of CRA and has proved highly effective in moving non-treatment seeking clients into support services. CRAFT operates by working with the concerned significant other in the user's life and teaches them how modifying their own behaviour to impact on the user's consumption. This is achieved through similar tools to those we have already explored.

The central aim of CRAFT is to support the problem using other into treatment. Its secondary aims are to improve the quality of life of the concerned other, who often experiences profound disruption and emotional pain in their role as carer. This sub-goal is maintained regardless of whether the problem user seeks help (See Smith and Meyers, 2004; Meyers and Wolfe, 2004). The basic assumption of the programme is that the concerned other is a substantial force of positive and negative reinforcement in the user's environment. Inevitably conflict regarding the using loved one's behaviour, driven by good and often desperate intentions, can inadvertently promote greater use as the problem using loved one sedates away these stresses. In this way the concerned other negatively reinforces consumption as use offers an escape from the confrontation.

CRAFT begins with a functional analysis of the loved one's use to identify triggers, behaviours and consequences of consumption. When the problem user's triggers and reinforcers are understood the concerned other can begin to manipulate these environmental factors. This demands they shift the balance of reinforcement away from using towards other behaviours that the concerned other desires. Based on their deep knowledge of the user, the concerned other can implement alternative positive reinforcers of non-using behaviours at risk times to compete with use. For example, the problem drinker who typically comes home and drinks after a bad day at work could be intercepted with the offer of a back rub and hot bath. In this way the concerned other is ideally placed to break the behavioural chain that results in inebriation.

The concerned other also explores the consequence of their loved ones use. This is done to specifically disable any established patterns of them trying to assuage the consequence of use. Enabling behaviour describes the way that the concerned other develops strategies to intercede and limit the damage caused by their loved one's use. This might include covering up; making good the damage that their loved one does whilst using; phoning in work sick; making excuses to others; taking care of the children or cleaning up the mess. The concerned other may see this as caring but are in fact protecting the user from the negative consequence of use. This will only sustain the behaviour. In CRAFT the concerned other is taught to allow the natural consequences of use to be felt. Here we see that they can begin to shift the balance of pros and cons of change in the user's environment by making non-use more desirable; reducing the negative reinforcement that encourages people to use; and allowing the consequences of use to create crisis and anxiety. Hence change can be prompted in the user by shifting their environmental balance rather than developing their conscious awareness through begging or pleading with them.

If, in the sequence of proving alternate positive reinforcement, the user decides to resume consumption, then the concerned other simply withdraws elsewhere without any conflict. Accepting use in this way prevents negative reinforcement and them being blamed for it. It becomes the user's activity which they do alone. This withdrawal is augmented by teaching the concerned other communication skills. These emphasise how the concerned other can relay their own feelings and show empathy for the other. This reduces conflict in their day-to-day interactions as well provides a gentle announcement of withdraw when the loved one uses.

At the same time the programme aims to increase the concerned other's access to wider social support in their own lives and reward systems, which are often decimated through the behaviour of their loved one. This uses a life audit for the concerned other, where they identify their own needs and set goals to improve their quality of life. A range of additional skills are taught to augment this process including problem–solving, social interaction and the management of domestic violence where this is an issue. Timing when to raise the issue of the need for treatment is also carefully assessed. Repeated functional analysis is also done to measure the impact of their efforts, because if the concerned other detects reductions in their loved one's use, their motivation increases too.

CRAFT has proven to be highly effective in reducing conflict, substance use and in getting non-treatment seekers into treatment services. It has demonstrated great efficacy regardless of the relationship between the concerned other and the substance using loved one. And it works regardless of the substance they use. Whilst many interventions of this kind try to impose the idea that the concerned other should end the relationship, CRAFT has the advantage that it aims to keep these relationships intact and improve on them. This is often much closer to the desires of parents, spouses and the offspring of problem users who seek help for their loved one. As a result, CRAFT has out-performed all other family therapy models in substance misuse (Meyers et al., 1999). In one study by Miller et al. (1999), comparing CRAFT with confrontational approaches such as Al Anon and the Johnson Institute method, the CRAFT treatment elicited over 60 per cent of problematically using loved ones into treatment. This compared to less than 30 per cent of the highly confrontational surprise party Johnson Institute method whilst the 'tough love' model of Al Anon only encouraged 10 per cent of drug using others into treatment. Those in the CRAFT arm of the study had also halved their use prior to treatment entry. Other research has put this figure higher (Meyers and Smith, 2004). As such, CRAFT represent the most promising intervention for families and partners of users, who historically, have been a much ignored treatment group.

Social behaviour and network therapy

Arising from the Project MATCH findings that treatment success was determined by the client reintegrating with pro-social relations a range of treatments have developed that focus not on the individual, or their relationships with the social environment, but the environment itself. Heavily influenced by CRA, a promising new treatment – Social Behaviour and Network Therapy (Copello et al., 2002) is being piloted. It delivers interventions with the focal client in combinations with individuals identified as both significant and supportive in the client's life. The treatment thus educates and strengthens this wider pro-social network in the individual's life and aims to create the self-sustaining environment which supports non-using behaviour. Treating the support structure and equipping them with core skills in relapse prevention creates a self-sustaining 'out of hours' support group of caring others that can cement gains. It also means that the focal client does not have to be present in every session for the treatment to continue to work. As long as these supportive others continue to attend the sessions, they can still learn and enact skills to sustain the changes. SBNT capitalises on these relationships and is currently in the early days of trials, but it has begun to show positive outcomes (see UKATT, 2001).

Conclusion

Natural remission studies of untreated users provide a rich insight into the final stages of the change process. Whilst addiction has been defined as the erosion of all relationships, recovery is closing the loop on social exclusion, and represents the reintegration of relationships. The most effective treatment provision, CRA, replicates this very process. Targeting the key domains of the individual's life, its pragmatic interventions strengthen connections to the wider social structures that we all inhabit. It offers the client the skills to meet these demands and even recreates the arenas where they can be refined, before being generalised into the wider world. It recognises that success and failure is not contingent on the abnormal individual but lies within the positive and negative rewards that reside in the environment. As such, when considering rehabilitation, one must consider the question of rehabilitation for whom? If we prevent access to the social structures that are the medium of life, we simply sustain the exclusion that is addiction. Families, partners, peers, employment, religions, housing providers and even the law have an intrinsic role in successful treatment because, for the most part, their attainment is treatment success. This demands that the individual's desire for reintegration must be met with the social networks receptiveness to it. It also means that if we are to help in this process we must revise our thinking whereby we stop treating dependence at the cost of resolving addictions. Instead, we must understand human beings in the fullness of their being, a fullness that can only be expressed in the cultural niches that they inhabit.

References

Abbot, P.J. et al. (1998) Community Reinforcement Approach in the Treatment of Opiate Addicts. *American Journal of Drug and Alcohol Abuse*, 24: 17–30.

Agosti, V. et al. (1991) Patient Factors Related to Early Attrition From an Outpatient Cocaine Research Clinic: A Preliminary Report. *International Journal of Addiction*, 26: 3227–334.

Alexander, B. and Hadaway, P. (1996) Opiate Addiction: The Case for an Adaptive Orientation. *Psychological Bulletin*, 92: 2, 367–81.

Allen, S.L. (2001) *The Devil's Cup: Coffee, The Driving Force in History*. Canongate Books.

Anderson, H. and Goolishian, H. (1992) The Client is the Expert: A Not Knowing Approach to Therapy. In Mcnamee, S. and Gergen, K.J. (Eds.) *Therapy as Social Construction*. Sage.

Annis, M., Herrie, M.A. and Watkin-Merek, L. (1996) *Structured Relapse Prevention*. Addiction Research Foundation.

APA (1995) *Diagnostic and Statistical Manual of Mental Disorders*. 4th edn. American Psychiatric Association.

Apsler, R. (1979) Measuring How People Control The Amount They Use. *Journal of Drug Issues*, 9: 2, 145–59.

Armor, D., Polich, J. and Stambul, H. (1978) *Alcoholism and Treatment*. New York: Wiley.

Ashton, M. (1999) NTORS: The Most Crucial Test Yet for Addiction Treatment in Britain. *Drug and Alcohol Findings*, 2: 16.

Auriacombe (2001) Deaths Attributable to Methadone Vs Buprenorphine in France. *Journal of American Medical Association*, 285: 45.

Ayllon, T. (1999) *How to Use Token Economies and Point Systems*. Pro-Ed.

Ayllon, T. and Azrin, N. (1968) *The Token Economy: A Motivational System for Therapy and Rehabilitation*. Appelton-Century-Crofts.

Azatian, A., Papiasvilli, A. and Joseph, H. (1994) A Study of The Use of Clonidine and Naltrexone in The Treatment of Opioid Addiction in The Former USSR. *Journal of Addictive Diseases*, 13, 35–52.

Azrin, N., Naster, B.J. and Jones, R. (1973) Reciprocity Counselling: A Rapid Learning-Based Procedure for Marital Counselling. *Behaviour Research and Therapy*, 11: 365–82.

Azrin, N.H. (1976) Improvements in The Community Reinforcement Approach to Alcoholism. *Behaviour Research and Therapy*, 14: 339–48.

Azrin, N.H. et al. (1982) Alcoholism Treatment With Disulfiram and Community Reinforcement Therapy. *Journal of Behaviour Therapy and Experimental Psychiatry*, 13: 105–12.

Bandura, A. (1992a) Self-Efficacy in Psychobiologic Functioning. In Schwarzer, R. (Ed.) *Self-Efficacy: Thought Control of Action*. Hemisphere Publishing Corp.

Bandura, A. (1992b) Exercise of Personal Agency Through the Self-Efficacy Mechanism. In Schwarzer, R. (Ed.) *Self-Efficacy: Thought Control of Action*. Hemisphere Publishing Corp.

Bandura, A. (1997) *Self-Efficacy: The Exercise of Control*. W.H. Freeman and Company.

Barkham, M. (1990) Research in Individual Therapy. In Dryden, W. (Ed.) *Individual Therapy: A Handbook*. Open University Press

Barrau, K. et al. (2001) Comparison of Methadone and High Dosage Buprenorphine Users in French Care Centres. *Addiction*, 96: 1433–41.

Battegay, R. (2000) Forty Four Years in Psychiatry and Psychopharmacology. In Healy, D. (Ed.) *The Psychopharmocologists*.

Bearn, J., Gossop, M. and Strang, J. (1998) Accelerated Lofexidine Treatment Regimen Compared With Conventional Lofexidine and Methadone Treatment for In-Patient Detoxification. *Drug and Alcohol Dependence*, 50: 227–32.

Belding, M. et al. (1998) Characterising 'Nonresponsive' Patients. *Journal of Substance Abuse Treatment*, 15: 485–92.

Bellack, A.S., Herson, M. and Kazden, A.E. (1990) *International Handbook of Behaviour Modification*, Plenum.

Berg, I.K. (1989) Of Visitors, Complainers, and Customers: Is There Really Such a Thing as Resistance? *Family Therapy Networker*, 13: 1, 21.

Berg, I.K. (1994) *Family Based Services: A Solution Focussed Approach*. W.W. Norton.

Berg, I.K. and Miller, S.D. (1992) *Working With the Problem Drinker: A Solution-Focused Approach*. W.W. Norton.

Berg, I.K. and Ruess, N.H. (1998) *Solutions Step by Step: A Substance Abuse Treatment Manual*. W.W. Norton.

Berridge, V. (1999) *Opium and the People: Opiate Use and Drug Control in Nineteenth and Early Twentieth Century History*. Free Association Books.

Bickel, W.K. and Degrandpre, R.J (1995) Price and Alternative: Suggestions for Drug Policy From Psychology. *International Journal of Drug Policy*, 6: 2, 93–103.

Bickel, W.K. et al. (1997) Effects of Adding Behaviour Treatment to Opioid Detoxification With Buprenorphine. *Journal of Consulting and Clinical Psychology*, 65: 803–10.

Bien, T.H., Miller, W.R. and Tonigen, J.S. (1993) Brief Interventions for Alcohol Problems: A Review. *Addiction*, 88: 315–36.

Biernaki, P. (1983) *Getting Off Dope: Natural Recovery From Opiate Addiction*. Manuscript.

Blackman, J.S. (2004) *101 Defences: How The Mind Shields Itself*. New York: Brunner-Routledge.

Bleuler, E. (1950) *Textbook of Psychiatry*. George Allen and Unwin.

Bordin, E.S. (1979) The Generalizability of The Psychoanalytic Concept of the Working Alliance. *Psychotherapy: Theory, Research and Practice*, 16: 3, 252–60.

Botvin, G.L. (1999) Adolescent Drug Abuse Prevention: Current Findings and Future Directions. In Glantz, M.D. and Hartel, C.R. (Eds.) *Drug Abuse: Origins and Interventions*. American Psychological Association.

Bowden, M. (2001) *Killing Pablo*. Atlantic Books.

Brehm, S.S. and Brehm, J.W. (1981) *Psychological Reactance: A Theory of Freedom and Control*. Academic Press.

Bry, B. H., Mckeon, P. and Pandina, R.J. (1982) Extent of Drug Use as a Function of Number of Risk Factors. *Journal of Abnormal Psychology*, 91: 273–9.

Budd, R J and Rollnick, S (1996). The Structure of Readiness to Change Questionnaire: A Test of Prochaska and Diclemente's Transtheoretical Model. *British Journal of Health Psychology*, 1: 365–76.

Budney, A.J. and Higgins, S.T. (1998) *Therapy Manuals for Addiction: Manual 2-A Community Reinforcement Approach: Treating Cocaine Addiction*. NIH Publication Number: 98-4309.

Burman, S. (1997) The Challenge of Sobriety: Natural Recovery Without Treatment and Self-Help Groups. *Journal of Substance Abuse*, 9: 41–61.

C'de Baca, J. and Wilbourne, P. (2004) Quantum Change: Ten Years Later. *Journal of Clinical Psychology.*

Cappell, H. and Greeley, J. (1987) Alcohol and Tension Reduction: An Update on Research and Theory. In Blance, H.T. and Leonard, K.E. (Eds.) *Psychological Theories of Drinking and Alcoholism.* Guildford.

Carere, S. and Gottman, J. (1999) Predicting Divorce Among Newly Weds From the First Three Minutes of Marital Conflict Discussion. *Family Process*, 38: 3, 293–301.

Carnwath, T. and Hardman, J. (1998) Randomised Double Blind Comparisons of Lofexidine and Clonidine in Outpatient Treatment of Withdrawal. *Drug and Alcohol Dependence*, 50: 251–4.

Carroll, K.M. (1997) Enhancing Retention in Clinical Trails of Psychosocial Treatment: Practical Strategies. In *Beyond The Therapeutic Alliance: Keeping The Drug Dependant Individual in Treatment.* Research Monograph No 165. Rockville, MD: NIDA.

Carroll, M.E. (1993) The Economic Context of Drug and Non-Drug Reinforcers Affects Acquisition and Maintenance of Drug-Reinforced Behaviour and Withdrawal Effects. *Drug and Alcohol Dependence*, 33: 201–10.

Carroll, M.E. and Lac, S.T. (1992) Autoshaping IV Cocaine Self-Administration in Rats: Effects of Non-Drug Alternative Reinforcers on Acquisition. *Psychopharmacology*, 110: 439–46.

Chan, M. et al. (1997) Client Satisfaction With Drug Abuse Day Treatment Verses Residential Care. *Journal of Drug Issues*, 27: 367–77.

Chaney, E.F., O'Leary, M.R. and Marlatt, G.A. (1978) Skills Training With Alcoholics. *Journal of Consulting and Clinical Psychology*, 46: 1092–104.

Chutuape, M.A., Silverman, K. and Stitzer, M.L (1998) Survey Assessment of Methadone Treatment Services as Reinforcers. *American Journal of Drug and Alcohol Abuse*, 24: 1, 1–16.

Cialdini, R.B. and Petty, R.E. (1979) Anticipatory Opinion Effects. In Petty, R. Ostrom, T. and Brock, T. (Eds.) *Cognitive Responses in Persuasion.* Erlbaum.

Cloninger, C.R. (1987) A Systematic Method for Clinical Descriptions and Classifications of Personality Variants. A Proposal. *Archives of General Psychiatry*, 44: 6, 573–8.

Coady, N.F. (1991) The Association Between The Client and Therapist's Interpersonal Processes and Outcomes in Psychodynamic Therapy. *Research Social Work Practice*, 1: 122–38.

Coggins, N. and Davies, J.B. (1988) Explanations for Heroin Use. *The Journal of Drug Issues*, 18: 3, 457–65.

Cohen, M. et al. (1971) Alcoholism: Controlled Drinking and Incentives for Abstinence. *Psychological Reports*, 28: 575–80.

Condon, W.S. (1982) Cultural Microrhythms. In Davies, M. (Ed.) *Interaction Rhythms: Periodicity in Communicative Behaviour.* Human Sciences Press.

Conners, G.J., Donovan, D.M. and DiClemente, C.C. (2001) *Substance Abuse Treatment and The Stages of Change: Selecting and Planning Interventions.* Guildford Press.

Connors, G.J., Maisto, S.A. and Zywiak, W.H. (1998) Male and Female Alcoholic's Attributions Regarding The Onset and Termination of Relapses and Maintenance of Abstinence. *Journal of Substance Abuse*, 10: 27–42.

Connors, G.J. et al. (1997) The Therapeutic Alliance and Its Relationship to Alcoholism Treatment Participation and Outcome. *Journal of Consulting and Clinical Psychology*, 65: 4, 588–98.

Copello, A, et al. (2002) Social Behaviour and Network Therapy: Basic Principles and Early Experiences. *Addictive Behaviours*, 27: 345–66.

Corrigan, P.W. (1997) Behaviour Therapy Empowers Persons With Serious Mental Illness. *Behaviour Modification*, 21: 45–61.

Corrigan, P.W. and Jakus, M.R. (1994) Behaviour Treatment. In Silver, J.M., Yudofsky, S.C. and Hales, R.E. (Eds.) *Psychiatric Aspects of Traumatic Brain Injury.* American Psychiatric Press.

Critchlow, B. (1986) The Powers of John Barleycorn: Beliefs About The Effects of Alcohol on Social Behaviour. *American Psychologist*, 41: 7, 751–64.

Cummings, C., Gordon, J.R. and Marlatt, G.A. (1980) Strategies of Prevention and Prediction. In Miller, W.R. (Ed.) *The Addictive Behaviours: Treatment of Alcoholism, Drug Abuse, Smoking and Obesity.* Pergamon.

Curry, S., Marlatt, G.A. and Gorden, J.R. (1987) Abstinence Violation Effect: Validation of an Attributional Construct With Smoking Cessation. *Journal of Consulting and Clinical Psychology*, 55.

Czarnecki, D., M. et al. (1990) Five Year Reliability of Self-Reported Alcohol Consumption. *Journal of Studies of Alcohol*, 51: 1, 68–76.

Darkes, J. and Goldman, M.S. (1993) Expectancy Challenge and Drinking Reduction: Experimental Evidence for a Mediational Process. *Journal of Consulting and Clinical Psychology*, 61: 344–53.

Davenport-Hines, R. (2001) *The Pursuit of Oblivion.* Weidenfeld and Nicolson.

Davies, J.B. (1993) *The Myth of Addiction.* Harwood Academic Press.

Davies, J.B. and Baker, R. (1987). The Impact of Self Presentation and Interviewer Bias on Self-Reported Heroin Use. *British Journal of Addiction*. 82: 907–12.

Dawe, S. et al. (1991) Should Opiate Addicts be Involved in Controlling Their Own Detoxification? A Comparison of Fixed Versus Negotiable Schedules. *British Journal of Addictions*, 86: 977–82.

De Jong, P and Miller, S.D. (1995) How to Interview for Client's Strengths. *Social Work*, 40: 6, 729–36.

De Shazer, S. (1985) *Keys to Solution in Brief Therapy.* W.W. Norton.

De Shazer, S. (1994) *Words Were Originally Magic.* W.W. Norton.

Deleon, G. (1989) Therapeutic Communities for Substance Abuse: Overview of Approach and Effectiveness. *Psychology of Addictive Behaviours*, 3: 140–7.

Deleon, G. (1996) Integrative Recovery: A Stage Paradigm. *Substance Abuse*, 175: 1–63.

Deshazer, S. (1995) Solution Building and Language Games. In Hoyt, M. (Ed.) *Constructive Therapies 2.* Guildford Press.

DiClemente, C.C. (2003) *Addictions and Change.* Guildford Press.

Dillon, P. (2002) *Gin: The Much Lamented Death of Madame Geneva.* Justin, Charles and Co.

Dixon, M. and Sweeney, K. (2000) *The Human Effects in Medicine: Theory, Research and Practice.* Radcliffe Medical Press.

Dole, V.P. and Nyswander, M.E. (1967) Heroin Addiction: A Metabolic Disease. *Archives of Internal Medicine*, 120: 19–24.

Dole, V.P. and Nyswander, M.E. (1976) Methadone Maintenance Treatment: A Ten-Year Perspective. *Journal of The American Medical Association*, 235: 19, 2117–19.

Dolon, M.P. et al. (1985) Contracting for Treatment Termination to Reduce Illicit Drug Use Among Methadone Maintenance Treatment Failures. *Journal of Consulting and Clinical Psychology*, 55: 549–51.

Dowrick, P.W. (1983) Self Modelling. In Dorwick, P.W. and Biggs, S.J. (Eds.) *Using Video: Psychological and Social Applications.* Wiley.

Draycott, S. and Dabss, A. (1998) Cognitive Dissonance 1: An Overview of The Literature and Its Integration Into Theory and Practice in Clinical Psychology. *British Journal of Psychology*, 37: 341–53.

Drummond, C. and Ashton, M. (1999) How Brief Can You Get? *Drug and Alcohol Findings*, 2.

Dunbar, R.I.M. (1992) Neocortex Size as a Constraint on Group Size in Primates. *Journal of Human Evolution*, 20: 469–93.

Duncan, B.L., Miller, S.D. and Sparks, J.A. (2004) *The Heroic Client*. Jossey-Bass.

Earlywine, M. (2001) Cannabis-Induced Koro in Americans. *Addiction*, 96: 11, 1663–6.

Edwards, G. and Gross, M. (1976) Alcohol Dependence: Provisional Description of a Clinical Syndrome. *British Medical Journal*, 1: 1058–61.

Edwards, G., Marshall, E.J. and Cook, C.C.H. (2003) *The Clinical Management of Alcohol Problems*. Cambridge University Press.

Elkin, G.D. (1999) *Introduction to Clinical Psychiatry*. Appleton and Lange.

Erickson, E.H. (1995) *Childhood and Society*. Vintage.

Erickson, M.H. (1959) Further Clinical Techniques of Hypnosis: Utilisation Techniques. *American Journal of Clinical Hypnosis*, 2: 1, 3–21.

Erickson, P.G. and Alexander, B.K. (1989) Cocaine and Addictive Liability. *Social Pharmacology*, 3: 249–70.

Evans, D. (2004) *Placebo: Mind Over Matter in Modern Science*. London: Harper-Collins.

Falk, J.L. (1981) The Environmental Generation of Excessive Behaviour. In Mule, S.J. (Ed.) *Behaviour in Excess*. Free Press.

Falk, J.L. (1983) Drug Dependence: Myth or Motive? *Pharmacology, Biochemistry and Behaviour*, 19: 3, 385–91.

Festinger, L. and Carlsmith, J.M. (1959) Cognitive Consequences of Forced Compliance. *Journal of Abnormal and Social Psychology*, 58: 203–10.

Festinger, S. (1957) *A Theory of Cognitive Dissonance*. Harper and Row.

Fisher, S. and Greenberg, R.P. (1993) How Sound is The Double-Blind Design for Evaluating Psychotropic Drugs? *Journal of Nervous and Mental Disease*, 181: 6, 345–50.

Foreman, S. A. and Marmar, C.R. (1985) Therapist's Actions That Address Initially Poor Therapeutic Alliances in Psychotherapy. *American Journal of Psychiatry*, 142: 8, 922–6.

Fox, R. (1967) A Multidisciplinary Approach to the Treatment of Alcoholism. *American Journal of Psychotherapy*, 123: 769–78.

Frankl, V. (1985) *Man's Search for Meaning*. Simon and Schuster.

Friedman, H.S. et al. (1980) Understanding and Assessing Non-Verbal Expressiveness: The Affective Communication Test. *Journal of Personality and Social Psychology*, 39: 2, 333–51.

Gately, I. (2002) *Le Diva Nicotina: The Story of How Tobacco Seduced The World*. Scribner.

Gilbert, P. (2003) *The Value of Everything: Social Work and Its Importance in The Mental Health Field*. Russell House Publishing.

Gold, M., Redmond, D. and Kleber, H. (1978) Clonidine in Opiate Withdrawal. *Lancet*, I, 929.

Goldman, M.S. et al. (1993) Alcoholism and Memory: Broadening The Scope of Alcohol-Expectancy Research. *Psychological Bulletin*, 110: 137–46.

Gossop, M. et al. (2000) Patterns of Improvement After Methadone Treatment: One Year Follow Up Results From The National Treatments Outcome Research Study. *Drug and Alcohol Dependence*, 60: 275–86.

Gossop, M. (1988) Clonidine and The Treatment of Opiate Withdrawal Syndrome. Drug and Alcohol Dependence, 21: 253–9.

Gossop, M. (2003) *Drug Addiction and Its Treatment*. Oxford University Press.

Gossop, M. and Grant, M. (1990) *The Content and Structure of Methadone Treatment Programmes: A Study in Six Countries, WHO/PSA/90.3* Geneva: World Health Organisation.

Gossop, M., Johns, A. and Green, L. (1986) Opiate Withdrawal: Inpatient Versus Outpatient Programmes and Preferred Versus Random Assignment to Treatment. *British Medical Journal,* 293: 103–4.

Gossop, M. et al. (1998) Substance Use, Health and Social Problems of Clients at 54 Drug Treatment Agencies: Intake Data From The National Treatment Outcomes Research Study (NTORS). *British Journal of Psychiatry,* 173: 166–71.

Greenstein, R.A. et al. (1981) Naltrexone: A Short Treatment for Opiate Dependence. *American Journal of Drug and Alcohol Abuse,* 8: 291–300.

Griffin, J.D. et al. (2000) Contingency Management in Outpatient Methadone Treatment: A Meta-Analysis. *Drug and Alcohol Dependence,* 58: 55–66.

Grilo, C.M. (1993) An Alternative Perspective Regarding 'Non-Compliance: What to Do?' *Behaviour Therapy,* 16: 8, 219–20.

Grund, J.P.C. (1993) *Drug Use as a Social Ritual: Functionality, Symbolism and Determinants of Self-Regulation.* Rotterdam: Instituut Voor Verslavingsonderzoek.

Haley, J. (1993) *Jay Haley on Milton H. Erickson.* Brunner Mazel.

Harding, W.M. (2000) Informal Social Controls and The Liberalisation of Drug Laws. In Coomber, R. (Ed.) *The Control of Drugs and Drug Users: Reason or Reaction.* Harwood Academic Press.

Harris, K.B. and Miller, W.R. (1990) Behavioural Self-Control Training for Problem Drinkers: Components of Efficacy. *Psychology of Addictive Behaviours,* 4: 82–90.

Harris, P. (2002) *Tutor's Manual: Evidenced Based Approaches to Substance Misuse. an OCN Accredited Counselling Programme.* Unpublished.

Harris, P. (2005) *Drug Induced: Addiction and Treatment in Perspective.* Russell House Publishing.

Harrison, L.D. (1995) The Validity of Self-Reported Data on Drug Use. *Journal of Drug Issues,* 25: 1, 91–111.

Haskell, R.E. (1994) Realpolitick in the Addictions Field: Treatment-Professional, Popular Culture Ideology and Scientific Research. *Journal of Mind and Behaviour,* 14: 3, 257–76.

Haynes, P. and Allcliffe, G. (1991) Locus of Control of Behaviour: Is High Externality Associated With Substance Misuse? *British Journal of Addiction,* 86: 1111–17.

Healy, D. (2002) *Psychiatric Drugs Explained.* Churchill Livingstone.

Heath, D.B. (1991a) Continuity and Change in Drinking Patterns of The Bolivian Camba. In Pittman, D.J. and White, H.R. (Eds.) *Society, Culture and Drinking Patterns Re-examined.* Rutgers Centre for Alcohol Studies.

Heath, D.B. (1991b) Drinking Patterns of The Bolivian Camba. In Pittman, D.J. and White, H.R. (Eds.) *Society, Culture and Drinking Patterns Re-Examined: Alcohol, Culture and Social Control Monograph Series.* Rutgers Centre for Alcohol Studies.

Heather, N. and Robertson, I. (1989) *Problem Drinking.* Oxford Medical Publications.

Heather, N., Rollnick, S. and Winton, M. (1983) A Comparison of Object and Subject Measures of Alcohol Dependence as Predictors of Relapse Following Treatment. *British Journal of Clinical Psychiatry,* 22: 11–17.

Heather, N., Stallard, A. and Tebbutt, J. (1991) The Importance of Substance Cues in Relapse Among Heroin Users: Comparison of Two Methods of Investigation. *Addictive Behaviours,* 16: 41–9.

Higgins, E., Rhodwalt, F. and Zanna, M. (1979) Dissonance Motivation: Its Nature, Persistence and Reinstatement. *Journal of Experimental Social Psychology,* 15: 16–34.

Higgins, S.T. et al. (1994) Incentives Improve Treatment Retention and Cocaine Abstinence in Ambulatory Cocaine Dependant Patients. *Archives of General Psychiatry*, 51: 568–76.

Higgins, S.T. and Abbot, P.J. (2001) CRA and Treatment of Cocaine and Opioid Dependence. In Meyers, R.J. and Miller, W.R. (Eds.) *A Community Reinforcement Approach to Addiction Treatment.* Cambridge University Press.

Higgins, S.T. and Budney, A.J. (1997) From The Initial Clinical Contact to After Care: A Brief Review of Effective Strategies for Retaining Cocaine Abusers in Treatment. In Onken, L.S., Blaine, J.D. and Boren, J.J. (Eds.) *Beyond The Therapeutic Alliance: Keeping The Drug Dependant Individual in Treatment.* National Institute of Drug Abuse Monograph Series, No 165. US Government Printing Office.

Higgins, S.T. et al. (2000) Contingent Reinforcement Increases Cocaine Abstinence During Outpatient Treatment and One Year of Follow Up. *Journal of Consulting and Clinical Psychology*, 68: 64–72.

Hofer, M.A. (1975) Survival and Recovery of Physiologic Function After Early Maternal Separation in Rats. *Physiology and Behaviour*, 15: 5, 475–80.

Hofer, M.A. (1987) Early Social Relationships: A Psychobiologic View. *Child Development*, 58: 3, 633–47.

Hollin, C.R. (1995) The Meaning and Implications of 'Programme Integrity'. In Mcguire, J. (Ed.) *What Works: Reducing Reoffending.* Wiley.

Hollister, L.E. (1998) From Hypertension to Psychopharmacology; A Serendipitous Career. In Healy, D. (Ed.) *The Psychopharmacologists*, 2.

Holmes, S. (1994) A Philosophical Stance, Ethics and Therapy: An Interview With Harlene Anderson. *The Australian and New Zealand Journal of Family Therapy.* 15: 155–61.

Holroyd, K.A. et al. (1984) Change Mechanisms in EMG Biofeedback Training: Cognitive Changes Underlying Improvements in Tension Headaches. *Journal of Consulting and Clinical Psychology*, 52: 1039–53.

Hovarth, A.O. (2001) The Alliance. *Psychotherapy*, 38: 365–72.

Howard, K.I. et al. (1986) The Dose-Effect Relationship in Psychotherapy. *American Psychologist*, 41: 2, 159–64.

Hunt, G.M. and Azrin, N.H. (1973) A Community-Reinforcement Approach to Alcoholism. *Behaviour Research and Therapy*, 11: 91–104.

Hunt, W.A., Barnett, L.W. and Branch, L.G. (1971) Relapse Rates in Addiction Programmes. *Journal of Clinical Psychology*, 27: 455–6.

Iguchi, M. et al. (1988) Contingency Management in Methadone Maintenance: Effects of Reinforcing and Aversive Consequences in Illicit Polydrug Use. *Drug and Alcohol Dependence*, 22: 1–7.

Iguchi, M.Y. et al. (1996) Contingent Reinforcement of Group Participation Versus Abstinence in a Methadone Maintenance Program. *Experimental and Clinical Psychopharmacology*, 3: 315–21.

Intagliata, J. (1976) A Telephone Follow-Up Procedure for Increasing The Effectiveness of a Treatment Program for Alcoholics. *Journal of Studies on Alcohol*, 37: 1330–5.

Isbell, L.M., Smith, H.L. and Wyer, R.S. (1998) Consequences of Attempts to Disregard Social Information. In Golding, J.M. and Macleod, C.M. (Eds.) *Intentional Forgetting: Interdisciplinary Approaches.* Erlbaum, Mahwah.

James, W. (1902) *Varieties of Religious Experience.* Cambridge, MA: Harvard University Press.

Janis, I.L. and Mann, L. (1977) *Decision Making: A Psychological Analysis of Conflict, Choice and Commitment.* Free Press.

Jellinek, E.M. (1960) *The Disease Concept of Alcoholism.* Hillhouse Press.

Johnson, R. et al. (2000) A Comparison of Levomethadyl Acetate, Buprenorphine and Methadone for Opioid Dependence. *New England Journal of Medicine*, 343: 1290–7.

Jones, R.T. (1992) Alternative Strategies. In Brook, G.R. and Whelen, J. (Eds.) *Cocaine: Scientific and Social Dimensions.* Ciba Foundation Symposium. Wiley.

Jones, S.L. and Lanyon, R.I. (1981) Relationship Between Adaptive Skills and Outcome of Alcoholism Treatment. *Journal of Studies on Alcohol*, 42: 521–5.

Julien, R.M. (1998).*A Primer of Drug Action.* New York: Freeman Press.

Kadden, R. et al. (1992) *Cognitive-Behavioural Coping Skills Therapy Manual. A Clinical Research Guide for Therapists Treating Individuals With Alcohol Abuse and Dependence.* Monograph 3. DHHS.

Kalant, H. (1987) Tolerance and Its Significance for Drug and Alcohol Dependence. In Harris, L.S. (Ed.) *Problems of Drug Dependence, 1986.* Monograph 61. DHHS.

Kandal, D. (1995) Ethnic Difference in Drug Use: Patterns and Paradoxes. In Botvin, G.J., Schinke, S. and Orlandi, M.A. (Eds.) *Drug Abuse Prevention With Multiethnic Youth.* Sage.

Kandel, D.B. and Raveis, (1989) Cessation of Illicit Drug Use in Young Adulthood. *Archives of General Psychiatry*, 46: 109–16.

Katz, S.H and Voigt, M.M. (1986) Bread and Beer. *Expedition*, 28: 23–34.

Katz, S.H. and Maytag, F. (1991) Brewing an Ancient Beer. *Archaeology*, 44: 4, 24–33.

Kegan, R. (1982) *The Evolving Self: Problems and Process in Human Development.* Harvard University Press.

Kelly, H.H. and Michela, J.L. (1980) Attribution Theory and Research. *Annual Review of Psychology*, 31: 221–36.

Kidorf, M. and Stitzer, M.L. (1993) Contingent Access to Methadone Maintenance Treatment: Effects of Cocaine Use of Opiate-Cocaine Users. *Experimental Clinical Psychopharmacology*, 1: 200–6.

Kidorf, M., Stitzer, M.L. and Giffiths, R.R. (1995) Evaluating The Reinforcement Value of Clinic-Based Privileges Through Multiple Choice Procedure. *Drug and Alcohol Dependence*, 39: 167–72.

Kidorf, M. et al. (1994) Contingent Methadone Take-Home Doses Reinforce Adjunct Therapy Attendance of Methadone Maintenance Patients. *Drug and Alcohol Dependence*, 36: 221–6.

Kirch, I. and Sapirstein, G. (1998) Listening to Prozac But Hearing Placebo: A Meta-Analysis of Anti-Depressant Medication. *Prevention Treatment*, 2a, (Http://Journals.Apa.Org/Prevention.)

Kirschenbuam, D.S. and Flanery, R.C. (1983) Behavioural Contracting: Outcomes and Elements. In Herson, M. Eisler, R.M. and Miller, P.M. (Eds.) *Progress in Behaviour Modification.* Academic Press.

Klein, A. (2001) Stirred and Shaken: Rank, Ritual and Reputation. *Druglink,*16: 1.

Klingemann, H.K. (1992) Coping and Maintenance Strategies of Spontaneous Remitters From Problem Use of Alcohol and Heroin in Switzerland. *The International Journal of Addictions*, 27: 12, 1359–88.

Klingemann, H.K. (1991) The Motivation to Change From Problem Alcohol and Heroin Use. *British Journal of Addiction*, 86: 23–5.

Kosten, T.R. and Kleber, H.D. (1984) Strategies to Improve Compliance With Narcotic Antagonists. *American Journal of Drug and Alcohol Abuse*, 10: 249–66.

Kosten, T.R., Morgan, C. and Kleber, H. (1992) Phase II Clinical Trials of Buprenorphine: Detoxification and Induction on Naltraxone. In Blaine, J. (Ed.) *Buprenorphine, an Alternative Treatment for Opioid Dependence*. Research Monograph, Rockville, MD: NIDA.

Kottler, J.A. and Carlson, J. (2003) *Bad Therapy: Master Therapists Share Their Worst Failures*. Brunner-Routledge.

Kraemer, G.W. (1985) Effects of Differences and in Early Social Experience on Primate Neurobiological-Behavioural Development. In Reite, M. and Fields, T. (Eds.) *The Psychobiology of Attachment and Separation*, Academic Press.

Labouvie, E. (1996) Maturing Out of Substance Use: Selection and Self-Correction. *Journal of Drug Issues*, 26: 2, 457–76.

Lambert, M.J (1992) Psychotherapy Outcome Research: Implications for Integrative and Eclectic Therapists. In Norcross, J.C. and Goldfreid, M.R. (Eds.) *Handbook of Psychotherapy Integration*. Basic Books.

Lambert, M.J. et al. (2003) Is It Time for Clinicians Routinely to Track Patient Outcome? A Met-Analysis. *Clinical Psychology*, 10: 288–301.

Lambert, M.J. (1989) The Individual Therapists Contribution to Psychotherapy Process and Outcome. Clinical Psychology Review, 9: 469–485.

Lankton, S.R. and Lankton, C.H. (1983) *The Answer Within: A Clinical Framework of Ericksonian Hypnotherapy*. Bruner Mazell.

Law, F.D. et al. (1997) The Feasibility of Abrupt Methadone-Buprenorphine Transfer in British Opiate Addicts in an Outpatient Setting. *Addiction Biology*, 2: 2, 191–200.

Lazarus, R.S. (1982) Thoughts on The Relation Between Alcohol Problems and The Anxiety Disorders. *American Journal of Psychiatry*, 147: 685–95.

Leake, G.J. and King, A.S. (1977) Effect of Counsellor Expectation on Alcoholic Recovery. *Alcohol Health and Research World*, 11: 16–22.

Ledermann, S. (1956) *Alcool, Alcoolisme et Alcoolisation. Institut National d'Etudes Demographiques, Travaux et Documents*. Press Universitaires de France.

Levett, S.D. and Dubner, S.J. (2005) *Freakonomics*. Allen Lane.

Levine, H.G. (1979) The Discovery of Addiction: Changing Conceptions of Habitual Drunkenness in America. *Journal of Studies on Alcohol*, 15: 493–506.

Levinson, D. (1978) *The Seasons of A Man's Life*. Random House.

Lewis,T., Amini, F. and Lannon, R. (2000) *A General Theory of Love*. Vintage Books.

Liebson, I., Bigelow, G. and Flamer, R. (1973) Alcoholism Amongst Methadone Patients. A Special Treatment Method. *American Journal of Psychiatry*, 130: 483–5.

Light, A. B. and Torrance, E.G. (1929) Opiate Addiction VI: The Effects of Abrupt Withdrawal Followed by Readministration of Morphine in Human Addicts, With Special Reference to The Composition of The Blood, The Circulation and The Metabolism. *Archives of International Medicines*, 44: 1–16.

Lillie-Blanton, M., Antonym, J.C. and Schuster, C.R. (1993) Proving The Meaning/Ethnic Group Comparisons in Crack Cocaine Smoking. *Journal of The American Medical Association*, 269: 993–7.

Lipchick, E. (2002) *Beyond Technique in Solution Focused Therapy*. Guildford Press.

Loberg, T. and Miller, W.R. (1986) Personality, Cognitive and Neuropsychological Dimensions of Harmful Alcohol Consumption: A Cross-National Comparison of Clinical Samples. *Annals of The New York Academy of Sciences*, 472: 75–97.

Losch, M. and Cacioppo, J. (1990) Cognitive Dissonance May Enhance Sympathetic Tonus, But Attitudes Are Changed to Reduce Negative Affect Rather Than Arousal. *Journal of Experimental Social Psychology*. 26: 289–304.

Lowinson, J. et al. (Eds.) (1992) *Comprehensive Textbook of Substance Abuse*. Williams and Wilkins.

Luborsky, L. et al. (1985) Therapist Success and Its Determinants. *Archives of General Psychiatry*. 42: 602–11.

Ludwig, A.M. (1985) Cognitive Processes Associated With Spontaneous Recovery From Alcoholism. *Quarterly Journal of Studies on Alcohol*, 46: 53–7.

Macandrew, C. and Edgerton, R.B. (1969) *Drunken Comportment: A Social Explanation*. Aldine.

Madge, T. (2001) *White Mischief: A Cultural History of Cocaine*. Mainstream Publishing.

Magura, S. and Kang S.Y. (1996) Validity of Self-Reported Drug Use in High Risk Populations: A Meta-Analytical Review. *Substance Use and Misuse*, 31: 9, 1131–53.

Mandelbaum, D.G. (1965) Alcohol and Culture. *Current Anthropology*, 6: 3, 281–93.

Marlatt, G.A. (1983) The Controlled Drinking Controversy: A Commentary. *American Psychologist*, 38: 1097–110.

Marlatt, G.A. (1985) Craving for Alcohol, Loss of Control and Relapse: A Cognitive-Behavioural Analysis. In Nathan, P.E. Marlatt, G.A.and Loberg, T. (Eds.) *Alcoholism: New Directions in Behavioural Research and Treatment*. Plenum.

Marlatt, G.A. and Gordon, J.R. (1980) Determinants of Relapse. Implications for The Maintenance of Behaviour Change. In Davidson, P.O. and Davidson, S.M. (Eds.) *Behaviour Medicine: Changing Health Lifestyles*. New York: Brunner Mazel.

Marlatt, G.A. and Gordon, J.R. (Eds.) (1985) *Relapse Prevention*. The Guilford Press.

Marlatt, G.A. and Rohsenow, D.J. (1980) Cognitive Processes in Alcohol Use: Expectancy and The Balanced Placebo Design. In Mello, N.K. (Ed.) *Advances in Substance Abuse (Vol 1)*. JAI Press.

Mars, G. and Altman, Y. (1987) Alternative Mechanism of Distribution in a Soviet Economy. In Douglas, M. (Ed.) *Constructive Drinking: Perspectives on Drink From Anthropology*. Cambridge University Press.

Marsh, P. and Fox, K. (1993) Alcohol Controls, Crime and Social Problems in The European Community. In The Amsterdam Group. *Alcoholic Beverages and European Society*. The Amsterdam Group.

Marshall, M. (1983). 'Four Hundred Rabbits': an Anthropological View of Ethanol as A Disinhibitor. In Room, R. and Collins, G. (Eds.) *Drinking and Disinhibition: Nature and Meaning of The Link*. NIAAA Research Monograph No. 12. United States Government Printing Office.

Matarazzo, R.G. and Patterson, D. (1986) Research on the Teaching and Learning of Therapeutic Skills. In Garfield, S.L. and Bergin, A.E. (Eds.) *Handbook of Psychotherapy and Behaviour Change*. Wiley.

Mattrick, R. et al. (1998) The Effectiveness of Other Opioid Replacement Therapies: LAAM, Heroin, Buprenorphine, Naltraxone and Injectable Maintenance. In Ward, J. Mattrick, R. and Hall, W. (Eds.) *Methadone Maintenance Treatment and Other Replacement Therapies*. Harwood.

Mccoy, A.W. (1972) *The Politics of Heroin: CIA Complicity in The Global Drug Trade*. Lawrence Hill.

Mclellan, A.T. et al. (1993) The Effects of Psychosocial Services in Substance Abuse Treatment. *Journal of The American Medical Association*. 269, 1953–9.

Mclellen, A.T. et al. (1988) Is the Counsellor an 'Active Ingredient' in Methadone Treatment? An Examination of Treatment Success Among Four Counsellors. *Journal of Nervous and Mental Disorders*, 176: 423–30.

Meichenbaum, D. (1992) *Stress Inoculation Training*, Allyn and Bacon.

Mello. N.K. and Mendleson, J.H. (1965) Operant Analysis of Drinking Habits of Chronic Alcoholics. *Nature*, 206: 43–6.

Meyers, R.J. and Smith, J.E. (1995) *Clinical Guide to Alcohol Treatment: The Community Reinforcement Approach*. The Guildford Press.

Meyers, R.J. and Wolfe, B.L. (2004) *Get Your Loved One Sober: Alternatives to Nagging, Pleading and Threatening.* Hazledean.

Meyers, R.J. et al. (1999) Community Reinforcement and Family Training: Engaging Unmotivated Drug Users Into Treatment. *Journal of Substance Abuse*, 10: 3, 291–308.

Miller, E.J. (2001) Practice and Promise: The Azrin Studies. In Meyers, R.J. and Miller, W.R. (Eds.) *A Community Reinforcement Approach to Addiction Treatment.* Cambridge University Press.

Miller, N.S. and Gold, M.S. (1994) Dissociation of 'Conscious Desire' (Craving) From and Relapse in Alcohol and Cocaine Dependence. *Annuals of Clinical Psychiatry*, 6: 2, 99–106.

Miller, S.D. et al. (2004) Using Outcome to Inform and Improve Treatment Outcomes. *Journal of Brief Therapy*. In Press.

Miller, S.D. et al. (2005) Making Treatment Count: Client Directed, Outcome Informed Clinical Work With Problem Drinkers. *Psychotherapy in Australia*, 11: 4, 42–56.

Miller, W.R. (1989) Increasing Motivation for Change. In Hester, R.K. and Miller, W.R. (Eds.) *Handbook of Alcoholic Treatment Approaches: Effective Alternative.* Pergamon Press.

Miller, W.R. (1998) Why Do People Change Addictive Behaviour? The 1996 H. David Archibald Lecture. *Addiction*, 93: 2, 163–72.

Miller, W.R. and Baca, L.M. (1983) Two Year Follow-Up of Bibliotherapy and Therapist-Directed Controlled Drinking Training for Problem Drinkers. *Behaviour Therapy*, 14: 441–48.

Miller, W.R. and C'de Baca, J. (1994) Quantum Change: Toward A Psychology of Transformation. In Heatherton, T. and Wienberger, J. (Eds.) *Can Personality Change?* American Psychological Association.

Miller, W.R. and C'de Baca, J. (2001) *Quantum Change: When Epiphanies and Sudden Insights Transform Ordinary Lives.* Guildford Press

Miller, W.R. and Rollnick, S. (2002) *Motivational Interviewing: Preparing People for Change.* Guildford Press.

Miller, W.R. et al. (1992) Motivational Enhancement Therapy Manual: A Clinical Research Guide for Therapists Treating Individuals With Alcohol Abuse and Dependence. Monograph 2. DHHS (ADM).

Miller, W.R. et al. (1995) What Works? A Methodological Analysis of The Addiction Treatment Outcome Literature. In Hester, R.K. and Miller, W.R. (Eds.) *Handbook of Alcoholism Treatment Approaches*. Allyn and Bacon.

Miller, W.R. et al. (2001) Community Reinforcement and Traditional Approaches: Findings of a Controlled Trial. In Meyers, R.J. and Miller, W.R. (Eds.) *A Community Reinforcement Approach to Addiction Treatment.* International Monographs in The Addictions) Cambridge University Press.

Miller, W.R., Benefield, R.G. and Tonigan J.S. (1993) Enhancing Motivation for Change in Problem Drinking: A Controlled Comparison of Two Therapists' Styles. *Journal of Consulting and Clinical Psychology*, 46, 74–86.

Miller, W.R., Meyers, R.J. and Tonigan, J.S. (1999) Engaging The Unmotivated in Treatment for Alcohol Problems: A Comparison of Three Intervention Strategies. *Journal of Consulting and Clinical Psychology*, 67: 5, 688–97.

Moss, B. (2005) *Religion and Spirituality.* Lyme Regis, Russell House Publishing.

Navjits, L.M. and Weiss, R.D. (1994) Variations in Therapist Effectiveness in The Treatment of Patients With Substance Use Disorders: an Empirical Review. *Addiction,* 89: 679–88.

Nelson, R.O. and Hayes, S.C. (1986) The Nature of Behavioural Assessment. In Nelson, R.O. and Hayes, S.C. (Eds.) *Conceptual Foundations of Behavioural Assessments.* Guildford Press.

Newcomb, M.D. (1995) Drug Use Aetiology Among Ethnic Minority Adolescence: Risks and Protective Factors. In Botvin, G.J. et al. (Eds.) *Drug Abuse Prevention With Multiethnic Youth.* Sage.

Newcombe, M.D. Maddahain, E. and Bentler, P.M. (1987) Substance Abuse and Psychological Risk-Factors Amongst Teenagers: Associations With Sex, Age, Gender, Ethnicity, and Type of School. *American Journal of Drug and Alcohol Abuse,* 13: 413–33.

Nutt, D.J. (1996) Addiction: Brain Mechanisms and Their Treatment Implications. *The Lancet.* 347: 8993.

O'Banion, D.R. and Whaley, D.L. (1981) *Behavioural Contracting: Arranging Contingencies of Reinforcement.* Springer.

O'Brien, C. (1994) Opioids: Antagonists and Partial Antagonist. In Galanter, M. and Kleber, H. (Eds.) *Textbook of Substance Abuse Treatment.* American Psychiatric Press.

O'Malley, S. et al. (1992) Naltrexone and Coping Skills Therapy for Alcohol Dependence: A Control Study. *Archives of General Psychiatry,* 49: 881–7.

O'Brien, C.P. and Mccellen, A.T. (1996) Myths About The Treatment of Addiction. *The Lancet,* 347: 8996, 237–40.

Olds, J. (1959) Studies of Neuropharmacologicals by Electrical and Chemical Manipulation of The Brain in Animals With Chronically Implanted Electrodes. In Bradley, P. Deniker, P. and Radouco-Thomas, C. (Eds.) *Nueropsychopharmacolgy.* Elsevier.

Onken, L.S., Blaine, J.D. and Boren, J.J. (Eds.) (1995) Integrating Behavioural Therapies With Medications in The Treatment of Drug Dependence. National Institute of Drug Abuse Monograph Series, No 150. US Government Printing Office.

Orford, J. and Edwards, G. (1977) *Alcoholism: A Comparison of Treatment and Advice, With a Study of The Influence of Marriage.* Maudsley Monographs No. 26. Oxford University Press.

Orford, J. (1999) Future Directions: A Commentary on Project MATCH. *Addiction,* 94, 62–6.

Orlinsky, D.E. and Howard, K.I. (1980) Gender and Psychotherapeutic Outcome. In Brodksy, A.M. and Hare-Mustin, R.T. (Eds.) *Women and Psychotherapy.* Guildford Press.

Oshodin, O.G. (1995). Nigeria. In Heath, D.B. (Ed.) *International Handbook on Alcohol and Culture.* Greenwood.

Panepinto, W.C. and Higgins, M.J. (1969) Keeping Alcoholics in Treatment: Effective Follow Through Procedures. *Quarterly Journal of Studies on Alcohol,* 22: 597–609.

Pape, H. and Hammer, T. (1996) How Does Young People's Alcohol Consumption Change During The Transition to Early Adulthood? A Longitudinal Study of Changes at Aggregates and Individual Level. *Addiction,* 91: 9, 1345–57.

Patterson, G.R. and Forgatch, M.S. (1985) Therapist Behaviour as a Determinant for Non-Compliance: A Paradox for The Behaviour Modifier. *Journal of Consulting and Clinical Psychology,* 53: 6, 846–51.

Peace, A. (1992) No Fishing Without Drinking: The Construction of Social Identity in Rural Ireland. In Gefou-Madianou, D. (Ed.) *Alcohol, Gender and Culture.* Routledge.

Peele, S. (1995) *Diseasing of America: How We Allowed Treatment Zealots and The Treatment Industry to Convince Us We Are Out of Control.* Jossey-Bass Publishers.

Peterson, K.A. et al. (1994) Determinants of Readmission Following Inpatient Substance Abuse Treatment: A National Survey of VA Programs. *Medical Care*, 32: 535–50.

Petrovic, P. et al. (2002) Placebo and Opioid Analgesia-Imaging A Shared Neural Network. *Science*. 295, 1737–40.

Petry, N. and Bickel, W. (1999) Therapeutic Alliance and Psychiatric Severity as Predictors of Completion of Treatment for Opioid Dependence. *Psychiatric Services*, 50: 2, 219–27.

Petty, R.E. and Cacioppo, J.T. (1979) Issue-Involvement Can Increase or Decrease Persuasion by Enhancing Message-Relevant Cognitive Responses. *Journal of Personality and Social Psychology*, 37: 1915–26.

Post, R.M., Wiess, S. and Pert, A. (1987) The Role of Context and Conditioning in Behavioural Sensitization to Cocaine. *Psychopharmacology Bulletin*, 23: 425–9.

Premack, D. (1965) Reinforcement Theory. In Levine, D. (Ed) *Nebraska Symposium on Motivation*. University of Nebraska Press.

Prochaska, J.O. (1994) Strong and Weak Principles for Progressing From Precontemplation to Action on The Basis of Twelve Problem Behaviours. *Health Psychology*, 13: 47–51.

Prochaska, J.O. and DiClemente, C.C. (1992) Transtheoretical Approach. In Norcross, J.C. and Goldfried, M.R. (Eds.) *Handbook of Psychotherapy Integration*. Basic Books.

Prochaska, J.O., Norcross, J.C. and DiClemente, C.C. (1994) *Changing for Good*. William Morrow.

Prochaska, J.O. et al. (1991) Patterns of Change: A Dynamic Typology Applied to Smoking Cessation. *Journal of Consulting and Clinical Psychology*, 56: 520–8.

Prochaska, J.O. et al. (1994) Stages of Change and Decisional Balance for 12 Problem Behaviours. *Health Psychology*, 13: 39–46.

Project MATCH Research Group (1997) Matching Alcohol Treatments to Client Heterogeneity: Project MATCH Post-Treatment Drinking Outcomes. *Journal of Studies on Alcohol*, 58: 7–29.

Rawson, H. et al. (1998) A 3 Year Progress Report on The Implementation of LAAM in The United States. *Addiction*, 93: 533–40.

Rawson, R.A. et al. (1999) Contingency Management and Relapse Prevention as Stimulant Abuse Treatment Interventions. In Higgins, S.T. and Silverman, K. (Eds.) *Motivating Behaviour Change Among Illicit-Drug Abusers: Research on Contingency Management Interventions*. American Psychological Association.

Ricks, D.F. (1974) Supershrink: Methods of a Therapist Judged Successfully on The Basis of Adult Outcomes of Adolescent Patients. In Ricks, D.F., Rolf, M. and Thomas, A. (Eds.) *Life History Research in Psychopathology*. University of Minnesota Press.

Robins, L. (1993) Vietnam Veterans' Rapid Recovery From Heroin Addiction: A Fluke or Normal Expectation? *Addiction*, 88: 8, 1041–54.

Robins, L.N., Helzer J.E. and Hesselbrock M. (1980) Vietnam Veterans 3 Years After Vietnam: How Our Study Changed Our View of Heroin. In Brill, L. and Winick, C. (Eds.)*The Yearbook of Substance Use and Abuse*. Human Sciences Press.

Rogers, C. (1957) The Necessary and Sufficient Conditions of Therapeutic Personality Change. *Journal of Consulting Psychology*, 21: 95–103.

Rogers, C. (2000) *Client Centred Therapy*. Constable.

Rollnick, S. and Heather, N. (1982) The Application of Bandura's Self-Efficacy Theory to Abstinence Orientated Alcoholism Treatment. *Addictive Behaviours*, 7: 243–50.

Rosenthal, H.G. (Ed.) (2000) *Favourite Counselling and Therapy Homework Assignments: Leading Therapists Share Their Most Creative Strategies*. Taylor and Francis.

Roth, A. and Fonagy, P. (1996) *What Works for Whom? A Critical Review of Psychotherapy Research.* Guildford Press.

Rounsavile, B.J. (1995) Can Psychotherapy Rescue Naltrexone Treatment of Opioid Addiction? in Onken, L., Blane, J. and Boren, J. (Eds.) *Integrating Behavioural Therapies With Medications in The Treatment of Drug Dependence.* NIDA Monograph No 150, NIDA.

Rudgley, R. (1993) *The Alchemy of Culture: Intoxicants in Society.* British Museum Press.

Safran, J.D. and Muran, J.C. (2000) *Negotiating The Therapeutic Alliance.* Guildford Press.

Saunders, B. (1985) The Case for Controlling Alcohol Consumption. In Heather, N., Robertson, I. and Davies, P. (Eds.)*The Misuse of Alcohol: Crucial Issues in Dependence, Treatment and Prevention.* Croom Helm.

Schachter, S. and Singer, J.E. (1962) Cognitive, Social and Physiological Determinants of Emotional State. *Psychological Review*, 69: 379–99.

Schaffer, H.J. and Jones, S.B. (1989) *Quitting Cocaine: The Struggle Against Impulse.* Lexington Books.

Schiffman, S. et al. (1994) Smoking Behaviour and Smoking History of Tobacco Chippers. *Experimental and Clinical Psychopharmacology*, 2: 2.

Schlosser, E. (2003) *Reefer Madness.* Allen Lane.

Schunk, D.H. and Hanson, A.R. (1989) Self-Modelling and Children's Cognitive Skills Learning. *Journal of Educational Psychology*, 81: 155–63.

Schwarzer, R. et al. (1992) Expectancies as Mediators Between Recipient Characteristics and Social Support Intentions. In Schwarzer, R. (Ed) *Self-Efficacy: Thought Control of Action.* Hemisphere Publishing.

Seleckman, M. (1993) *Pathways to Change: Brief Therapy Solutions With Difficult Adolescents.* Guildford Press.

Seligman, M.E.P. (1975) *Helplessness.* Freeman.

Silbertfeld, M. and Glaser, F.B. (1978) Use of the Life Table Method in Determining Attrition From Treatment. *Journal of The Studies on Alcohol*, 39: 1582–90.

Silverman, K. et al. (1996) Sustained Cocaine Abstinence in Methadone Maintenance Patients Through Voucher Based Reinforcement Therapy. *Archives of General Psychiatry*, 53: 409–15.

Silverman, K. et al. (1998) Broad Beneficial Effects of Cocaine Abstinence Reinforcement Among Methadone Patients. *Journal of Consulting and Clinical Psychology*, 66: 811–24.

Simpson, D.D. (1981) Treatment for Drug Abuse: Follow Up Outcomes and Length of Time Spent. *Archives of General Psychiatry*, 38: 875–80.

Simpson, D.D. and Sells, S. (1983) Effectiveness for the Treatment of Drug Abuse: An Overview of the DARP Research Programme. *Advances in Alcohol and Substance Abuse*, 2: 1, 7–29.

Simpson, D.D. et al. (1997) Programme Diversity and Treatment Retention Rates in the Drug Abuse Treatment Outcomes Study (DATOS). *Psychology of Addictive Behaviour*. 11: 279–93.

Smith, D. and Wesson, D. (1999) Benzodiazepines and Other Sedative-Hypnotics. In Galanter, M. and Kleber, H. (Eds.) *Textbook of Substance Abuse Treatment.* American Psychiatric Press.

Smith, J., Conchitta, C. and Lane, J.D. (1984) Limbic Muscarinic Cholinergic and Benzodiazepine Receptor Changes With Chronic Intravenous Morphine and Self-Administration. *Pharmacology, Biochemistry and Behaviour*, 20: 443–50.

Smith, J. and Dworkin, S.I. (1990) Behavioural Contingencies Determine Changes in Drug-Induced Neurotransmitter Turnover. *Drug Development Research*, 20: 337–48.

Smith, J.E. and Meyers, R.J. (2004) *Motivating Substance Abusers to Enter Treatment: Working With Family Members.* New York, Guildford Press.

Smith, J.E., Meyers, R.J. and Delaney, H.D. (1998) The Community Reinforcement Approach With Homeless Alcohol-Dependant Individuals. *Journal of Consulting and Clinical Psychology*, 66: 541–8.

Sobell, M.B. and Sobell, L.C. (1978) *Behavioural Treatments of Alcohol Problems*. Plenum.

Solomon, K.E. and Annis, H.M. (1989) Development of a Scale to Measure Outcome Expectancy in Alcoholics. *Cognitive Therapy Research*, 13: 409–21.

Spitz, R. (1945) Hospitalism: an Inquiry Into the Genesis of Psychiatric Conditions in Early Childhood. *Psychoanalytic Study of the Child*, I: 53–74.

Stall, R. and Biernacki, P. (1986) Spontaneous Remission From Problematic Use of Substances: An Inductive Model Derived From a Comparative Analysis of the Alcohol, Opiate, Tobacco, and Food/Obesity Literatures. *The International Journal of Addiction*, 21: 1, 1–23.

Stastny, D and Potter, M. (1991) Alcohol Abuse by Patients Undergoing Methadone Treatment Programmes. *British Journal of Addictions*, 86: 307–10.

Stewart, D. et al. (2000) Variation Between and Within Drug Treatments Modalities: Data From The National Treatment Outcomes Research Study. *European Addiction Research*, 6: 106–14.

Stitzer, M.L., Bigelow, G.E. and Liebson, I. (1979) Reinforcement of Drug Abstinence: A Behavioural Approach to Drug Abuse Treatment. In Krasnegor, N.A. (Ed.) *Behavioural Analysis and Treatment of Substance Abuse*. Research Monograph No. 25. National Institute of Drug Abuse.

Stitzer, M.L. and Bigelow, G. (1978) Contingency Management in a Methadone Maintenance Programme. *International Journal of Addiction*, 13: 5, 1737–46.

Stitzer, M.L. et al. (1977) Medication Take Home as Reinforcer in Methadone Maintenance Program. *Addiction Behaviour*, 2: 9–14.

Strang, J., Bearn, J. and Gossop, M. (1999) Lofexidine for Opiate Detoxification: Review of Recent Randomised and Open Trials. *American Journal of Addiction*, 8: 337–48.

Strang, J. et al. (1997) Methadone Treatment for Opiate Addiction: Benefits in The First Month. *Addiction Research*, 5: 71–6.

Streatfeild, D. (2002) *Cocaine*. Virgin Publishing.

Sugarman, L. (2001) *Life-Span Development: Frameworks, Accounts and Strategies*. Psychology Press.

Sullivan, M.A., Comer, S.D. and Nunes, E.V. (2006) Pharmacology and Clinical Use of Naltrexone. In Strain, E.C. and Stitzer, M.L. (Eds.) *The Treatment of Opioid Dependence*. John Hopkins University Press.

Sutton, S. (2001) Back to The Drawing Board? A Review of The Applications of The Transtheortical Model to Substance Abuse. *Addiction*, 96: 1, 175–86.

Talmon, M. (1990) *Single Session Therapy: Maximising The Effect of The First (And Often Only) Therapeutic Encounter*. Jossey-Bass.

Tennant, F.S. et al. (1984). Clinical Experience With Natlrexone in Suburban Opioid Addicts. *Journal of Clinical Psychiatry*, 45: 41–5.

Toma, F. (2000) A Comparison of The Perception of Drug and Alcohol Misusers on The Helpfulness of Therapeutic Attitudes Used by Counsellors. *The European Journal of Psychotherapy, Counselling and Health*, 3: 1, 103–10.

Tuchfield, B.S. (1981) Spontaneous Remission in Alcoholics: Empirical Observations and Theoretical Implications. *Journal of Studies on Alcohol*, 42: 626–41.

United Kingdom Alcohol Treatment Trial Team (2001) UKATT Hypothesis, Design and Methods. *Alcohol and Alcoholism*, 36: 1, 11–21.

Unnithan, S., Gossop, M. and Strang, J. (1992) Factors Associated With Relapse Amongst Opiate Addicts in an Outpatient Detoxification Programme. *British Journal of Psychiatry.* 161: 657–67.

Vaillant, G.E. (1995) *The Natural History of Alcoholism – Revisited.* Harvard Academic Press.

Valins, S. and Nisbett, R.E. (1972) Attribution Processes in The Development and Treatment of Emotional Disorders. In Jones, E.E. et al. (Eds.) *Attribution: Perceiving The Causes of Behaviour.* General Learning Press.

Van Bilsen, H. (1994) Learning Controlled Use: A Case Study. *Behavioural and Cognitive Psychotherapy*, 22: 87–95.

Van Kalmthout, M.A. (1991) Spontaneous Remission of Addiction. In Schippers, G.M. et al. (Eds.) *Contributions to the Psychotherapy of Addiction.* Swets and Zeitlinger.

Velicer, W.F. et al. (1985) A Decisional Balance Measure for Assessing and Predicting Smoking Status. *Journal of Personality and Social Psychology*, 48: 1279–89.

Velicer, W.F.et al. (1998) Smoking Cessation and Stress Management: Application of Trans-theoretical Model of Behavioural Change. *Homeostasis*, 38: 216–33.

Volpicelli, J.R. et al. (1995) Effect of Naltrexone on Alcohol 'High' in Alcoholics. *American Journal of Psychiatry*, 152: 613–15.

Walach, H. (2003) Placebo and Placebo Effects-A Concise Review. Focus on Alternatives and Complimentary Therapies. *Pharmaceutical Press*, 8: 2, 178–87.

Wallace, B.B. (1989) Psychological and Environmental Determinant of Relapse in Crack Cocaine Users. *Journal of Substance Abuse Treatment*, 6: 95–106.

Walter, J.L. and Peller, J.E. (1992) *Becoming Solution-Focussed in Brief Therapy.* Brunner Mazel.

Walters, G.D. (2000) Spontaneous Remission From Alcohol, Tobacco and Other Drug Abuse: Seeking Quantitative Answers to Qualitative Questions. *American Journal of Drug and Alcohol Abuse*, 26: 3, 443–60.

Wampold, B.E. (2001) *The Great Psychotherapy Debate: Models, Methods and Findings.* Erlbaum.

Warburton, H., Turnbull, P.J. and Hough, M. (2005) *Occasional and Controlled Heroin Use: Not a Problem?* Joseph Rowntree Foundation.

Waterhouse, J.M., Minors, D.S. and Waterhouse, M.E. (1990) *Your Body Clock: How to Live With It Not Against It.* Oxford University Press.

Watson, P. (Undated) *Does Abundant Supply of Drugs Lead to Heavy Consumption? A Papua New Guinea Case Study.* Www.Drugtext.Org/Library/Articles

Wegner, D. (1991) Transactive Memory in Close Relationships. *Journal of Personality and Social Psychology*, 61: 6, 923–9.

Weinberg, R.S., Gould, D. and Jackson, A. (1979) Expectations and Performance: an Empirical Test of Bandura's Self-Efficacy Theory. *Journal of Sport Psychology*, 1: 320–31.

West, R. (2005) Time for a Change: Putting the Transtheoretical (Stages of Change) Model to Rest. *Addiction*, 100: 1036–9.

WHO (1992). *International Classification of Diseases and Health Related Problems, Tenth Revision (ICD-10).* World Health Organisation.

Williams, M. (2001) *Suicide and Attempted Suicide.* Penguin Books.

Wilson, G.T. (1982) Alcohol and Anxiety: Recent Evidence on the Tension Reduction Theory of Alcohol Abuse. In Polivy, J. and Blankstein, K. (Eds.) *Self-Control of Emotional Behaviour.* Plenum.

Wolgin, D.L. (1989) The Role of Instrumental Learning in Behavioural Tolerance to Drugs. In Goudie, A.J. and Emmett-Oglesby, M.W. (Eds.) *Psychoactive Drugs: Tolerance and Sensitization.* Humana Press.

Wood, R.E. and Bandura, A. (1989) Social Cognitive Theory of Organizational Management. *Academy of Management Review*, 14: 361–84.

Woods, J.H. (1990) Abuse Liability and the Regulatory Control of Therapeutic Drugs: Untested Assumptions. *Drug and Alcohol Dependence*, 25: 229–33.

Woody, G. et al. (1983) Psychotherapy for Opiate Addicts: Does It Help? *Archives of General Psychiatry*. 40: 639–45.

Wortman, C.B. and Brehm, J.W. (1975) Response to Uncontrollable Outcomes: An Integration of Reactance Theory and the Learned Helplessness Model. In Berkowitz, L. (Ed.) *Advances in Experimental Social Psychology*. 8: 275–336.

Wyer, R.S. and Srull, T.K. (1986) Human Cognition in Its Social Context. *Psychological Review*, 93: 322–59.

Zeig, J.K. and Munion, W.M. (1999) *Milton H. Erickson*. Sage.

Zimbardo, P.G. and Leippe, R. (1991) *The Psychology of Attitude Change and Social Influence*. McGraw-Hill.

Index

Also by the same Author

Drug Induced
Addiction and treatment in perspective

By Phil Harris

'It would be difficult for anyone involved in working with addiction whether as a practitioner, or manager, or policy maker to come away from reading this informative and interesting book without some spur to reflecting on and changing their own thinking and practice.' *VISTA.*

'Should be essential reading . . . his critique of peer pressure, the importance of relationships throughout adolescence and why some young people are more prone to drug dependency than others are brilliant . . . **an excellent book** . . . Much to my own surprise I thoroughly enjoyed *Drug Induced* and found myself repeating to colleagues much of what I read. I found it to be a refreshing, courageous book that radically challenges many of our widely held beliefs about addiction and treatment: it is just up to you now to read it.' *Youth & Policy.*

'This **thought-provoking** book challenges many aspects of the theoretical base and clinical practices prevalent in the addictions field today . . . The disease concept, motivational interviewing, stages of change and dual diagnosis are all examined in a way which will, hopefully, **encourage alcohol and drug workers to re-evaluate their 'sacred cows'**. The authors' clinical experience shines through what I largely experienced as a social-science perspective with a developmental and environmental focus.' *Addiction Today.*

'He supports his arguments with a comprehensive array of references from both friend and foe of his stance . . . it hangs together well . . .' *Journal of Mental Health.*

160 pages 978-1-903855-53-9 2005 £15.95

Available from www.russellhouse.co.uk

Secret Lives: Growing With Substance

Working with children and young people affected by familial substance misuse

Edited by Fiona Harbin & Michael Murphy

Containing a chapter by Phil Harris entitled *Where it all begins: growing up and the helping relationship,* this book offers new and challenging insights into the task of working with children and young people who are affected by substance misuse, particularly those who are:

- brought up in substance misusing households
- beginning to misuse substances themselves in this context.

'Packed with useful research quotes, references and counselling tips . . . First, you could use the cornucopia of research to consolidate funding applications, to back up training or lectures, or to substantiate points you wish to make elsewhere. Second, you can use the therapeutic advice given just after the research to guide your own practice: the authors aim to help practitioners and managers in the identification, assessment, treatment and support of the children and siblings of substance misusers. Buy this book as a reference and investment – **any good clinician will have a need to call on it some time.**' *Addiction Today.*

'Most books of this genre discuss either how to assess the issue or how to work with it: this book does both, leaving the reader with a sense of confidence as to how they might go about working with this group of service users, as well as why they are working with them in this way . . . **I recommend this book for all concerned about substance misuse.**' *Community Care.*

160 pages 978-1-903855-66-9 £15.95

Available from www.russellhouse.co.uk